# What Should We Tell
# Our Daughters?

*Also by Melissa Benn*

# What Should We Tell Our Daughters?

## The Pleasures and Pressures of Growing Up Female

### MELISSA BENN

JOHN MURRAY

First published in Great Britain in 2013 by John Murray (Publishers)
An Hachette UK Company

1

A CIP catalogue record for this title is available from the British Library

ISBN 978-1-84854-627-1
Ebook ISBN 978-1-84854-629-5

Typeset in Bembo 11.5/14 pt by Palimpsest Book Production Limited, Falkirk, Stirlingshire

Printed and bound by Clays Ltd, St Ives plc

John Murray policy is to use papers that are natural, renewable and recyclable
products and made from wood grown in sustainable forests. The logging
and manufacturing processes are expected to conform to the environmental
regulations of the country of origin.

John Murray (Publishers)
338 Euston Road
London NW1 3BH

www.johnmurray.co.uk

For Hannah and Sarah – who else?

# Contents

# Introduction

Around midnight. My daughters and I are slouched on the living-room couch watching a quiz show on television, the kind where a pack of youngish men in loud shirts and wacky spectacles show off − endlessly − to their mates. Suddenly, as if out of nowhere, they begin to mock one of (only two) female guests. Their verbal ribbing has no connection to authentic comedy but is, instead, a falsely sugared version of contempt, and is directed at the female guest's estuary accent, her Essex background, and − oh, the jokes within jokes! − her apparent failure to understand that she *is* being mocked. And this is supposed to be *funny*? A brewing irritation is shaking me from my slumped weariness. My daughters are also fed up although they keep a slight distance from my middle-aged certainty: just in case I should betray signs of a generational inability to 'get it'. It's true, I *don't* get this craftily understated, apparently cool but nonetheless blatantly misogynist spectacle. Why is this young woman − who has, so far, gamely colluded with every stereotype of desirable and adaptable femininity − now gamely colluding in her own humiliation?

Late Saturday evening. A tube carriage. A group of young men, teetering on the edge of drunkenness, take up a ring of seats around two teenage girls, entering into a form of banter that, to the attentive listener, clearly employs various code words about the sexual desirability of women in general and these young women in particular. The men are either not drunk enough or are sufficiently canny to keep their stream of talk this side of rude or threatening, aware, possibly, of adult onlookers, tuned in to their tactics. Yet one of the more uncomfortable aspects of the scene, which lasts for the eternity of four stations, is the way the girls laughingly 'play along' − whether out of innocence or spirited self-defence is hard to tell. If they had

I

not done so, the scene might well have turned ugly, possibly brutal. They saved themselves, as the woman on the TV panel show saved herself, by playing the feminine game.

Two passing moments: signifying everything and nothing. But there are plenty like them. Crude, cruel, casual misogyny – the darker, angrier sibling of simple old sexism – is increasingly a feature of modern culture. In January 2013, Cambridge classics professor Mary Beard appeared on BBC's *Question Time* where she made the reasoned and reasonable claim, to largely polite applause, that immigration might bring some benefits to local areas, including the town playing host that night to the programme. Soon after, she was subject to an avalanche of sexualised and violent comments posted online. 'Internet trolls [posted] dozens of horrifying sexual taunts, in language too offensive to reprint. The level of the abuse was so shocking that even those accustomed to the cut-and-thrust of online debate were appalled. In one of the milder examples, Beard was called "a vile, spiteful excuse for a woman, who eats too much cabbage and has cheese straws for teeth". . . [and her] features were even superimposed on an image of female genitalia.' Beard said such generic, violent misogyny left her feeling 'a sense of assault', as if reeling from a 'punch'.[1]

In this case, Beard attracted a great deal of support and solidarity in part, perhaps, because of her noted intellectual achievements and high public profile. But for many women, derided or threatened within more private arenas, to take a stand might be less rewarding or even risky: hence the girly going-along-with; the flirty deference – the default position of many a young woman, in innocence, in trouble, or in wordless fury.

But all this begs the much bigger cultural question: how do we reconcile this nasty new, and not-so-new, sexism, with a genuinely unabashed celebration of female competence at so many levels? During the course of researching and writing this book I have stored a small mountain of clippings, and filled multiple folders on my computer with news and features about dozens of high-achieving women in any field you care to mention: women like Nicole Cooke, the UK's leading woman cyclist, who retired aged twenty-nine early in 2013 (with a powerful attack on the lack of support for women in the sport, and the rewards showered on her often corrupt male equivalents such as Lance Armstrong); sixteen-year-old Laura Dekker, from the Netherlands – one of only five teens, two of them female – to have sailed solo round the world; Abi Morgan, the prolific TV and film screen-writer; Zaha Hadid, the fierce, female star of global architecture; Gillian Tett, the ice-cool assistant editor of the *Financial Times*, one of a growing number of scarily impressive women who regularly appear on *Newsnight*, talking about world finance and politics; Marissa Mayer, newly-appointed CEO of Yahoo, who declared that her maternity leave would be 'a few weeks long and I'll work through it'; Mary Beard – academic, author, broadcaster – herself.

On the 200th anniversary of the publication of *Pride and Prejudice*, possibly the most famous novel ever written about gender, property and family, a survey conducted by Scottish Widows of a thousand British parents found that 37.3 per cent believe their sons will be financially secure for the rest of their lives if they marry a good woman while less than a third of parents (31.9 per cent) think their daughters will be secure if they wed. The survey suggested that 'priorities for families have also drastically changed since Austen's time. Today more than half of parents' top goal for their daughters is getting a good education.'[2] Soon after, Radio Four's *Woman's Hour* set out to find the top hundred most powerful women in the country in 2013, accompanied by vigorous debate on the changing nature of women's leadership roles; although, interestingly, the woman who effortlessly topped the list inherited every part of her power: property, privilege and far-reaching influence.

> On the 200th anniversary of *Pride and Prejudice*, a survey conducted by Scottish Widows of a thousand British parents, found that 37.3 per cent believe their sons will be financially secure for the rest of their lives if they marry a good woman, while less than a third of parents (31.9 per cent) think their daughters will be financially secure if they wed.

It is no wonder that a series of disconnected words – contradiction, the emergence of extremes, achievement and attrition – begin to ricochet round my head as I pore over the statistics about the future direction of politics or the economy, watch the news or talk to academics, politicians, women in business or young women themselves. Something about our current age encourages me to think in un-matching pairs. Girls in crisis: Women on top. Chief Executives: Benefit Queens. Slut shaming: One Billion Rising. Christine Lagarde (the first woman head of the International Monetary Fund): 'We saw your boobs' (the appallingly crass opening song of the 2013 Oscar ceremony). 'It's a Man's World': *The End of Men*. Rising female unemployment: *The Richer Sex*. In 1995, the nation was gripped by a drama called *The Politician's Wife*, about a woman devastated by her husband's affair: in 2013 we were riveted by *The Politician's Husband*, a series about a man devastated by his wife's greater career success. It is hard to push through all this and see exactly what kind of world we are making for our daughters or how we should help them to negotiate it − or fight it. Or both.

Certainly there is a degree of public worry, a kind of constant anxious scrutiny directed at the girls and young women of today. Their young years are deemed more 'edgy and fragile' than their mothers' or grandmothers'.[3] Advertising, celebrity culture, film and television, the internet, all apparently pose a real danger to the mental health and stability of young, growing females. According to the author Kate Figes, 'It has never been harder to bring up a daughter.'[4] I have lost count of the number of books now published on the unvarying theme of girls on the edge/girls in crisis. Two books published over the last year − Steve Biddulph's *Raising Girls* and Sue Palmer's *21st Century Girls* − take as their starting point the problems of 'toxic' and 'over-sexualised' young women, frequently suffering from 'bullying' and 'low self-esteem'.

There are thousands of titles like this now available for worried parents. *Girls Adrift, Adolescent Girls in Crisis: Intervention and Hope, My Big Fat Teen Crisis, The Triple Bind: Saving Our Teenage Girls from Today's Pressures*. The top seller here is Steve Biddulph, who had a strong message to convey about a 'sudden and marked plunge in girls' mental health' and more striking yet, the ways in which 'The world today does not seem to care about girls at it should, and sees them just as a way to make money'. Soon after the publication of *Raising Girls*, a *Huffington Post* article that asked the question 'What Should We Teach Our Daughters?' went viral.

Several things immediately strike me about this new wave of girl-concern. It risks, as all generalised gender alarms do, neglecting the sheer variety of Girl Land (the title of yet another recently published book), not to mention the extraordinary energy, purposefulness, humour and hope of so many young women today. Anyone who only read the paper or perused Amazon best-seller lists could easily be forgiven for thinking that today's girls were either engaged in the anguished and unwilling exchange of sex texts or performing serial blow jobs before starving themselves out of misery at their failure to get into one of the higher-ranking universities.

> Anyone who only read the papers or perused Amazon best-seller lists could easily be forgiven for thinking that today's girls were either engaged in the anguished and unwilling exchange of sex texts or performing serial blow jobs before starving themselves out of misery at their failure to get into one of the higher-ranking universities.

Of course, out in the real world, teenage girls enjoy an extraordinary diversity of ordinary pleasures: friendship, food, music, sport, reading, travel. They can do virtually anything on a computer, and as they move into the late teens many start to negotiate the world of festivals, cheap trains and flights, and hostels, with consummate ease; they will read novels, talk about politics, be hilariously funny about the vagaries of other human beings, particularly adults. They develop and pursue highly individual passions – for a vocation, a writer, a TV series, a language, a cause. As the young feminist journalists Rhiannon Lucy Cosslett and Holly Baxter note, 'the teenage years are the time when many of us begin to develop social consciences, hence the startling upsurge in girls announcing at the breakfast table, aged thirteen, that they have decided to become vegetarians. They have a keen sense of injustice.'[5]

However, even when we turn to consider the genuine difficulties of a substantial minority it feels odd to consider Girl Land as a territory somehow separate from Woman Land. It is not as if girls spend their entire adolescence in their bedrooms and therefore fail to witness, on a daily basis, the complex emotional or employment trajectories of their elder sisters, mothers or aunts; nor do they grow up separate from boys or men. Most young women are acutely sensitive to the world as it is experienced *by*, rather than the ways in which it is represented *to*, themselves and all the women in their lives.

What, then, if our daughters' 'crisis' and 'distress' is ours too? What if their over- (or under-) eating, anxiety about school performance, or absence from broader public participation, is only an early or exaggerated – or both – logical response to what they see around them? Do girls pick up on the fact that from an earlier and earlier age they are now likely to be divided between those considered capable of achieving professional success and those who are heading for lower-status, often badly paid, work? Can we one minute 'affirm' a girl's autonomy, according to the laudable dictates of the latest how-to manual, while, the next minute, demanding that she do more around the house or be more emotionally nurturing than her brother? Can we really advise her to head straight for a bright future when all around her she observes the complex struggles of women trying to manage finances, friendship and family? When Steve Biddulph declared on *Woman's Hour* that one of the most important things we should tell our daughters is that 'looks don't matter hardly at all' I swear I heard the collective hollow laughter of the nation's women in the eerie radio silence that followed.

And, increasingly, we have to be aware that some lives contain far, far fewer chances than others. Researcher Tess Lanning examined the experiences and expectations of women over three generations, and argues:

> To construct a narrative of progress, or a broad argument about 'gender equality' is to ignore the ways in which the economic, social and political changes of the last 30 years have been experienced very differently by women of different backgrounds . . . inequality within the sexes is far greater than the difference between men and women.[6]

Recent research by the Institute for Public Policy Research (IPPR) has found the wage gap between graduate/high-skilled and non-graduate/low-skilled women has grown at a far faster rate than the same gap between men. It has recently been estimated that up to 70 million women, in professional and managerial occupations, worldwide have, in recent decades, joined their countries' elite.[7] In the UK a professional women in her thirties and forties is now likely to earn nearly three times as much as her unskilled female counterpart.[8] The number of women in absolute poverty is growing at an alarming pace. According to the Poverty Site, around 5 million women live in low-income households, and are more likely to be in poor households aged between sixteen and forty-five and then when pensioners. By 2015, almost 7.1 million of the nation's 13 million youngsters will be in homes with incomes judged to be less than the minimum necessary for a decent standard of living; a truly shocking statistic.[9] This does not mean that poorer women do not share in the broadest ambitions for themselves and for their daughters but it does mean, to use another IPPR term, that better-off women are acting as a kind of 'decoy': diverting attention from the widespread and rapid pauperisation of perhaps the majority of their sex.

> Better-off women are acting as a kind of 'decoy': diverting attention from the widespread and rapid pauperisation of perhaps the majority of their sex.

This is a book about young women, viewed through the prism of an older generation. It is about what we pass on, from our personal, political and cultural past, and what we are at risk of losing, if we are not vigilant. At the outset, then, I believe we have a duty, both to ourselves and our daughters, to recall just how far we have come and how fragile all progress is. At a recent cross-generational conference about feminism, one participant made the point that you need to 'curate' a political movement, just as you curate a range of artistic, political or cultural artefacts that have survived from the past.[10] Natasha Walter has observed what she sees as an unhelpful a-historicism among up-and-coming activists:

> I am shocked when I read young feminists today blithely admitting that they don't know what second-wave feminists wrote or being apparently unaware of their history or the way that feminism connects to other philosophies of rights and equality. I worry that young women today – unless they come from a very particular class and background – are not being encouraged to aim high intellectually, to read deeply, and to be earnest and thoughtful if they want to.[11]

The artist Judy Chicago was clearly irritated by parts of Caitlin Moran's best-selling book *How To Be a Woman*. According to Chicago,

'There's a chapter where she says: let's admit it, girls, for the last 100,000 years women have basically done fuck all. I'm like: excuse me?'[12] An understanding of, and interest in, the ideas and struggles of our past is not just a precious resource but a necessary one, particularly in a world of instant reaction and disposable dissent.

So I begin this book insisting on two political truths. First, we must acknowledge and celebrate the slow, halting but definite advance of women's rights and freedoms over the past century, within the relatively wealthy West, and recognise the way in which they have benefited all women to some degree. Kate Middleton's fate may be too confined to be of general relevance, but she will be the first consort of a monarch educated to university level; her daughters will have the same rights of inheritance as her sons. At the same time, a teenage girl born to a poorer family today will have far greater expectations of her own life, in every way, than her grandmother, whether she is supplied with, or can wrest for herself, the means to realise those possibilities.[13]

In Britain, the steady expansion of state schooling since the historic 1944 Education Act, and the increasing numbers of women going into further education have launched successive generations of women into more rewarding paid and professional work and, in its turn, generated higher expectations. Now, in 2013, girls and young women outnumber and out-perform men at every level of education from primary school right up to undergraduate and postgraduate studies. While I will argue that there are different ways of looking at the oversimplified 'girls on top' education narrative, I would never dispute the importance of intellectual development, particularly when one considers the struggle of young women around the world to get even a basic education.

The expansion of paid work has been an equally important, if double-edged, advance. Of course, women have long worked 'outside the home' and, in fact, the boom-time in women's paid labour began in the 1970s and peaked in the 1990s; the rate of expansion of women at work has been slowing down ever since. While we have a lower percentage of women in the workforce in Britain than, say, in France or Denmark, 12 million women went out to work of some kind in 2012 even if the majority of these work in relatively poorly paid, service occupations – call centres, shops, offices, restaurants, in personal beauty or hair care, as cleaners, carers and cooks. For some, their jobs are rewarding and enjoyable. For others, the chance to earn money and to have a life outside home and family represents a more limited kind of liberation.

A large minority of women have risen to well-paid managerial or professional positions: some earn very well indeed. As increasing numbers of young women become more qualified, their progress through the ranks of their chosen professions seems to be more rapid. Many make a big professional impact in their early twenties; in earning terms, this cohort appears to have pulled parallel to their male peers (although we may need, later, to quarrel with these simplistic headlines). But the mood music has undoubtedly changed, over the generations; as one highly successful woman, still only in her late twenties, said to me, 'The biggest change in our lives from that of our mothers is that we can have careers and think of ourselves as feminine. They couldn't. They had to struggle with the idea that this it was possible. It's perfectly normal to us.'

The second truth I will insist on – and here, the story lines inevitably blur and overlap – is that feminism, in all its diverse forms, has changed the world. Steve Biddulph put it rather well. 'Your daughter needs to know she is part of a bigger story; a fight that has been fought on her behalf, long before she was born, and that she needs to keep fighting.' When, on International Women's Day in 2012, writer Linda Grant tweeted a story about how, as a twenty-eight-year-old, in 1979, she could not apply for a store credit card, at a now defunct department store in Canada, unless the form was signed for by her husband or father, she caused a minor explosion on Twitter. Grant wanted to 'remind young women that the rights they take for granted were achieved by those feminists with whom they feel they have nothing in common, rights which did not always exist, even in their own lifetimes.' Her observation was retweeted many times, encouraging reports from others about their own experiences of the 'often casual, low-level, everyday sexism' directed at women, and how they had been treated as second-class citizens over the years. @Rosebudia wrote, 'Earlier than that I wanted a washing machine and I had to sign that my husband or male figure would guarantee my payments.' Carissa Mason noted, 'I know a woman who, just 40–45 years ago, was required to have a man provide consent for her emergency caesarean!' @harrietvde said, 'My mum was a thirty-nine-year-old well-respected journalist on a national newspaper when she married my father and was forced to quit.'[14]

There was a time, not that long ago, when a woman couldn't vote or stand for political office; she could not get a mortgage in her own name, nor be taxed separately from her spouse; if she were ever unlucky enough to get pregnant outside marriage she might have to risk her life in a back street abortion. As recently as the 1960s, in some areas of work, a woman had to give up her job if she married; some women 'passed' for single, in terms of employment, in order to retain a much-needed income. Once upon a time, a woman pilot or political leader or surgeon or film director or newspaper editor or car mechanic was an exotic rarity. (Now she is just a rarity). Feminism fought for equal pay – and equal pay for work of equal value, one of the most radical economic concepts of our time. Feminism fought for more women in local government and Parliament, for the minimum wage, for better childcare, for fairer rape laws. It still does. It is a movement that has transformed our very language, altered the ways we interpret and think and feel about the world. When I think of feminism I think not just of Emmeline Pankhurst or Gloria Steinem but of Rozsika Parker, the art historian and psychotherapist, whose book on maternal ambivalence broke new ground, or of the American literary and political essayists Vivian Gornick or Audre Lorde or contemporary journalists like Kira Cochrane and Tanya Gold. Feminism's voices are vivid and various.

Every woman, whatever her family, whatever her social class, will be able to register the impact of these changes over several generations. My father's mother, Margaret Eadie, born in 1897 to Scottish 'puritan agnostic Humanist' parents, and strong supporters of the Liberal party, was not sent to school until she was seven; this, despite the fact that her father was Head of the English Department at Paisley Grammar

School, and later a Liberal MP. 'Had I been a boy he would have sent me to school early and kept me hard at it, but he had no interest in the education of daughters.'[15] (Her father was also profoundly, if puzzlingly, opposed to women's suffrage.)

Although used to discussing politics and religion at the family dining-table, young Margaret was unable to read or write and 'suffered the indignity of being put with the babies of five years old. I was nearly eight and could hardly squeeze into the little seat.'[16] At fifteen she began to think seriously about her future: 'Did I want a career or a family? In those days hardly any middle-class women contemplated both. It was felt that the two could not be combined without grave risk of strain for a marriage and neglect for the children.'[17] Although a natural scholar with a passion for theological study and discussion, my grand-mother 'chose' marriage; she did not receive a university education nor was she able to become a priest although she spent much of her adult life tenaciously campaigning for women to be admitted to the priest-hood. As the mother of four sons – two of whom died: one in a still-birth, the other, of a broken neck, incurred on his last ever oper-ational flight in the Second World War – she never undertook any paid work. To the last, her role as wife and mother came first.

My own mother, Caroline de Camp, born in 1926, the eldest child of a well-off family from Cincinnati, USA, came to adulthood post war; this was a time in which women's beauty, domesticity and fecundity were prized: a period brilliantly dissected by Betty Friedan in *The Feminine Mystique* and creatively evoked in Mary McCarthy's *The Group* or Sylvia Plath's *The Bell Jar*. My mother completed both an undergraduate degree and a Masters, the latter researched and written when pregnant with her first child, my eldest brother, but there was no serious expectation that she would have a career. Women of this era were not in serious worldly competition with men; and, for many, the price of not exposing their ambition to the outside world meant there was inevitably an air of dabbling, and associated depression, about their 'good works' – resulting in what Simone de Beauvoir scathingly dissects as a form of bad faith in her monumental work *The Second Sex*.[18] (In contrast, several women of my generation have spoken rather more kindly about the thwarted aims and ambi-tions of their own mothers.) My mother was one of the lucky ones.

Her intellectual and work life really took off once we children had left home; she became a respected scholar and campaigner.

Growing up in the sixties and seventies, I was one of the last generation of girls to be schooled at a time when male educational superiority was taken for granted. At the same time, second-wave feminism, led by a generation of educated young women and mothers, gave voice to a brooding sense of existential injustice on a range of personal and political fronts. I was fortunate to have a mother who thought it important to encourage intellectual ambition in girls although there was an unspoken ambiguity about what I might do with my intellect or my education. I expected to work but somehow not to pursue anything as deliberate or apparently arid as a career. It was only in the 1980s, by which time I was in my early twenties, that women in general were encouraged to seek power and high salaries. 'Careers' for women suddenly became not just acceptable but admirable, the chutzpah of this generation matched by the outsize shoulders of the time. Thatcherism encouraged, by example, a cohort of women into the higher ranks of law, finance, the media, and politics. If they were mothers they were deemed, in the soon-to-be exhausted language of that decade, to 'have it all'. The period also enabled the rise of a new generation of working-class girls to a lifestyle, influence and personal wealth that their forebears would only have dreamed of. I had mixed feelings about the 1980s. I admired, and envied, the new refusal of traditional feminine self-denial even as I disdained so much of the 'me first' selfishness of the period.

Looking back, however, I can now grasp some of the salient differences between the life patterns, and choices, of my grandmother, my mother and myself. Firstly, whereas both of them had completed their families by their early thirties (a relatively late age compared to most of their contemporaries) I did not have my first child until I was thirty-seven, and my second at thirty-nine; I also stopped at two, whereas they had larger families. Secondly, although I longed to take time off after both my daughters' births, and was acutely aware of the years that my mother had had 'at home' after the birth of the four of us, I felt I could not afford, in various senses, to drop out of sight, professionally speaking – and so lose all the benefit of my hard work up to that point. So I worked through both my pregnancies, was back at (writing and teaching) work within a short period of the birth of my elder daughter and completed a significant work project about eighteen months after my younger daughter was born. Throughout their early years, I felt as if I was perpetually balancing anxiety, at the prospect of falling behind, with exhaustion, at the effort of keeping up; I preferred to deal with the fatigue than the fear. Thirdly, my partner (who later became my husband) and I have always shared child-related and household tasks. Far from being in the vanguard of social change, as might once have been thought, his willingness to give up full-time work (the classic male career pattern) now appears as more of an exception, a product of a particular political moment – the influence of 1970s feminism on a particular group of egalitarian men – rather than the start of a fundamental shift in men and women's roles. As I argue in Chapter 6, women still carry an unacceptably heavy, yet oddly invisible, domestic – and emotional – load. Yet 'domestic democracy' remains a vital key to the genuine freedom of women.[19]

Nowadays, I look around and think – who will share the load with my daughters? Are today's young men being brought up to see that the work of the home *is* work, a form of labour they should recognise, value and share?

> 'Domestic democracy' remains a vital key to the genuine freedom of women.

When the BBC recently hosted an Expert Women's Day, at which were gathered a range of experts from cosmochemists, nanoscientists and maritime archaeologists, 'women who, between them, had more double firsts, PhDs and awards than Simon Cowell has had Number 1 hits', one of the most striking facts was the number of those admitting to so-called impostor syndrome and questioning whether they were 'expert enough' to warrant a place.[20] According to Professor Frances Ashcroft, who helped discover a pioneering treatment for diabetes, 'Not until I'd published 100 papers did I feel like a scientist. What I've learnt from today is that *many people* feel like that' [my emphasis]. What the BBC day confirmed was that even when approached by broadcasters as experts, it seems that women are 'far more likely to turn them down, often due to lack of confidence and training'.[21]

It's not really *people* though, is it? As the reasons for the 'Expert Day' itself suggested, there's a particular problem for women in confirming and celebrating their work. Why do so many of us – even the manifestly high-achieving ones – end up feeling like frauds? When market research consultant, and part-time doctoral student, Jill Armstrong asked a group of successful career women what they most wanted for their daughters many of them answered 'confidence'. At the same time, some feared that this was the one quality that their daughters did not possess.

I don't find it hard to understand why confidence is so tricky for women, in particular, to feel, or to sustain. Confidence is a slippery, elusive quality: a complex mix of hard-won achievement and a more nebulous spirit of hope and daring. With luck, it grows with age. But I think we are missing an important part of the puzzle if we tell ourselves that, with our children, it is innate, a matter of temperament or even luck. Does it simply emanate from within? Or is it the product of structures of support that help draw out inner resources, support experimentation and confirm further self-sufficiency and competence and creativity: a constant cycle of action, affirmation, encouragement to further efforts and greater boldness? As one of the many dictionary definitions put it, confidence is the 'feeling or belief that one can rely on someone or something; firm trust . . .' Too many young women today cannot claim their necessary portion of support, material or emotional, for reasons that this book explores. And judging from the statistics on income and capital, their material resources often dwindle as they age although their emotional resources may grow, creating an interesting paradox and supplying, as I suggest, some important lessons for younger women.

For now, despite all the rights won and advances made, the bald figures are there before us: reminders of how far we have not come, of the realities our daughters may yet stumble over. Oh – and how well rehearsed are the statistics on unequal pay! The average annual salary for all full-time employees in the UK is £25,900 full time but men earn £28,091, compared to £22,490 for women: a marked difference of 19.9 per cent. (Sadly, percentages never quite manage to get us in the political gut.) Sixty-four per cent of the lowest paid workers are female. Nine out of ten lone parents are women but the median gross weekly pay for male single parents is £346, while for female single parents it is £194.4. Professor Tom Schuller is currently investigating the Paula Principle, asking why women 'tend not to occupy jobs commensurate with their experience, aptitude and raw talent'. On his blog of the same name, he states the problem with an appealing baldness and boldness: 'Most women work below their level of competence.'[22]

> 'Most women work below their level of competence.'
> Tom Schuller

We also know that most women end their lives in relative poverty. What I did *not* know, until I started researching this book, was that half of all women over the age of 50 in the UK work part time and that the majority of them earn less than £10,000 a year or that women in their fifties earn less than women in their thirties.[23] Many professional women see their work, and opportunities, diminish in early middle age. According to one eponymous study by Women in Journalism, *The Lady Vanishes at 45*.[24] Turning to other equally depressing facts: the UK government estimates that an astonishing 80,000 women are raped and 400,000 sexually assaulted in this country every year. One out of three women will be hit by a partner, a figure that makes me scrutinise my neighbours, my friends, and indeed my own history, with a tender, slightly voyeuristic, care.

For all this, could there be some Pollyanna-ish element at work in our collective psyches, some buried hope that the next generation will be the one to gracefully but magically sidestep these profound and persistent structural barriers? After all, so many of today's girls are abrim with the exuberance and plans of youth. We read the constant coverage – much more cheering, this – of the apparently irresistible rise of girls' academic achievements: the headlines in the papers about how women in their twenties may now – or soon – be earning more than men in their twenties. We see that many women postpone motherhood, and take a generally more efficient attitude to the whole childbearing process. I am always passing groups of mothers, exercising, en bloc, with babies in prams, in my local park, led by a scary-looking woman with a whistle. We are inundated with coverage of the Exceptional/Decoy Women, some – the lawyers, bankers,

> We are inundated with coverage of the Exceptional/Decoy Women.

journalists, politicians – the direct heirs of Thatcher's twin-headed revolution (capitalism and individualist feminism). Add to these the formidable academics, head teachers, scientists, architects, sports-women of whom we often read in the newspapers; in terms of salary, status and all round self-possession, these women seem to be flourishing. And then there is the growing army of high-achieving glamorous women in their fifties, sixties and seventies – actresses, political figures, writers – who seem to hold the centre stage effort-lessly – claiming experience as an attractive and bankable asset, just as men have always done.

On every level, then, culture soothes us and raises our hopes. But does it also deceive? Yes and no. Contradiction – the emergence of extremes – achievement and attrition. In terms of the future direc-tion of women's lives, we simply cannot know if things will get a lot better or a lot worse – or perhaps a little of either? Many of the signs are not encouraging. I was struck, during my reading and interviews, by just how many people made note of the new girlifi-cation and sexualisation of childhood and the subtle and catastrophic effects this is having on young women. Senior academic Kate Purcell, co-researcher and author of a key study on graduate experience in the early twenty-first century, was an 'idealistic' young mother in the 1970s, and raised her son and daughter under the influence of ideas of 'non-sexist' childrearing. Like many women who came up through feminism, and saw the changes that it brought, she is convinced of the importance of early socialisation in creating, or holding back, possibilities for girls and boys, 'ideas that push them into one way of being, or distort their development'. She is now a grandmother and says, 'When I go into shops and see the way that young girls' clothes and toys are marketed – the whole pink, girly thing – I am absolutely horrified by how much worse it has become.'

In her recent book *Living Dolls*, Natasha Walter took to task a new wave of scientifically based gender essentialism, with its easy assumptions and underwriting of stifling, conventional norms. So we are told: girls are hard-wired for empathy and therefore more suited to the human complexities of private life; men are hard-wired to build systems, and rule the world. Like Walter, I won't have any of it. History shows us, again and again, that biology has too often been used to invoke social and political ends, be it to underwrite crass racism or brute classism or the suppression of women's public and social talents. The point, it seems to me, is not to find in science or biology where 'essential' masculinity or femininity lies but to identify, build on, and help develop, the latent individual talents of every girl or boy, without prior presumption of either who they are or what they can do.

Linked to that – no news this, either – is the continuing importance of appearance in our daughters' lives and how it spills over into neurosis, excess and illness. Anorexia. Bulimia. The exponential growth in female genital cosmetic surgery including 'vaginal rejuvenation', designer vaginoplasty, G-spot amplification and the horrific-sounding re-virgination. To this, we should now add nipple tattoos (the deliberate darkening of nipples) and thigh gap surgery.[25] A study of nearly 2,500 American women, in 2012, revealed that among the 18–24 age group, two-thirds had totally or partially removed their pubic hair over the previous month and a fifth had been hairless during that entire period.[26] More and more young women are opting for Botox. A vast range of magazines zoom in – literally – on parts of women's bodies. It's as if young women are being broken up into bits before our very eyes, the commercial obsession with surfaces further their diminishment as whole, rounded, multi-dimensional human beings.

> A vast range of magazines zoom in – literally – on parts of women's bodies. It's as if young women are being broken up into bits before our very eyes.

Statistics and moral panics are one thing. But it is only when they become part of a human story that we may grasp what they really mean. Anorexia is a somewhat abstract proposition until a previously happy, healthy teenage daughter takes all evening to eat a piece of toast, both her parents hovering, sick with anxiety, around the kitchen table, to make sure she finishes at least half of it. Violence against women takes on breath and flesh and meaning when it is *your* daughter, coming home, bruised and shaken from an encounter with a boy (or man) she is seeing – all the while steadfastly refusing to acknowledge that there is even a problem.

★

As the mother of two smart, outgoing, teenage girls, I take the paucity of women in public life particularly personally: I am offended by the imbalance, the startling unequal ratios. Just over one in five MPs in Britain are women (although the insult is perhaps better conveyed by saying 4 out of 5 MPs are men: that's some block vote). According to a recent report by Deloitte, 20 per cent of companies in the FTSE 100 have no women in their boardrooms at all and just 5 per cent of executive positions are held by women. (The proportion of women on boards has only increased from a mere 5 per cent to a still mere 9 per cent in ten years.) I had never thought much about street names until BBC *Woman's Hour* did a feature on how few are named after women; it set me ruminating on what impact, if any, it may have (in our collective or individual unconscious) to see our sex rarely marked, let alone honoured, on the roads we walk along every day or when arriving in an unfamiliar place. Recently, I went to speak at Grantham, the birthplace of Margaret Thatcher. I was no fan of Britain's first female Tory Prime Minister but on my way into the town, I asked the taxi driver in what way the town had marked its most famous resident. He presumed I was talking about the scientist Isaac Newton who was also born in the area. After a successful feminist campaign in spring 2013, the Bank of England rescinded its decision to remove the only woman (bar the Queen) on the face of a banknote; nineteenth-century prison reformer Elizabeth Fry is to be replaced by novelist Jane Austen. Female authors have recently protested at the way in which their novels are so much more likely to have a 'girly' cover and be marketed in an un-serious way, leading best-selling author Jodi Picoult to ask recently, 'Why is it "domestic fiction" if a woman writes about family/relationships, but if a man does that, it's Pulitzer-worthy?'[27]

> What impact does it have on our collective or individual unconscious to see our sex rarely marked, let alone honoured, on the roads we walk along every day?

When Kira Cochrane of the *Guardian* surveyed a month's worth of broadsheet and broadcasting coverage, she found that every single major newspaper featured far greater numbers of male voices than female ones. BBC Radio 4's *Today* programme had an astonishing 83.5 per cent of male contributors to just 16.5 per cent of female ones. For any girl who might have been listening to the *Today* programme on Tuesday 5 July 2011, between 6.15 a.m. and 8.20 a.m., she would have caught only one female contributor alongside twenty-seven male contributors: correspondent Rebecca Jones talking about the Hampton Court Palace flower show. In late 2012 *Today* hosted two conversations on consecutive days, about teenage contraception, and breast cancer, featuring men only.[28] In early 2013, writer and activist Marina Cantacuzino analysed a month's worth of 'Thought for the Day', again on *Today*: apparently twenty-two men had thoughts of a moral, spiritual or religious nature deemed worth sharing but only three women. And I thought women were the guardians of emotional and private life!

Of course, once you start on this track, of looking for where other people's daughters are, out there in the world, you can't easily step off it. Female conductors? You'd be lucky to catch one of *those* on a podium: just 1.6 per cent of them are female (and let's just hope that 0.6 per cent is the baton-wielding half). Thinking of going to Glastonbury? There, performances by men outnumber performances by women 6:1. Just 7 per cent of the winners of the BAFTA award for best original or adapted screenplay have ever been women.[29] A parent of daughters then can't help brooding on which comes first: the attention boys get that drives them to out-perform girls, literally, on pretty much every single marker or the range of markers that stake out the possibilities for our daughters before they have even reached adulthood? And quite how, as I come on to ask, does this fit with the endless publicity about females out-performing males at every point from Year 2 to postgraduate degrees?

There is one final question – of a general kind – that I want to raise. It concerns a kind of ethical or emotional absence that is, in part, summed up by the term 'celebrity culture', if we take celebrity culture as a shorthand for empty showiness, an all-pervading status anxiety. I love a lot of popular culture – its wit, speed, irreverence – but I've also tired, as a parent of daughters, of the endless parades of girls on television, in music, in films, who seem to spend a large part of their time honing a 'perfect' body or face (often of a peculiarly orange hue) before hooking up with, or unhooking from, an equally tangerine man, all the while keeping their face in the 'news'. There is surely a posher, high-culture, version too? Sheila Heti has a very funny line in her novel *How Should A Person Be?* in which she says, 'I want to be famous without being famous but for everyone to know that I am famous.' Melanie Strickland, a young lawyer in the charity sector, who became active in the Occupy movement, describes the problem for some of her peers as follows: 'There's this obsession with stuff. It's important for people to have the latest gadget or fashion accessory and to be seen to be keeping up. It's a problem across society, but young people especially who have grown up in a "status anxious" society.'

Sheila Rowbotham accurately pinpoints a 'diffuse but widespread distress which has arisen in response to the recurring short-termism which contemporary capitalism displays towards nature and the environment, human life, work, values, culture and relationships'.[30] When I went to see psychotherapist Susie Orbach, she talked about a 'monosodium glutamate version of happiness'. She named this unease to me, as follows:

> I often see clients who are young, successful and female. They come to me and say, 'I have the flat, the boyfriend, the job. So why do I feel empty?' They mimic the demands of consumer society in which they are encouraged to see themselves as both consumers and producers of an acceptable self.

All these pressures, and assumptions, dangerously narrow the options for our naturally curious and possibly impressionable daughters. One of the slogans of the campaign group All Walks Beyond the Catwalk is 'You can't be what you don't see'. The group's argument is simple and powerful; if when they are growing up girls do not see a wide range of women doing a wide range of things – in life, in magazines, on television – but are instead subject to a dull diet of the same old thin, pretty, girls doing their thin, pretty, thing, then this will limit their imaginations and daring. Southwark councillor and broadcaster Rowenna Davis, twenty-eight,

> . . . used to live in a mixed block and there was a little girl whom I helped with her reading. One day she said to me, 'I want to be a judge.' And I thought that was amazing . . . I could see her, with her wig and her hammer. And then she said, 'Yes I want to be like Cheryl Cole.' Oh – right, I suddenly saw what she meant. *That* kind of judge.

Academic Nina Power berates a new generation (or part of a generation) for managing to reduce even feminism to an activity akin to liking chocolate or sex: a pick 'n' mix sort of politics.[31]

This may be one reason for the recent popularity of a spate of autobiographical books, particularly those exploring personal confusion or celebrating imperfection. We have a collective craving to read about authentic lives, and the full rainbow of experiences and emotions. Utter failure. Crease-up laughter. Undramatic, daily, sibling affection. The vagaries of friendship. Dull parties. The reality of body hair. Dancing, smoking, sex, meandering conversations: the pleasures of . . . Love, arriving out of nowhere. Love, draining away into domesticity. To me, this explains the recent celebration, albeit in very different ways, of works such as Rachel Cusk's dark *Aftermath* (the story of her divorce), Caitlin Moran's super-light *How To Be a Woman*, (a laugh-out loud memoir), and Sheila Heti's dark and light account of twenty-something artistic anxiety, a mix of autobiography and fiction, *How Should a Person Be?*

One definition of parenting is that it involves a continual balancing of the wisdom of experience with the rashness of hope. Optimism of the Will: Pessimism of the Intellect. You will find this mix throughout this book. Each chapter is loosely organised around certain key stages in a young woman's life. In each one, I try to address a familiar question from a different angle, to home in on some unresolved political and cultural issues, and to pose new questions, connections and directions. The first section, *Uneasy Beginnings*, opens with 'Think Yourself Thin', an investigation of the dominant contemporary narratives concerning girls and exam success, and girls and body distress, and attempts to find new connections between them. In 'Name, Shame – and Blame', I explore the new cultural obsession with the pornification of society, finding both sanity and some ominous silences in public concern. 'The Myth of Perfection' grew out of my work on the previous two chapters, reflecting my strong belief that the uncovering and affirmation of girls' voices – emotional and intellectual – is still an important, but very much unfinished, task.

In *Promises, Promises* I go to the main menu of a woman's life; work, sex and love, and motherhood. Obviously, all of these are interconnected, in multiple ways, so I have had to separate them out again, in order to try and make sense of changing patterns. 'Lean In? – Or Lose Out?' questions recent popular assumptions that women in their twenties and early thirties are actually overtaking men, and interrogates the recent arguments of Sheryl Sandberg as to how this work narrative should now develop. 'Love in a Cold Climate' tries to dig beneath both the cheap celebration and conservative concern about a new sexual freedom – and test the state of modern partnerships, as far as women are concerned. In 'The Breakpoint' I try to look at why motherhood is going to become more and more of a shock for women of the future and so make them even more unprepared for the unfair labour that parenthood loads on them; again, I try to suggest a broader way out of the impasse.

In the third section of the book, Rebellions and Resources, I look at how we might facilitate change: in particular, the importance for women of establishing their own personal truths and political priorities. 'How Should a Woman Be?' is a rumination on the issues of anger, ambition and – a bit of fun, this – the age-old problem of male condescension. 'Stand Up and Stand Out' looks at the exponential, but often unheralded, growth in feminist campaigning, as well as changes, and stasis, in mainstream politics.

In many ways, this is a deliberately hybrid work. It draws on a variety of research materials, many interviews, hundreds of conversations, a great deal of reading but also my own experience as a woman, writer, partner, friend, daughter, sister, and, of course, as a mother. It is personal, in places, but never confessional. Rachel Cusk argues,

> As I have grown older, it is experience that has become radical. . . . Sex, marriage, motherhood, work, domesticity: it is through living these things that the politics of being a woman are expressed, and I labour this point because it is important to understand that the individual nature of experience is essentially at odds – or should reserve the right to be – with any public discourse.[32]

I am not so sure. Autobiographical work is one way of tunnelling through to universal truths: it can feel essential and fascinating but it is not necessarily radical. It can gloss over or even divert us from important truths as much as it can illuminate. In a recent lecture on the interrelationship between generations of feminists, Lynne Segal said of the poet Adrienne Rich, whose personal writings are exceptionally powerful,

> Rich became sceptical about some of her earlier visions of feminism, noting 'the uncomfortable fit between the marketing of feminist-sounding solutions to personal problems and a corporate system that mocked collective action as pointless and sterile.' Continuously self-critical, Rich mentioned her own involvement in helping to unleash the 'demon of the personal' in feminist celebrations of women's experience, unaware then of how words of personal liberation could be 'taken hostage' to become what she refers to as a 'horribly commoditized version of humanity'.[33]

Natasha Walter makes the same point, when she explains why she did not use her own experience when writing *Living Dolls*: 'if we are to create a genuine challenge to inequality, we cannot just talk about ourselves.'[34]

To change things, it is vital that we *do* investigate the 'public discourses', to ask questions about more general social and economic patterns and the direction of lives. And we can learn a great deal from doing so. It is only now, in middle age, that I am able to understand that many of the things that seemed 'just to happen' or 'just to be' in my teens and twenties were, in their complex, infinitely subtle, form, part of the prevailing mores of the time; the personal was indeed the political in more ways than I could then grasp.

Similarly, in today's world, where we are constantly told that private choices are just that, I can see, at every turn, the way that the public world shapes the choices – or lack of them – that our daughters face. As one single parent, in intermittent, underpaid part-time work, said to me, 'I think I just made the wrong moves – bad choices – somewhere along the line.' In fact, it was not her 'choice' to bring up her children alone, to adapt her work to the joyful burden of care and to find that work less well-paid because she had to have flexibility in terms of schedules, nor her 'choice' to face numerous ordinary problems in regard to the children that she took sole care of, from a young age. If anything, her problem was that she bought into the 'choices' argument when she was younger and did not insist, or have any means of insisting, on fairer treatment, at various points in her life.

Throughout the book, I try to stay close to some of my deeper themes, too: the importance of the idea of *variety* in relation to what a human and particularly a female life might be: the need for authenticity – that is, attention and respect paid to the inevitable complexity of every existence and recognition of the inevitable difficulty of life (two separate but related questions); a respect for history, in particular the intellectual and political debt we, and our daughters, all owe feminism and more collective ways of thinking through our lives; the need to move beyond self-interest; finally, the importance of getting up and doing things, taking part, trying to change things.

This book is an assessment of where we are now but it also attempts, from time to time, to second guess the shape of things to come. Four factors seem key to the shaping of the future; these permeate the narrative throughout. Firstly, the internet, new technology and all things digital, for all the obvious reasons. But for now a small snippet. The US broadcaster and activist Laura Flanders reminded me that when the activists of Greenham Common, who campaigned against the siting of nuclear weapons on British soil by the American government, first started organising their 'peace camp' and mass actions at the base, in the early 1980s, they contacted other women through chain letters! Jump forward to the Arab spring or virtually any other demonstration you care to think about, and one sees how vital was the role of texting, Twitter and Facebook.

Secondly, everything is being changed, all the time, by the accelerated pace of globalisation: from the instant accessibility of news from around the world to the increased opportunities for travel, to the intensifying of human traffic across continents to the rapid and impressive link-ups of movements of people and protests. Not for nothing is Steve Biddulph considered a 'global author', employing teams of researchers to gather evidence and anecdotes from around the world. TED talks – in which experts in a vast range of topics speak to a chosen audience of globally relevant people, their speeches beamed across the world via the net – are another example of this new, often weirdly context-free, worldwide embrace.

Of course, the shrinking of the world affects the powerful and powerless in diametrically opposed ways. While the wealthy gather in Davos, once a quiet meeting spot for the movers and shakers of the financial and political world and now yet another glitzy, well-publicised (and tweeted upon) international event, the desperate or dragooned of the poorer nations scramble to get into wealthier countries or are smuggled across borders in order to be brutally exploited for their labour or their bodies. Worldwide, it is estimated that somewhere between 700,000 and four million women, children and men are trafficked each year, and no region is unaffected.[35]

One of the most interesting things about globalisation from a gender perspective is that it aggrandises the potential of an exceptional minority. A certain kind of woman now bestrides the globe like a wondrous giantess. Often multilingual, with a life and career built on several continents, such a creature travels and networks widely, consolidating her cultural capital at every turn: women such as Arianna Huffington, founder of the hugely influential *Huffington Post*, born in Greece, educated in England, who then settled in America and became a political power-broker and publisher, or the current head of the International Monetary Fund, Christine Lagarde, who was educated in France and America, and spent much of her early professional life working as a political aide and corporate lawyer in America before moving back to France. There's a feminist version too. Writing of her decades-long friendship with the activist and playwright Eve Ensler, Laura Flanders describes their relationship as follows:

> As the 1990s advanced, Eve drew more into theater, I into journalism. We slept in the streets less and traveled the world more, on criss-crossing tracks; I to Northern Ireland, Central America, Haiti, the Middle East, Croatia, Berlin; she to Berlin, Bosnia, Croatia, Kosovo, Haiti, later Afghanistan.[36]

The Exceptional Woman has a trickle-down effect too. Increasing numbers of students from emerging nations such as India or China will come over to the UK or to the USA to be educated, and launch, or consolidate, their careers in the West. From Russia to Poland, Iran to Europe, professional women of the future are likely to have greater awareness of, and contact with, their peer equivalents from other nations than any generation before them. Several of my interviewees had continent-hopped in their young or not so young lives: one woman I interviewed was born in Australia, grew up in Korea then, after a brief spell living in Japan, spent her twenties in London. Research for this book involved me in a number of across-the-world conversations – as more and more people find their writing and activism touches those at the other end of the globe.

The third factor that will surely have an increasing impact on young women's lives is economic stagnation and austerity. According to a poll conducted by the *Observer* in 2011 almost two-thirds of people (64 per cent) believe that this current generation of children will have a lower standard of living than their parents. In 2010, Yvette Cooper, shadow Home Secretary and one of the Labour Party's most prominent female figures, claimed: 'For the first time we risk seeing the clock turned back. I know I have had more opportunities in life than my mother and grandmother before me. But now for the first time I worry about my daughters.'[37]

Women are in the front line of austerity. In December 2011, the number of women out of work across the country hit a twenty-three-year high of 1.09 million. By February 2012 this had reached a record twenty-five-year high, with women's unemployment up a staggering 18 per cent since the recession began compared to just 1 per cent for men. Women are estimated to make up two-thirds of the public sector workers expected to lose their jobs by 2015. These figures come on top of severe budgets cuts affecting everything from child care costs, benefits, withdrawal of already sparse funding for domestic violence services, and extension of the retirement age. According to Yvette Cooper, 30,000 women have had to give up their jobs in the last year because of lack of childcare.[38] And the pressure on women is only likely to be increased by Big Society emphasis on voluntary and third-sector effort, plugging the gap once state services have been withdrawn.

Anna Bird, of the Fawcett Society, the leading campaign group for women, spoke of

This toxic triple jeopardy [which] is laying waste to women's equality: women typically start off poorer, they tend to earn less, own less, and have less financial security than men. Taking away their jobs, while also cutting their benefits and cancelling the vital services that enable them to juggle jobs with families undermines women's ability to act independently, to provide for themselves, to be financially self-reliant.[39]

Slipping living standards. The struggle to survive. Columnist Suzanne Moore, writing in early 2013, put it more bluntly, 'Everything I wanted for my daughters and yours is being denied them: housing, free education, employment.'

Finally, we have to take account of the renewed rise of feminist protest; in some ways

> 'Everything I wanted for my daughters and yours is being denied them: housing, free education, employment.'
> Suzanne Moore

more discreet, less dramatic, than previous waves of women's liberation, but in other ways more extensive and powerful. I gained an insight into the character of this new wave at three events over the past months. The first, a packed conference looking at the cross-generational impact of feminism, which attracted old and young, black and white, national and international speakers – and many men. The second was, again, a crowded event led by the activist group UK Feminista: a meeting and lobby of the House of Commons on an agreed set of key measures to improve women's lives. Hundreds crammed into a meeting room in Church House, Westminster, to listen to speakers from across the political parties, including Tory MP Amber Rudd, who bravely claimed, to largely good-tempered barracking, that David Cameron's Coalition government was improving the lives of women. Early in 2013, I joined hundreds of men and women outside the Indian High Commission in protest at official inaction in the face of the notorious Delhi rape case. Again, men, women, black, white, black, old, young, mingled on the narrow pavements of the Aldwych.

Time and again, collective action brings in broad groups of individuals, across cultures and countries. The writer and campaigner Selma James has described how a London SlutWalk march in 2011 'was light years ahead of the 1970 women's liberation march, which made way for it. I was at both. Most of the women forty years ago were a bit older and less grassroots than the Slutwalkers . . . there were no wheelchair users in 1970. But last weekend, women with disabilities were an integral part of the protest.'[40] In a letter to the *Guardian*, following a wave of attacks on women such as the Delhi case, the sexual assault of journalists in Egypt, the shooting of Pakistani schoolgirl Malala Yousafzai, a group of public figures headed by Annie Lennox and Elton John declared:

> In the wake of such atrocity, men and women have united to stand for equality and change. We know the support of men and boys is also an important part of the solution, that we're more powerful together. Across the globe, bells have chimed, people have converged in peaceful protest, communities have congregated online and men and women have danced in the street in the name of change. In 2012 the power of the internet and social media gave us an opportunity to unite. This year could provide the moment to act.[41]

And act they did on 14 February 2013, when hundreds and thousands of women – and again, men – around the world, in dozens of cities – Hyderabad, Oakland, Miami, Jerusalem, New Delhi, Khartoum, Hawaii, Manila, Byron Bay, Australia – rose up as part of the One Billion Rising movement against violence against women.[42] There is no reason not to think this kind of protest will continue, down the decades. Who knows what power it will unleash?

When my daughters were young, I longed to give them enough intellectual and emotional battery power, to keep them going through life. When she was only a few months old, I would take my elder daughter out in the pram and tell her stories about everything from the battle for votes for women to the rise of Britain's first woman prime minister. (And she was the first person to text me to tell me that Margaret Thatcher had died.) Like many mothers, I often considered leaving both my girls a letter, or two or twenty, telling them everything I thought they needed to know or that I wanted to pass on. I never did, of course, and have now only a few of the short notes that I wrote when they were younger – each one packed with detailed loving guidance on everything from the importance of getting a good night's sleep to eating enough fresh fruit to the having of fun.

Oddly enough, my accumulated wisdom has been less in demand

during their teenage years. But it is not strange at all: adolescence is, by definition, the process of slow managed separation of parent and child. At the same time, all parents, because they were once children, understand the lasting impact we are likely to have on our offspring, the many ways that our words – and more hauntingly – our deeds live long within our children's lives, for good or ill. My mother died thirteen years ago and yet many of her thoughts and stories remain vivid to me, still providing comfort in times of difficulty. My experience has convinced me that sound judgement is not only one of the most vital human arts but is a skill that can be learned and, in some measure, passed on.

But no mother offers advice without trepidation. I have not forgotten the way I felt, when young, about older people: 'What do they know? And what do they know of what we know?' (Interesting, how one comes to think, when older, much the same about younger people!) But there is, I am afraid, no stopping most mothers, with our blind, primitive urge to defend and improve our children's lives, in whatever way we can, as well, perhaps, as our own need to do something useful with our experience. At a special memorial service for those who died in the 1989 Hillsborough disaster, Everton football club chairman Bill Kenwright said the two greatest words in the English language were 'my mum': testament to the remarkable tenacity and moving endurance of those like Anne Williams who fought for nearly a quarter of a century to find out the truth about what happened to her son that day.

During conversations and interviews for this book, I was struck by the fact that several women, having told me a story about their own experience in a neutral, even passive, tone, would react quite strongly when I asked what they would feel should the same thing happen to their own daughter. It may be that strategies we have long employed to keep ourselves safe, behaviour we have put up with or silences that have become ingrained look not wise, but weak, when we imagine our daughters adopting them.

Following the Delhi rape atrocity, the novelist Sohaila Abdulali wrote in the *New York Times* about her experience of being gang-raped when she was seventeen and her struggle, in the decades that followed, to come to terms with it. I got in touch with her after I read the article, it moved me so much, and we talked about how her story had affected her life, and her politics. One thing she said in that *New York Times* article has stayed with me. 'At 17, I thought the scariest thing that could happen in my life was being hurt and humiliated in such a painful way. At 49, I know I was wrong: the scariest thing is imagining my 11-year-old child being hurt and humiliated.'[43]

Here, then, is a 'tiger mother' mentality I can admire and applaud. Here is a woman drawing on one of the most terrible ordeals anyone could experience as force for both private and public good. It reminds me why I decided to write this book: not just because I believe we need to think about our collective future but because I want to contribute to a new alliance across the generations in order to make real change. This much, we owe our daughters.

# PART I

## Uneasy Beginnings

# I

# Think Yourself Thin

*In which we speculate upon the strange, twisted relationship between the rise and rise of girls' academic achievements and the parallel emergence of a cultural obsession with extreme thinness, and how the theme of female obedience might just link both story lines.*

At some point in the mid 1990s, when I was bundled up with a toddler and new-born baby on the couch in front of Disney videos at dawn, something important was happening out in the world from which I was temporarily, but profoundly, detached. There, upon the billboards, in the shiny pages of the magazines, a new kind of model was born; thin, androgynous, wasted. This was the birth of what was called 'heroin chic', a look signifying the opposite of just about everything I wanted for my own pink-cheeked baby daughters: health, robustness, laughter, freedom from the male gaze. At the same time, another far more positive, if slow building, change within our schools had become consolidated into incontrovertible truth. Girls were now the new high achievers in British society; their lead in GCSE results (exams taken at sixteen) was now so well established as to confirm it as a long-term shift. Soon, they would overtake boys at every stage of education from reception class to postgraduate degrees.

This, then, was the world my daughters were born into and would grow up in, a world shaped by two distinct narratives that are (now) both so well aired as to have passed into mainstream common sense but that, taken together, don't quite add up or, at the very least, beg a great many further questions. No matter: both story lines continue to make great copy – including visual copy – as stories about girls always do. Pretty girls suffering: pretty girls celebrating; they're still young, pretty girls. One story line does not begin or end with heroin chic; rather, it is that image, of a dwindling female frame, and the associated idea that this is how a girl should be, that stands at the symbolic heart of a grim modern fairy tale concerning the exponential rise in eating disorders and self-harm in young women today, often leading to long-term damage to body and soul. By contrast the other story line is an apparently heartwarming tale of a nation of hard-working Cinderellas finally made good as, in educational terms at least, today's adolescent girls soar past successive generations of increasingly marginalised and middling boys.

Of course, neither narrative – nor indeed, both – adequately captures the complex reality of most teenage lives, lived in far greater balance, vibrancy and ordinary contentment than suits a theme-voracious media.[1] Even so, I can clearly recognise the direct and more subtle impact of these entwined stories on my own daughters' upbringing, and the ways they have shaped the lives of their own, and subsequent, generations now emerging into young adulthood. At their most worrying, they risk presenting our daughters with frighteningly mixed messages about what is required of them, right with them, wrong with them.

Is there anything but praise and pride to be offered in terms of Story Line One, the apparent unstoppable rise in girls' educational achievement, as measured by both academic results and levels of participation: the so-called 'gender cross-over'? Current major changes planned to GCSE and A-level examinations in England may make a dent in this unbroken story of female success but it is unlikely to put the story of endless female improvement in the last two or three decades into reverse: nor does it detract from extraordinary gains that girls have made, academically speaking, over this same period.

Even for someone, like me, schooled in the 1960s and 1970s, the scale of the revolution in terms of expectations of girls is astonishing and generally heartening. Miriam David, an expert in gender and education, describes the long-term shift in Britain, as follows: 'If you look at the Robbins report of 1963 you find in there a clear reflection of the idea that to give a girl an education was to give her a "negative dowry". That education would not serve her well in terms of what society later expected of her.' What made the difference, David says, is feminist pressure over a sustained period, which helped to close the gender gap in schools between the 1970s and the 1990s. 'The education of girls became one of the key issues considered by Equal Opportunities Commission set up under the Sex Discrimination Act of 1975. Studies done by the EOC found very clearly that while, in some senses, girls were doing very well they were also being excluded from educational opportunities.' Seminal work was done by feminists on everything from inherent prejudice against girls in the classroom to a masculine bias in maths.[2]

What's extraordinary is the way that girls have continued to make gains at every level of schooling. Girls have now overtaken boys in almost every subject, at GCSE and A level, and have far higher rates of participation in undergraduate and postgraduate courses. And even when they are in work, they take up more chances to gain further qualifications and further their professional development. Tom Schuller has recently collated all the evidence on women's educational performance. He has found that 'Girls have been doing better than boys at school for quite a long time. In school tests for ages seven, eleven and fourteen (the latter now phased out), girls have been out-performing boys across all three areas of English, Maths and Science for the last dozen years or more.' Boys have narrowed the gap between the genders in some subjects, such as English at the end of primary school, but the gaps are still large, particularly in English in secondary school tests.

> Girls have now overtaken boys in almost every subject, at GCSE and A level, and have far higher rates of participation in undergraduate and postgraduate courses. And even when they are in work, they take up more chances to gain further qualifications and further their professional development.

This early lead is consolidated in results in public examinations. Since the late 1980s, girls have outperformed boys on the 'threshold' measure of five A–C GCSEs and, in subsequent years, the gap has increased and become stable at around a 10 per cent point difference, with little variation since 1995. According to a Department of Education document, 'While girls had long outperformed boys in the arts, humanities and religious studies, they now established a lead in mathematics, were creeping ahead in geography, and even in history (a subject where there has been "fluctuation") girls now outperformed boys.' Girls also sweep greater numbers of top – A star – grades in GCSEs while boys 'are a little more likely to gain a G grade'. This pattern has continued into A levels, girls outperforming boys in significant ways here, with boys gaining a little ground in terms of A stars in recent years; in 2011, the percentage of boys and girls gaining A stars in 2011 was 8.2 but, in absolute numbers, girls gain far more A stars, and if you take A and A stars together, 29 per cent of girls achieve this figure, compared to just over 26 per cent of boys. And once again, boys take a larger percentage of the lower grades.

Women are not just enrolling in greater numbers in higher and further education: they are doing so at elite universities. Women have overtaken men, by a substantial margin, at both first degree and Masters level, at these institutions. According to the latest figures, British women are applying to universities in even higher numbers than their male peers. Applications to universities have fallen overall, with the introduction of higher fees. This has exacerbated the long-standing gap between males and females. The fall in the numbers of young men applying now stands at about twice that of younger women: with entry rates for both at 24.6 per cent and 32.5 per cent respectively.[3] Just 30 per cent of male school-leavers applied to university in 2012, compared with 40 per cent of their female counterparts, according to UCAS (the Universities and Colleges Admission System).[4]

Higher rates of enrolment have led, in turn, to women outperforming men here too, with more women achieving a 2.1 or higher: the so-called top degree now considered an essential passport to most forms of graduate employment. In Britain, nearly 30,000 more women than men leave higher education every year with a qualification that will enable them – in theory, at least – to get a job. More women are now enrolled in full-time postgraduate education, particularly at part-time level. The figures for 2011/12 confirm that the female/male gap at Masters level has increased very sharply. For 2010 the gap in women's favour was 11 per

> In Britain, nearly 30,000 more women than men leave higher education every year with a qualification that will enable them – in theory, at least – to get a job.

cent; for 2012 it was 17 per cent: that is, 40,334 women taking a Masters degree compared to 33,577 men.[5] As Tom Schuller observes,

> This is a really major widening of the gap, at the level at which people increasingly jump off into high grade professional lives. Far more women than men are about to graduate from Britain's elite universities qualified to this key Master's level. And, once in work, women are also more likely to pursue further qualifications . . . To revert to the ungraceful language of economics, at the upper end of the human capital market women now dominate.

And this is a trend that has been repeated across the OECD countries over the past decades.

Critics of modern education, at school level but increasingly at university level too, point to the growingly mechanistic nature of modern education in which testing, data and other forms of measurement play an ever bigger part in deciding the value of an institution and individual. According to former education journalist Hilary Wilce, universities and schools are increasingly raising 'the alarm about how today's "satnav" students now seemed less able to think for themselves or manage their lives':

> A toxic combination of teaching to the test at school and parents hovering over their lives at home, was starting to mean that even those headed for the most prestigious universities in the world were proving to be as helpless as babies when they first found themselves fending for themselves.[6]

'The essence of being a good child is taking on the perspective of those who are more powerful than you,' writes Carolyn Steedman in her wonderful not-quite-autobiography, *Landscape for a Good Woman*. By today's standards, a successful student will be one that learns how to imbibe large amounts of knowledge, and can regurgitate it in the required forms; and it could be that this kind of approach suits girls more than boys. One English mother, watching her quick-witted daughter approach GCSEs, described the process to me as follows:

> Without ever discussing it with me, she methodically went through every syllabus for every course she was studying and discovered exactly

what the 'assessment objectives' of each relevant unit were, what ground they covered and exactly how they would be marked. Not surprisingly she came out with 100 per cent in a lot of her exams. It was very impressive, in its way, but I have to admit that, knowing that she possessed this capability, which counts for a lot, I am always delighted – and relieved – when she comes home at the end of the day bursting with enthusiasm or irritation at a debate she has had in class – usually about some finer point of modern history. It's a much better way to learn surely – by arguing different points of view, taking up a position, changing your mind and so on? I want her to have *fun* rather than to think of education as something coldly and efficiently executed or a, hurdle to be got over in order to consider herself a success.

Another reason put forward for girls' extraordinary rise up the English educational league tables has been the prevalence of coursework which rewards not just those children with parents who can 'help' (usually but not exclusively middle-class girls and boys) but the kind of hard slog that keen-to-achieve girls, in particular, are often prepared to put in. When coursework was scrapped from maths GCSE in the late 2000s, boys came out on top in exam results for the first time in a decade and are still fractionally ahead. In 2010, coursework was replaced by controlled assessments – basically, coursework done in class, under supervised conditions – but this innovation will be dropped with the reform of GCSEs, that will now be taken all at once, with no modules or re-sits possible, at the end of Year 11. This reform – one among a mass of changes introduced, often hastily and without due consultation with the teaching profession, by the Coalition government since 2010 – will undoubtedly pile on the pressure, particularly for conscientious or anxious girls. However, informal early soundings taken from experts in education suggest that adolescent girls will conquer these new demands with relative ease.

Does the exam success of girls make them 'on top' in all respects, during adolescence? Of course not; as we shall see, the power balance between the sexes in the teenage years – within classrooms, social settings, on the internet, not to mention more intimate spaces and places – is as tricky and temperamental, and as mediated by class, temperament and cultural difference, as ever. But the powerful sense of girls' competence – confirmed by league tables, encouraged by teachers, celebrated by newspapers – has shaped a generation of young women in interesting and positive ways. It has revised, and reversed, centuries-long assumptions of how girls should defer to men, on the intellectual front. In her major study of femaleness *The Second Sex*, written in the middle of the twentieth century, Simone de Beauvoir observed that in adolescence girls 'must give up *emerging* beyond what is given and asserting themselves *above* other people'.

> The powerful sense of girls' competence – confirmed by league tables, encouraged by teachers, celebrated by newspapers – has shaped a generation of young women in interesting and positive ways.

Look where we are now. In many respects, girls *have* emerged; they *are* often deemed 'above' other people. Well, above boys. And that has a knock-on effect. Exam success is a form of pre-preparation for all kinds of jobs of work and worldly success. It shows girls how achievement is, so often, a one-foot-in-front-of-another kind of business, rather than a vague abstract glory that can be dreamed into being. In a wonderful essay on what early feminism gave her, the American writer Vivian Gornick described how, at a key moment in her life, she gave up the romance of love for the romance of work: the classic path of the clever woman.[7] But, as Gornick persuasively argues, she soon fell into an equally unproductive vacuum, for she came to realise that work was no more 'romantic' than romance itself; it was not an abstract idea that could replace obsessing over a man. It was, instead, a moment-by-moment grind with long periods of unproductiveness, many small and large failures, and endless revisions.

My point is: girls today are well placed to understand this early on. Slog is not – quite – all, but it is the bedrock beneath many a triumph; step-by-step effort might lead to a kind of conquest. To know that you can actually win, be the best at something, even in subjects traditionally colonised by boys, is very satisfying. For high-achieving girls in mixed-sex schools, individual success at exams – or tests in general – provides a useful early lesson in the limits of male *braggadocio*. Girls report how months or years

> Girls report how months or years of boys' patronage or disdain is quietly undercut on results days.

of boys' patronage or disdain is quietly undercut on results days. The boys are more likely to march out of exams yawning how 'easy' it was while the girls reflect anxiously on their performance in the exam room. So that moment of exam results reckoning sets down a useful template for the future, as each briefly grasps the felt meaning of the difference between arrogance and confidence.

Success breeds success. It is easier to tell girls who have done well that intellectual development matters, and that they should keep working at it individually and collectively; a collaborative approach which can further reinforce their performance. Many parents report, if with slightly amused suspicion, the way that girls revise together before exams. Tom Schuller is the father of two daughters, and believes:

> Girls help each other more than boys to do the necessary at school. Take teenagers doing homework. My experience is that girls will call or text each other in the evening, partly to chat about fashion, music, boys and so on, but also to sort out what they think needs to be done for school. This just does not happen for boys to anything like the same extent. It's not just about pooling ideas and helping each other on specific tasks; it's also about saying to each other that school-work is something which matters – even though it may be a drag, and may not be the most important thing. So girls far more than boys reinforce for each other the value of education, and that pays off for them individually and collectively. Female social capital – communicating about norms and values to achieve shared objectives – generates higher female human capital.

This unofficial mentoring continues to be an important element throughout young women's lives – in further education and beyond, into the world of work.

Access to greater educational opportunity may also keep some girls safe, if it deflects pressure from boys to get entangled in potentially threatening or dangerous relationships. A major UK study from the National Society for the Prevention of Cruelty to Children (NSPCC) and Bristol University analysed what factors made girls vulnerable to emotional and sexual pressures. It found that 'providing an opportunity to focus on more long-term goals . . . may subsequently offer some protection against factors that may impede this ambition, including violence and controlling partners. This supposition is supported in interviews with girls who had not experienced any form of partner violence. For many of these girls their priority centred on their education and longer-term career aspirations. Most felt that their education was more important than having a serious boyfriend. Thus, although most had been in a relationship at some point, this was viewed as significantly less important than their education. This provided protection against experiencing partner violence, not simply as they had fewer relationships, but because the ones they did enter were less serious. They also clearly stated that they were likely to terminate a relationship if any concerns arose due to the potential impact this may have had on their educational aspirations.'[8]

For all this, I think we should be careful in Britain about attributing too much to recent developments or misjudging the superficial brightness of this educational picture. Firstly, we are clearly talking about some girls, not all. There is certainly still a strong class element at work in education, even if determined individuals can buck the difficulties of a particular background. The benefit tends to go to girls in selective and private education or from more affluent homes to begin with than to girls – or boys – in poorer backgrounds and schools: an idea I explore in more detail in the next chapter. When the Equality and Human Rights Commission did a major survey of girls aged 14–18 years old they found a depressing lack of self-belief among working-class girls. According to Trevor Phillips, former head of the EHRC,

The majority of young women who come from working-class backgrounds believe they will fail. They believe the best they can do is to be a hairdresser or work in one of the three Cs: catering, childcare or cleaning. These are proper careers and I don't want to do them down. The problem is we have a society where young girls who aren't from well-off professional families can't see themselves as successful in anything but a limited range of jobs Within education and careers services, the expectations for these girls are pretty low. Even well-meaning teachers and careers advisers are saying, 'You could be a very good hairdresser.' They should be saying, 'Why don't you want to be a doctor or lawyer?' It's wrong if girls are told they can only do certain things.[9]

> 'The majority of young women who come from working-class backgrounds believe they will fail.'
> Trevor Phillips

At the same time, there is a definite downside to our test-obsessed culture for both boys and girls, if in different ways. For girls, the problem is that it can put intolerable pressure on them to be intellectually conscientious rather than bold and innovative. It may also conceal, as I argue in the next chapter, their lack of confidence and openness in other areas. Indeed, following the drastic fall in the number of applications received from young men to British universities, the relative failure of white working-class boys within our education system has become a new target of concern, including among senior politicians.[10] For now, Miriam David's perceptions seem apt:

> The rise in educational achievement has been a limited success story. What we have done is give everybody more education, but class and ethnic difference remain. Everyone may achieve more qualifications than they did a generation ago but they will all end up in roughly the same position within the given educational hierarchy.

Enter Story Line Two: a narrative that has also been building and banking in western culture for decades and has, too, more general application beyond the UK. Only this is a story about bodies – not brains. In the early 1990s, the American Association of University Women undertook 'the most extensive national survey on gender and self-esteem ever conducted' asking questions of 3,000 boys and girls between the ages of nine and fifteen on their attitudes towards self, school, family and friends. According to the journalist Peggy Orenstein, the results 'confirmed something that many women already knew too well. For a girl, the passage into adolescence is not just marked by the menarche or a few new curves. It is marked by a loss of confidence in herself and her abilities . . . and a scathingly critical attitude towards her body and a blossoming sense of personal inadequacy.'[11]

'For a girl, the passage into adolescence is not just marked by the menarche or a few new curves. It is marked by a loss of confidence in herself and her abilities'
Peggy Orenstein

We cannot say if this 'blossoming sense of personal inadequacy' preceded or reflected the rise of a new kind of body type. But it was during this period that heroin chic emerged: a starved, smudged-eye, look of available derangement. Androgyny was the new name of the game, including the chiselling away of curves to raw, jutting bone. But frailty was at the heart of it. Kate Williams of Mumsnet, Britain's leading online parents' discussion forum, described the new female of this period rather brilliantly to me as 'like a kind of faun, fracturable and droopy'. The journalist and TV presenter Caryn Franklin saw it in more clear-eyed industry terms:

> Fashion became more and more focused on this one body ideal. At least with supermodels, during the 1990s, there was some individuality there and more womanly figures . . . women like Cindy Crawford, but from about this time, the 1990s onwards, models began to shrink in size and age. It was not about robust, proactive femininity . . . but all about passive, wan, girlish adolescent energy . . . models began to have less personality.

Less personality? Never good news for women.

This process of downsizing, or cutting down to size, was deftly analysed in a thoughtful feature by journalist Polly Vernon in upmarket women's magazine *Grazia* in mid 2012. 'Have we become size-blind?' asks Vernon, who admits during the course of the feature that as a size 6, she was ahead of the curve – pardon the pun, here – in first enjoying a super skinny body. In the piece, she compares the body of actress Kate Winslet – aged twenty-one in 1997, at the time she made the blockbuster *Titanic* – to the ideal image of womanhood in 2012. Talking of Winslet's 1997 body she observes:

> It's, well – bigger. Winslet's old body curves, it slopes, it undulates . . . from some angles, it actually looks . . . chunky. Her 1997 upper arms are not toned and tautly slender, they're unaltered, possibly (gasp) un-worked out, and her 1997 belly is – well, just that. A (small, girlish, but undeniable) belly! Winslet was perhaps a UK dress size 10 – maybe a 12 – when she took on the role of Rose, and while that didn't seem like a big deal at the time, it would be *borderline astonishing now*. At some point over the last 15 years we have gone 'size blind'. We've lost any reasonable idea of what constitutes fat, curvy, slim and thin . . . Now we can only really accept some variation on incredibly skinny. It's as if we've developed visual anorexia; we see extremely skinny girls on TV but they look normal to us. We see normal girls . . . and we think they're big.[12] [My emphasis.]

Vernon's argument was alarming but plausible, its message visibly underscored by her own picture by-line showing an attractive, feminine woman, androgynous in style and super lean. Looking at Vernon, a real woman, who embodies a new ideal, I realise that one sees this sort of person everywhere in fashionable urban spaces and places: young – or young middle-aged – men and women in skinny jeans and well-cut jackets. 'Frail', 'Fracturable', 'Shrinking', 'Super skinny'. They fill art galleries and cinemas and newspaper and TV production offices with their self-denying and hungry silhouettes – but hungry for what exactly? Even the subsequent rise of *Mad Men* style curves has not diminished the ubiquity or popularity of this particular prototype. She – and occasionally he – is there in girls' and women's magazines, in which everything from style to sex to self-improvement has stepped up a notch or ten in the years since I was a regular reader of such publications. It is not just that the whole parade seems more relentless, making me feel at times as if I am caught on a fast-whirling gaudy carousel. The camera itself seems to have moved in closer, as if it can longer keep its distance. 'Fit to flab or wobbly to toned. *Now* brings you all the new showbiz body shocks.' There are cruel shots of double chins; 'booze bloats'; emaciated rib cages, endless befores and afters of leopard-skin clad thighs. (As my younger daughter acutely observed, looking at a particularly crude photo-spread over my shoulder, 'It's as if every woman in those things is either two stone too thin or two stone too fat. Whatever it is, she is in the *wrong*.') Certainly, the body, rather than a person who inhabits a body, has taken centre stage, robbed of its connection to character or circumstance; subject to relentless, obsessive scrutiny. In fact, the camera – or its metaphorical equivalent – has gone in even closer; now it zooms in, and stays, on body parts. 'Cheryl's Hot Booty' – 'Return of the Curves'. 'I'm happy with my small boobs'. 'A bum lift has finally made me happy'. (Except it hasn't – quite.) 'Coleen's flat tum body blitz'. As philosopher Nina Power fiercely notes,

> 'It's as if every woman . . . is either two stone too thin or two stone two fat. Whatever it is, she is in the *wrong*.'

All of this marks a very serious transformation in the relationship between women and their bodies. Far from flaunting their assets in the hope that the refracted attention will filter back to their person as a whole . . . it is the 'assets', the parts, that take on the function of the whole. The all-pervasive peepshow segmentarity of contemporary culture demands that women treat their breasts as wholly separate entities, with little or no connection to themselves, their personality, or even the rest of their body.[13]

It is not uncommon in these magazines to have a woman talk in the following slightly crazy way about herself:

I have a bit of cellulite, which I'm not too stressed about. I'm actually noticing my wrinkles more lately. Some friends have been getting Botox and I can't help feeling tempted now I'm nearly 30 . . . I know my body isn't perfect and if I scrutinise it hard enough I'll always find something wrong – *but I feel comfortable in my own skin*. [My emphasis.]

As if. There are endless references to surgical intervention; botox and liposuction, implants and bum lifts – pretty much unheard of, even a decade ago. Back then, it was the exceptional, eccentric practice of the super-rich or the super-famous. Now it is part of the repertoire of the ordinary, if, desperate (but 'hey I'm not desperate, I feel good about myself') woman. No surprise then that teenagers talk about bits of their bodies with astonishing specificity and contempt. 'I *hate* my thighs,' says a fifteen-year-old with the passion one should really reserve for a personal enemy. 'I've got a big ribcage,' says another, with the solemnity of a scientist taking an objective measurement. But then, I remember this same kind of self-scrutiny at that age; it went with the overwhelming self-consciousness of teenage years. The only difference back then? There simply weren't as many ways of encouraging and exaggerating it.

So here we are, at the portal of Story Line Two: The Battle for Thinness as a Cultural Problem or how Girls Got Downsized – and in an age when obesity is increasingly the real social problem. The only consolation in the thin epidemic is that there is now a widespread sense of mass emergency. The problem has become official. The authorities are alerted to it. We know what is wrong, even if we don't know what to do. Awareness of eating disorders, statistics on this same problem, commentary on the multiple issues around size and self (plummeting weight, plummeting confidence) has moved from intense, politicised feminist sidelines to mainstream discussion. It is striking, in fact, this industry of worry that has grown up around girls and weight. It can feel, in a surreal way, as if it is, itself, an adjunct of the food or fizzy drinks industry, part of some vast plot to have it all ways at once. Capitalism, after all, markets a certain look: it markets good and bad foods; it markets self-denial; so why not market the analysis and the solution as well?

Of course, each of us will judge the meaning, and impact, of the super-skinny, high-anxiety distress differently depending on our own experience. For many the danger feels akin to those of foreign wars; the thunder is worrying but it is pretty far away. For others, as I have said, the nightmare can become personal; it invades their house, their family, their sleep, their every conversation. For one mother whose daughter became anorexic at fourteen, and then tried, within months, to commit suicide, the questions are still there. 'Why this form of rebellion? Why this wish to strip herself right down to her bones? If I'd been asked how she would rebel, I'd have had her down as reckless, expressing it through drink and drugs, not through starving and cutting herself.' Her daughter had done her own exaggerated version of a 'Kate Winslet': a lush, curvaceous young woman melting away before her family and community's eyes, her angry bones revealed. In the crazy months that followed, her mother melted away to dangerous skinniness too. It often happens.

There is no limit to the official figures that show us the crisis we're in – and its ever-extending reach. A recent survey showed that the majority of young and old women admit eating in secret which strongly suggests that eating itself is felt to be some kind of aberrant behaviour. And a UK all-party parliamentary group, reporting in May 2012, declared in its anodyne official way that 'body image dissatisfaction is high and on the increase and is associated with a number of damaging consequences for health and wellbeing. Around a half of girls and up to one-third of boys have dieted to lose weight.' Statistics released from thirty-five NHS hospitals, in May 2011, hinted at the worrying new reach of the issue, indicating that more than 2,000 children had received treatment for eating disorders in the previous three years. Of these, six hundred were hospitalised when their weight fell to dangerous levels. This, in turn, confirmed the findings of a study conducted by experts from the Institute for Child Health at University College London, that about three in every 100,000 children under the age of thirteen in the UK and Ireland have some sort of eating disorder. There is an alarming growth of incidents of anorexia among young males.[14]

On the face of it, we are looking at a global phenomenon: a crisis of enduring power and proportions. An Australian website confidently asserts:

> Eating disorders are estimated to affect 9% of the Australian popula-
> tion – therefore more than 2 million people are estimated to be
> experiencing an eaten disorder . . . Approximately 15% of women
> experience an eating disorder at some point during their lives. An
> estimated 20% of females have an undiagnosed eating disorder. Younger
> adolescents tend to present with Anorexia, while older adolescents
> may present with either Bulimia or Anorexia. Eating disorders are
> the third most common chronic illness in young females.[15]

The US 'Alliance for Eating Disorders Awareness' which lists an alarmingly rich variety of eating malfunctions, including Orthorexia, Bigorexia, Body Dysmorphic Disorder, and Night Eating Syndrome, asserts that 'Eating disorders currently affect approximately 25 million Americans, in which approximately 25% are male. Anorexia has the highest mortality rate among all psychological disorders.'

There is, of course, a big difference between a woman – or girl – who diets on and off all her life – and the evidence suggests that most do – and an anorexic who starves herself, risking health and threatening her own life. Or is there? According to the therapist and writer Susie Orbach, the problem is much deeper and begins much earlier, than statistics and surveys convey:

> Problems that might have been sub-clinical are now considered normal.
> Take any year group of 160 girls. Ten per cent will have a really
> serious eating disorder. God knows how many have been cutting
> themselves and throwing up or not eating in the week but at the
> weekend. Even with my daughter's year at school there wasn't one
> girl who ate when they were hungry and who stopped when they

were full. When I do a workshop with girls and I ask them who feels OK about their body and their eating the basic stance of everyone is critical. Their eating is disturbed – and I believe it has been from the time they were babies. It's a generational legacy which is now reproducing unstable bodies. It is passed down. Women whose bodies are assaulted consistently come to mothering with conflicts, confusions and often distress about their own bodies. They want to give their daughters (and their sons) the best they can but inadvertently their own destabilised bodies are passed on to them.

How then, might we piece together these two story lines, triumph and disaster, and treat these two impostors both the same?

On the face of it, the super-skinny, couldn't-give-a-toss, blank-stared girl could not be more different from the keen, eager-to-please girl teen, poring over her revision timetables or her exam papers. Yet a number of connections, or questions, immediately present themselves.

Firstly, should we view the rise and rise of cultural attention to the weight and bodies of girls as a form of complex backlash, a long-running, low-grade, mean-minded sort of punishment of – as well as a means of keeping in check – the parallel rise in their intellectual achievements? It makes a cold and crazy sense. As their achievements grow, their bodies (have to) diminish. Caryn Franklin sees it like that. Dieting is a 'potent, political sedative. Worrying about what's on her plate, they don't look out at the world beyond. As women have started achieving academically, where does this lead? So, let's hold them back.' And maybe the men grasp that too, if in a different way. In a recent angry article about the British online magazine *Uni Lad* Rhiannon Lucy Cosslett writes:

> Should we view the rise and rise of cultural attention to the weight and bodies of girls as a form of complex backlash, a long-running, low-grade, mean-minded sort of punishment of – as well as a means of keeping in check – the parallel rise in their intellectual achievements?

In a society where women are excelling more and more academically, these privileged young men are asking their readers to conform to a vision of masculinity that is practically Stone Age, and rather than resorting to 'boys will be boys' it's high time we start asking why they seem so keen on dragging women back into the caves of the past, just as their futures have started to seem so promising.

Cosslett notes that much of this misogyny comes from well-educated middle-class boys who use language and imagery that would shock their nice middle-class families.[16]

Certainly, history teaches us that each time women pose a serious challenge to power, there is counter-cultural reaction or more direct political reaction. The long years of battling for the vote gave way to the light-hearted flapper. The involvement of women in heavy industry and the economy in general during the Second World War did not result in increased employment rights post war, but a widespread cult of domesticity and the rise

> History teaches us that each time women pose a serious challenge to power, there is counter-cultural reaction or more direct political reaction.

of the housewife and 'the problem that has no name' – domestic boredom and intellectual passivity. Second-wave feminism with its complex connections forged between women's oppression and class inequalities was followed by a harsh, having-it-all post-feminism and then by the return of the loud-mouthed girl – the ladette? – and, in general, the unstoppable rise of individualist, rather than collective, approaches to the problems of women in our economy and society.

So it makes sense. As girls step out, literally, into the limelight; as they learn and earn more than ever before, what more useful weapon to defend a once set-in-stone masculine superiority is there than to ratchet up concern about their appearance on a daily basis? Recently Fraser Nelson, the editor of *The Spectator*, spoke – with or without irony, it really doesn't matter – of his concern that his two sons might suffer from the indignity of 'erectile dysfunction' in the face of newly powerful graduate woman. What better way to keep the smart girl down than have her obsessing over her weight or worrying that she is never quite pretty enough? As Mary Pipher, the wise and thoughtful American therapist, put it, 'Girls lose IQ points as they become feminised.' A number of studies have found a clear correlation between the sexualising of girls and a loss of confidence in their own intellectual capacities.[17]

The reverse may also be true: that some girls are forced to seek a more feminine, or sexual, identity, as alternative avenues for self-development and paid work are limited. If, as I have argued, working-class girls are offered fewer opportunities within the current educational hierarchy (although more opportunity than they once would have had) the appearance-obsessed, sexualised wider culture may have a disproportionately greater influence on them – and offer a dangerous new role. Some working-class girls may turn more readily to forms of sex work or self-display in order to earn money or a sense of self, an issue that Natasha Walter explores in *Living Dolls*. Looking at the glamour modelling industry, she observes:

> Other people in the industry also admit that many of the women who set out into this industry may have few other routes in front of them which they feel will lead to any equivalent success. As Phil Hilton (editor of *Nuts* magazine) said to me at one point: 'In reality, if you're a young working-class woman from the provinces who sends your pictures into these magazines, you're not likely to become incredibly successful . . .' The mainstreaming of the sex industry has coincided with a point in history when there is much less social mobility than in previous generations. No wonder, then, if the ideal that the sex industry pushes – that status can be won by any woman if she is prepared to flaunt her body – is now finding fertile ground among many young women who, as Phil Hilton says, would never imagine a career in, say, politics.[18]

But excessive body anxiety also has a preventative, self-limiting, function, particularly for clever middle-class girls who have more options and choices. Displacing worry about life – its freedoms, its risks, its very possibilities – onto the body, can have a twisted kind of logic. I have read enough accounts of anorexia to understand it is often the blight of highly intelligent girls who have not yet figured out the simple–complex question of how to be themselves. Anorexia, after all, is a way of channelling a formidable organising capacity, only one turns the power inwards, until that terrible point where the distress takes on a life of its own, and the body, in crisis mode, sets up its own potentially deathly rules.

There's a vibrant passage in *The Beauty Myth* by Naomi Wolf (a former anorexic) in which she describes the function of self-starvation in her case, and riffs about what she might have done if she had not spent her time counting calories and trying to keep warm.

> What if she (the young woman) doesn't worry about her body and eats enough for all the growing she has to do? She might rip her stockings and slam-dance on a forged ID to see the Pogues, and walk home barefoot, holding her shoes, alone at dawn; she might baby sit in a battered-women's shelter once a month; she might skateboard down Lombard Street with its seven hairpin turns or fall in love with her best friend and do something about it, or lose herself for hours gazing into test tubes with her hair a mess, or climb a promontory with the girls and get drunk at the top, or sit down when the Pledge of Allegiance says stand, or hop a freight train, or take lovers without telling her last name, or run away to sea.[19]

Drinking while *rock climbing*? The mother in me shies away from such a crazy idea. (And as for those seven hairpin turns on Lombard Street!) But Wolf is right. To spend one's time preening over straight hair, producing the right kind of pout, in place of exploring ideas, places, other disciplines, is to limit one's intellectual and practical self to an absurd and depressing degree; and this is happening to too many of our girls, despite all the advances we have made. One mother whom I interviewed in my research for this book about her daughter's growing eating problems found the incipient anorexia checked, only to be replaced by what she perceived as 'reckless' behaviour. Her daughter had given up giving up food, and grabbed her freedoms instead. More mother-worry, obviously, but I took it as a definite sign of progress.

It may go against every bit of contemporary conventional rhetoric but the theme of female obedience, deference to external norms, can still be perceived − as faint but as definite as the sugar-pink line running through a stick of rock − in the lives of middle-class young women today. Looking good which means looking thin: being clever which means getting good exam results. To achieve these 'measures' is above all to be doing what one is told to do, conforming to an outer directed idea of who one should be. As I have said, I do not decry female academic achievement but to succeed in what is generally agreed to be something of a tick-box culture, educationally speaking, is quite separate from pursuing one's own thoughts or interests, speaking up, speaking one's mind and learning to trust one's own perceptions and impulses. When Sheryl Sandberg was a student in leading economist Larry Summers' Harvard class, she has admitted that she never raised her hand or participated. She never 'leaned in'. She just did what a lot of women in companies do, she worked hard and got the best grade.[20]

Girls are often conscientious. They want to do the life thing right. Until the point that they leave school, there is a clear template laid down about what getting it 'right' means: a string of A stars, being pretty (in one particular standard symmetrical way) and having a lean silhouette. Increasingly, being good at sport (and music, art and drama) is considered part of the all-round perfect package, particularly in the eyes of middle-class parents.[21] It seems to embrace all that a human can be or does. What of the girl who questions the way her school is organised or bunks off to go to art-house cinemas, who stands up to boys' harassment or who challenges her parents' stifling materialism or finicky cruelty? We find little mention, or approval, of this sort of assertiveness.

> Girls are often conscientious. They want to do the life thing right. Until the point that they leave school, there is a clear template laid down about what getting it 'right' means . . .

Put it another way: if doing all these expected and approved things – and not much else – was the route to genuine autonomy, why do so many girls find life so difficult? Caryn Franklin, founder of All Walks Beyond the Catwalk, put it like this: 'Young women have so much more chances and choices and yet all we are hearing is "Am I good enough?"' Kate Mosse – Co-Founder of the Women's Prize for Fiction (formerly the Orange Prize) and best-selling author – fears there is a new pressure of perfectionism in young girls in recent years:

In our day, we were safe being in one group or another – the brainy gang, or the sporty gang, or you might be arty or into science. You were, up to a point, able to choose your tribe. Everyone had their place. Now when I go to school prize-givings, I see girls thinking they have to deliver on all fronts. I think it's incredibly hard. The underlying suggestion is that *any* successful person is attractive, person-able, gifted in all things. It's the dark side of the idea of Renaissance man or woman and it doesn't give young people of 15 or 16 time to grow into their own skins and find out who they really are.

★

It would be hard to explain to that always useful outside arbiter, a visitor from Mars, quite how all-encompassing and pressuring the whole panoply of educational success has become – from tests at school, to public examinations, to college or university entrance and then employment. As Alison Wolf observes, with a degree of under-statement: 'The upside of a meritocratic society is that girls can compete equally. On the downside are the consequences for every-one's childhood of a society built round exams and certificates.'[22] Increasingly, I think, it is becoming about the creation of an entire package – learning and looks, emotional discipline and educational outcomes – that will play well in the chill, demanding marketplace. For one English mother of an anorexic, it was clear that one of the – many – triggers of her daughter's illness was the onset of Year 10, and GCSE courses. 'It was not a coincidence that it began then, I am sure of it,' she said. Her daughter had become more and more worried that she would not match, or catch up with, an academically clever sister or a peer group that included girls who seemed to demonstrate all-round academic and athletic ease, and were also thin and pretty. Schools feel the pressure with increasing force: there are always new forms of measurement, new standards to reach. Good results will bring in the right sort of parents which will then attract the right sort of teacher – a form of virtuous circle. With the intro-duction of performance-related pay, teachers will now feel the pres-sure personally. And parents certainly feel it, as a clutch of 'good' results is essential to the transition to the next stage; good, or indeed excellent, exam results an essential, if only preliminary, prerequisite, for access to a prestigious university.

As always, class and cultural differences shape parental response in different ways. Studies of some working-class parents suggest that, given their own unhappy experiences at school, they put more emphasis on their children being happy at school and exert far less pressure in terms of exam results than their middle-class equivalents.[23] Aspirational migrant families are more focused on exam results and less concentrated on the 'extra-curricular' activities which form such an important part of what the established British middle-class parents perceive as a good education.[24]

In fact, the single most positive conversation I had, during many long discussions with teachers and academics, was with a pastoral care officer at a comprehensive in Speke, one of the most deprived areas of Liverpool. A few years ago, Parklands was described by a Conservative MP as 'the worst school in the country' on account of its low rate of GCSE passes. Under a new, dynamic head, the school was 'turned around', although it still struggles to meet national benchmarks. Visiting the school, I was struck by its happy, purposeful atmosphere and the unwavering commitment to teaching and learning, and determination to do well by each and every one of its students. In our appallingly divided education system, few middle-class families would choose a school like Parklands nor see anything good in it. Yet in my conversation with Karen Townson – and in my earlier visit to the school itself – I received an impression of upbeat confidence and constant activity. 'Our girls are very confident. They take part in the arts – and they enjoy it. No one puts them down, certainly not the boys. They know who they are and what they are worth.'

Could it be, then, that the more 'successful' the institution is deemed to be, in terms of objective markers – first-rate facilities, top results, high levels of entrance to elite universities – the more likely one is to find in it a certain kind of female distress? I am not saying that high-achieving middle-class girls stand outside ordinary happiness or that their parents are joy-denying dragons. But I would assert that for many of them, anxiety about how to ensure the right kind of future – through university entrance, social networks, intern-ships and all the rest – is particularly marked, and creates a sometimes dangerous form of hothouse environment (at school, at home; a mix of both). This, in turn, can create a type of girl vulnerable to eating disorders or other forms of self-harm that seem completely senseless to the outsider, who perceives only shining success.

Leonard Sax, an American doctor and author of *Girls on the Edge*, observes:

> In my experience, boys who are deliberately hurting themselves usually fall in a narrow demographic. Bluntly, those boys tend to be the weirdos, the losers, the lonely outsiders. Not so for girls. The most popular girl, the pretty girl, the girl who seems to have it all together, may also be the girl at greatest risk for cutting herself.[25]

Sax poses the interesting idea that some girls cut themselves not because they are depressed, but because they want to 'feel real'. Maybe they feel under pressure to become a 'perfect girl'. In the words of psychologist Carol Gilligan, such a creature is an 'incredible construct who is always nice, always generous, who has only good feelings and is good at everything'.[26] Perfectionism is such a pressure, says Gilligan, not because it involves unrealistic striving but because it means suppression of a true self; the desire to do or be it all has an odd effect on girls; it makes them go inward, deny what they really feel.[27]

> The perfect girl is an 'incredible construct who is always nice, always generous, who has only good feelings and is good at everything'.
> Carol Gilligan

Other writers, more recently, have identified what is hauntingly called an 'anorexia of the soul' in which girls are exhausted and depleted, over-extending themselves by pursuing success in every area of personal achievement – sport, music, the arts, as well as straightforward academic achievement. They have to get As in everything, get into a top college, develop extra-curricular interests. In addition, in order to complete this portfolio, they have to be 'hot' or in the words of one interviewee, 'effortlessly hot'.

In a *New York Times* piece on this issue, Sara Rimer quotes one girl, Esther, as saying, 'If you are free to be everything, you are also expected to be everything' . . . 'You want to achieve,' Esther said. 'But how do you achieve and still be genuine?' (Genuine? Real? An alternative lexicon is already building . . . to this we shall return.) As Rimer correctly identifies, this anxiety directly links to the economic – and is surely exacerbated by the credit crisis, recession and now austerity:

There is something about the lives these girls lead – their jam-packed schedules, the amped-up multitasking, the focus on a narrow group of the nation's most selective colleges – that speaks of a profound anxiety in the young people, but perhaps even more so in their parents, about the ability of the next generation to afford to raise their families (in the same places as they now live.) Admission to a brand-name college is viewed by many parents, and their children, as holding the best promise of professional success and economic well-being in an increasingly competitive world.[28]

More subtle pressures are evident in a sympathetic academic study by Dr Claire Maxwell and Professor Peter Aggleton, of a group of girls in four private schools within one geographical area. Here, the emphasis is all on 'concerted cultivation'.

At Rushby (not the school's real name) those few young women who were not so heavily committed to extra-curricular activities as some of their peers felt this made them relatively uninteresting or even 'lazy'. Alice (Year 12), for instance, felt that she was 'not a very interesting person, I'm just kind of standard' because although she was good at sport – 'I do lacrosse, hockey, netball, athletics (and tennis) . . . I'm not incredible at Drama, I'm not performing for a local company.' Expectations of accomplishment – across a number of spheres – were therefore promoted by the school community through teachers and peers. According to another student, Elizabeth (Year 13), 'Well, when people are like, "Oh I'm good at this" – I wouldn't actually say I'm good at anything in particular, because . . . because there are kind of a few people in my year that strive at everything and you can't really beat them.'[29]

Some academics see a clear connection between the rise in eating disorders and recent changes in contemporary schooling. John Evans and Emma Rich believe that the damaging effect of academic and educational pressure, particularly on certain groups of middle-class girls, 'are sometimes masked by wider "celebratory discourses" which espouse only the positive effects of educational achievement on the well-being and development of girls.'

> Such discourses are connected to claims concerning the growing opportunities for young women to access higher education and employment, girls outperforming boys in A levels in almost all subjects, and recent claims of the emergence of 'alpha girls'. Within these cultures, 'excellence and success' are normalised, in the sense that it is taken as a given that those 'achieving' these things are the 'winners' in the educational arena.[30]

They go on:

> Our thesis is that, in the lives of young women suffering from anorexia nervosa, we can vividly see not only the embodiment of damaging, wider (extra school) social forces but also *some of the problematic,*

*intensified work conditions of contemporary schooling*; specifically, the commingling of what we refer to below as *performance and perfection* codes endemic in contemporary western societies and schools.[31] [My emphasis.]

And again:

All the young women in our study suggested that schooling played a strong part in the development of their eating disorder, highlighting to various extents, problematic experiences with competition, between individuals for grades, achievement status, sporting recognition, popularity, bullying 'cliques', groups, stereotyping and lack of individual recognition.[32]

They quote a young anorexic called Carrie who says, 'Even if you work really hard and get an A, and then someone else gets an A star, it doesn't matter any more because they have taken it [the achievement] away from you.'[33]

> 'If you work really hard and get an A, and then someone else gets an A star, it doesn't matter any more because they have taken it [the achievement] away from you.'
> Carrie

What this study, and similar and subsequent ones, makes clear is that the codes of 'performance and perfection' damage more than just the Performer or the Perfectionist; excessive dieting, chasing the ideal body ('white, slender, fit and sexy') can become a way for a wide range of girls to find recognition, in a system that does not seem to recognise them for – simply – being who they are. 'The body becomes a "voice" through which to convey a message through which to ultimately subvert "performativity", their embodied action saying, "look; now I have NO body, now see and treat me as a person, for who I really am."'[34] Another girl is quoted as saying, 'If I don't eat it's a way of people seeing how much I am hurting.'[35] For girls who are not particularly academic or sporting, not eating could be the way of having a defined personality.

And just as eating disorders themselves are creeping back, chronologically speaking, into childhood and affecting more and more young people, so anxiety about achievement is now starting earlier and earlier. When Amy Chua, a high-flying Chinese-American legal academic, published *Battle Hymn of the Tiger Mother* in 2011, one woman's account of parenting as an extreme sport, it set off alarmed discussion among many middle-class parents. Amy Chua knew what she was doing. In her opening declarative sentences she challenged relaxed, bohemian parents everywhere, those deluded creatures who have mistakenly come to believe that childhood is a time for enjoyment and exploration or just for being, rather than regimented discipline and the drive to succeed.

On the very first page of her book, Chua threw down the gauntlet:

> Here are some things my daughters, Sophia and Louisa, were never allowed to do: attend a sleepover/ have a playdate/be in a school play/complain about not being in a school play/ watch TV or play computer games/ choose their own extracurricular activities/ get any grade less than an A/ not be the number one student in every subject but gym or drama/ play any instrument other than the piano or violin/ not play the piano or violin.

When *Battle Hymn* was published in this country it was the talk of the middle-class dining table for a week or two (for we live in a fast-ideas culture as surely as we live in a fast-food one; nothing lingers in the broadsheet tract for long). Many parents dismissed its cold, cruel, constrained approach while possibly checking their own parenting 'rules' – and failures – against this riveting account of rigid policing and inter-generational warring, albeit a struggle that yielded spectacular results. To Chua's credit, she is brutally honest about her battles with her younger daughter in particular and the ways in which her best-laid plans – for hours and hours of violin practice in particular – eventually broke down and she had to come to a synthesis of sorts between Western parenting and the super-strict, directed Chinese version. 'Phew!' said the Western parents. 'So we were right all along.'

Well, not quite. For just as Chua has made her accommodation with Western freedom or laxness, in her own parenting style, so the middle class in the UK have nudged closer to Chua's model. The way we bring up our children has changed enormously over the years, with many negative consequences. Interestingly, working parents spend more time with their children than stay-at-home mothers (for they *were* all mothers) of the 1950s, 1960s, and 1970s, but that time is structured differently.[36] Parents scrutinise, direct, hover over and generally try to intervene in and control their children's lives far more than they once did. And it has the paradoxical result, particularly with girls, of creating outwardly more obedient and successful daughters, while at the same time robbing them of the freedom of youth and the responsibilities that develop when children are required to be part of wider groups, families or communities, rather than agents of a parental plan for the survival of the fittest.

> Parents scrutinise, direct, hover over and generally try to intervene in and control their children's lives far more than they once did. And it has the paradoxical result, particularly with girls, of creating outwardly more obedient and successful daughters, while at the same time robbing them of the freedom of youth.

Two things strike me about the current moment and how it affects our daughters in particular. Firstly, it is clear that we can put much of it down to mounting economic anxiety and the fear of downward mobility. I read *Battle Hymn of the Tiger Mother* as a bible, or handbook, for both the aspirant immigrant parent, first or second generation, and a warning to the once comfortable middle class who fear being over-taken by the success-hungry millions, now offered greater mobility, and access to education systems, around the world. They are right to be worried. If we are going to compete with the tiger economies, we are going to become increasingly influenced by their punishing work ethic and their relentless schooling. In South Korea, for example, there are reports filtering through of anxious parents trying to emigrate, such is their fear of the impact of long days of rote learning, in order to access the next stage on the educational ladder.

According to a special report in *The Economist* entitled 'We don't need quite so much education':

> Results of a survey released last week by the Institute for Social Development Studies at Seoul's Yonsei University show that Korean teenagers are by far the unhappiest in the OECD. This is the result of society's relentless focus on education – or rather, exam results. The average child attends not only regular school, but also a series of *hagwons*, private after-school 'academies' that cram English, maths, and proficiency in the 'respectable' musical instruments, i.e. piano and violin, into tired children's heads. Almost 9% of children are forced to

attend such places even later than 11pm, despite tuitions between 10pm and 5am being illegal.[37]

Our system is edging ever closer to this picture, as demonstrated by the dramatic rise in extra-school tutoring across all classes and school sectors.

But the emphasis of a book like Chua's, coupled with the irresistible rise in girls' educational achievement, speaks to a new role for girls as potential weapons in the battle to retain, or augment, family status. Historically, girls always have had an important social and economic function within and between families, largely on the grounds of their potential marriageability. But today, I suspect, many parents – unconsciously perhaps? – scrutinise their daughters on a double level: assessing both their attractiveness and potential employability and earning power. Let us recall that Scottish Widows survey of a thousand parents conducted on the 200th anniversary of the publication of *Pride and Prejudice*, by Jane Austen, which found that 37.3 per cent believe their sons will be financially secure for the rest of their lives if they marry a good woman – while less than a third of parents (31.9 per cent) think their daughters will be secure if they wed. Hanna Rosin's *The End of Men* and Liza Mundy's book *The Richer Sex* both work from a similar premise, that a significant minority of young women – the top highly educated 30 per cent – have the potential to be big earners, to outstrip their male peers, particularly before they are thirty years old. But in order to live well – or indeed really well – these top female graduates will need to merge their lives – and incomes – with a similarly successful male peer, particularly if they hope to have children at some point in their lives when, inevitably, their income will fall relative to men's.

Today's parents, particularly those of a worldly, ambitious cast of mind, will be acutely aware of this double pressure. So they might well be hoping – requiring? commanding? – that their daughter will not just do well, but will also conform to the dictates of modern femininity (and the age-old rules of a Jane Austen novel) and 'attract a mate' which will also, of course, double their earning and purchasing power. In today's world, looking good, 'being attractive', tends to mean being thin, with long, ironed hair and a vaguely androgynous look. There is clearly a perceived link in many people's minds between the self-discipline of the academic star, and the desirable 'super-skinny' body. Many of today's mothers surely buy into the prevailing view that, in the words of Hilary Mantel, 'overweight people are lazy, undisciplined slobs'.[38] Some writers have gone further and made clear their belief that fat is a form of a failure.[39]

They may also perceive a not quite fully articulated link between a daughter's ability to control her weight and her ability to manage the very many pressures that now exist, in education and work, in a highly competitive world. Evans, Rich and Holroyd put it like this: 'Effectively, perfection code principles of "slenderness" become "the" credential for recognition and belonging and diet (talking about and trying it) becomes "a rite of passage", a means of achieving and displaying what individuals have in common (the "right" body, the "right" commitment and attitude) with high status others.'[40] And again, 'fat is thus interpreted as an outward sign of neglect of one's corporeal self, a condition considered either as shameful or being dirty or irresponsibly ill.'[41]

In short, appearing sleek and 'together' are vital elements in the modern marketplace as is deferred gratification and high levels of self-discipline. Who knows? A girl who lets her flesh 'hang out' might wish to 'hang out' in other ways. Any unseemly self-display or tendency to unfettered enjoyment simply will not cut it in the highly competitive slimmed-down modern workforce. Here we certainly find a clear link – of a nightmarish kind – between Story Line One and Story Line Two: the life project and the body project ease ever closer, making authenticity and freedom appear ever more a utopian dream of old. For me, this fits with a generally narrowed view – in all senses – of what it is to be a human being or a happy, fulfilled (I know, I know – such terms seem to travel from another time and place) woman. It leads to the kind of bizarre and deeply sad question put by one of the interviewees in Rich, Evans and Holroyd's study, 'Do you think it's seen as a weakness to eat?'[42] The modern answer, I'm afraid, could well be: yes.

> Appearing sleek and 'together' are vital elements in the modern marketplace, as is deferred gratification and high levels of self-discipline. Who knows? A girl who lets her flesh 'hang out' might wish to 'hang out' in other ways . . .

# 2

# Name, Shame − and Blame

*In which we consider the pornification of our world, and the surprising consensus arising between progressives and conservatives, and wonder why society remains incapable of protecting our daughters from real harm − or helping them think intelligently about their sexuality.*

There's an advertisement for an online lingerie company that I often see on my journeys up and down tube escalators in London. It is an air-brushed poster of a beautiful woman stripped down to her underwear, and you are supposed, I presume, to want to buy the lacy bra and the panties because you think you, and your flesh, will look like that, if you bought the same or similar items. I can't say that what I feel when I see this advertisement is simple but I know I tend to feel the same things in roughly the same, faintly surprised, order. First of all, I think, 'Gosh, that's a very sexy picture for a public place.' Then I think, 'It's almost like a painting, it's rather arresting.' Often, I feel a brief spasm of nostalgia for the young woman I once was and the loveliness I might have possessed but did not − quite − know I possessed: so that lowers my mood a little, puts me in my biological place.

Next, I think about my daughters and how they might react to such image. A picture of a lovely young woman always looks different when you *are* a lovely young woman − even if you do not, quite, know it − for you are, in some sense, a peer judging a peer, or perhaps anxiously wondering if you are a match for the half-naked figure in the painting splashed on a public wall. And surely any young woman might wonder what it would be like if it was *her* splashed half naked on that wall. I mean, supposing you were heading off for a job interview and needed to feel competent and together, how might it affect you to contemplate a young woman — rather like yourself — offered up, like that, for the public to feast upon you, minutes before you had to go into a room, and present yourself as a self-possessed woman to a room full of strangers?

By this time, I have emerged, as if from Hades, blinking into the light of day.

Not surprisingly, women can react very differently to this sort of sexualised imagery. TV director Anna Coles told me, 'It just doesn't affect me — I just can't imagine feeling put down by an objectifying culture. I guess this is to do with my age — I feel as if those Victoria's Secret models only really affect teenagers. In my experience, men are not overly bothered about the "ideal woman" images forced down their throats.' But when Kat Banyard, the founder of UK Feminista, was at university, one of her lecturers illustrated a talk about a memory function using pictures of the tennis player Anna Kournikova in a bikini. 'I remember feeling very uncomfortable about those pictures being used by someone who had authority over me. I started wondering, "What does he think of me? What does he think of other women?"'[1]

It is one thing to look at a picture and to mobilise all one's young-adult defences against it. It is another to soak up these images as part of the apparently neutral wallpaper of your babyhood and impressionable youth, part of the reason that parents are so concerned about contemporary culture. Certainly, when I compare the sexualised hard sell of today's world to the rather prudish, post-post-war world in which I grew up, I am struck most by the noise and gaudiness of the change: the fact that almost everything is for sale, all the time — including images of women. In the words of journalist and fellow London-dweller Simon Jenkins, our freedom poses the danger that 'London buses become one vast crotch shot (like London phone-boxes) . . . the Thames is lined with ads . . . and Hyde Park is one industrial estate.'[2] Batteries or bodies, blow jobs or take-aways, images or insurance. One can purvey or purchase all of it, 24/7. There's also no hiding from it and much of the hideousness it spawns.

The 'pornification' of culture is an extension of Story Line Two; a relatively new, but related, dimension of female distress. According to teacher Chloe Combi, 'There was a time when the biggest body issue for teenage girls was thinness, and the biggest worry was that they might develop eating disorders . . . Now, however, this body dysmorphia has extended to plastic surgery and body alteration.'[3] In recent years, a once marginalised and deeply derided feminist argument has edged slowly but inexorably, into the mainstream, where it is now deployed to explain (almost) everything that is going wrong with young women's lives today. The current consensus − spanning left and right, liberal and Tory − is that girls growing up in the early twenty-first century are subject to a barrage of demeaning images and practices which is harming their well-being. From Nick Clegg, the Deputy Prime Minister (we have 'such a highly sexualised culture at the moment and there are huge pressures' on girls),[4] to parenting guru Steve Biddulph, from UK Feminista's Kat Banyard to *Daily Telegraph* journalist Allison Pearson, all are united in condemnation of this turn of cultural events. There is growing concern at the increasingly pornographic ways of representing women's bodies in the more 'ordinary' world of film, TV and magazines, as well as in the marketing of everything from clothes to computer war games: the whole lot of it 'turbo-charged', in the words of Labour MP Diane Abbott, by new technology and social media.[5]

There's nothing new in pretty girls being used to sell things. Consider those hilarious advertisements in the 1970s where lovely girls in Laura Ashley dresses perform blurred fellatio on chocolate bars or sleek women in sports cars bring a gear stick to a state of purring arousal. Today's pretty girls wear fewer clothes; parts of their bodies blown up or stripped down or away. Girls are half naked on tube escalators, but men, too, bulge in their briefs on the backs or sides of buses. Advertisements for clothing clearly mimic the codes of soft core pornography. Male or female, everyone is more likely to be more pouting, thrusting, enticing, than they once were, as if in a state of semi-permanent arousal; the bedroom door is now perpetually open to the street or indeed the boardroom.

According to Rita Clifton, former Chief Executive of global conglomerate Interbrand,

It's strange how it's worked out. There's all this equality and maternity legislation. But in a way things have gone backwards. Young women feel pressured to present themselves in a certain way and its happened over the last ten years . . . All these Californian teen programmes – girls with fake tans. *OC/The Hills/90210* . . . All the girls want to look like that. Playing the game to get the boys. Breasts have got to stand up at 90 degrees; girls have to have no hair; fake tans. I worry about that pressure on them. Does it matter what you look like as much as you being current, interested and curious . . . caught up with the modern world?

'In a way things have gone backwards. Young women feel pressured to present themselves in a certain way and it's happened over the last ten years . . .'
Rita Clifton

Clearly, it does, or they wouldn't do it.

In the late 1990s women posting on the parenting website Mumsnet began to notice a change in the marketing of certain merchandise. In the words of Mumsnet's Kate Williams,

> They wanted to discuss the kind of products that were available for pre-teens such as seven- or eight-year-olds, like Playboy stationery. It was just after the rise of Lad culture – and there was this idea that it was empowering for young women – that brash sexuality is an act of self-determination.

Mumsnet supporters thought otherwise although different contributors approached the issue from different political viewpoints. Some were angry at the loss of innocence that the marketing of these products presented, and were protective about the idea of authentic girlhood. Others – 'and these were the most ferocious in their criticism,' says Williams – came from a broadly feminist angle. 'What they were saying in effect is that "it's up to us to show girls that this is not the only kind of adulthood available" – this kind of "pornified" pastiche of female sexuality which seemed in effect to be shutting down girls' choices about what sexuality could or should be. The idea was to empower girls in terms of their sexuality and their freedom – not to take it away.'

Their campaign showed the power of protest, of whatever kind.

It differed in character from the more outright political approach of a group like Object – a third wave feminist movement, protesting at women's objectification. From the outset, Williams says,

> We felt that we could use our perceived 'heft' – but we were also aware that we were more likely to make a bigger impact if we got retailers on board, and if there was no finger pointing. What we wanted to say to retailers was 'work with us'. We put up a couple of pages on the site and wrote to retailers.
>
> We called our campaign *Let Girls be Girls*. We asked retailers to commit to look at all the products through that lens: in other words, not just tick off a few boxes, but to scrutinise their retailing through a completely new perspective. We contacted Tesco, George at Asda, John Lewis and lots of others. Most had corporate governance policies which meant they could show us that they were already broadly 'in compliance' with our aims, but we wanted them to really change their thinking. We also wanted to create a tipping point; so that it was riskier for retailers not to be in on it than to be in on it. Many of them, of course, had noticed this cultural shift – although to be fair it was not always so straightforward. I mean take padded bras. On the face of it, one might not like the fact that they appear to draw attention to the breast size of even very young girls – but of course, padded bras also serve another function, which is as modesty layers; young girls can feel self-conscious about their nipples showing as they hit puberty, so there was an argument for that kind of padding, as a form of protection.

The campaign had plenty of coverage in the press, and was perceived to be a success, although overall Williams is cautious. 'The issue was raised effectively – it definitely had an impact on the products available, and in practical terms, it diminished the problem by drawing attention to the issue. On the other hand, there was a fear that retailers might think "been there – done that – don't have to think about that any more".'

According to Williams, it's an ongoing campaign, 'although we think it has achieved its main objective, which was to raise awareness and really get people thinking – and subsequently both Tesco and Asda have run potential product lines by Mumsnet users to canvass their views.'

★

It may be, in part, thanks to that Mumsnet campaign, but the marketing of lap-dancing poles in supermarkets and push up T-shirts for seven-year-olds seems like mild stuff compared to the 'real' pornography that can be accessed, with just a touch of a button, via the internet. Increasingly, pornographic images will just 'pop up' on screen. These internet versions of 'Readers' Wives' are painfully amateur shots of young women, in various forms of self-display. It's pretty raw stuff: labias held open with thumb and forefinger, bottoms bare, bar the thin, painful slice of a thong, and thrust towards the outsider's gaze. My first inevitably mumsy thought: surely it is risky for the women to expose themselves in this public manner? The images are ineradicable; their faces are easily identified. It saddens me, the fact that the domestic scenes behind them are so ordinary; an overcoat hurriedly thrown over a rather collapsed-looking sofa, a bedsit clearly mocked up to look like a boudoir. It is impossible to tell if these women, who appear to be in various states of arousal, are projecting sexual desire or, indeed, mimicking it for the sake of an aroused or arousable viewer. And then there are their bodies, largely shorn of inconvenient and animalistic pubic hair; revealing the slits and folds of their own flesh, like overgrown baby girls.

Of course, pornography has always existed. Everyone in my generation makes much of the fact that, back *then*, *we* had to hunt out our pleasures. It's true. Sexual images had to be sneaked off a top or back shelf, whether in the pages of naturist magazines, the bawdy storylines of historical fiction, or the centre pages of *Playboy*. If you were curious about pornographic cinema, as my friends and I were, in our late teens, you had to go in search for it, in seedy cinemas in designated parts of town. We stuffed tissues down our bras to make us look eighteen (the age at which you would be admitted to an X film) while the girl with the best nails bought the tickets and we all shuffled into the auditoria of special cinemas in Soho or King's Cross. Here, cheap European imports with laugh-out-loud titles like *Danish Dentist on the Job* played to dark cinema interiors groggily thick with the sense of brewing or (it was hard to tell which was worse) already spent, viscous longing. I can still remember my raw shock, and a parallel thrill, at what these people could do with their bodies without either apparent shame (or indeed sense of comedy). But it was also

amazing how rapidly both shock and thrill could fade into a profound
if tainted tedium. I was not tempted to go back.

Now, with access to broadband and an adult credit card, and
without moving from your living room or bedroom, you can access
anal, oral, group sex, within moments. Caitlin Flanagan recommends
that all parents take the Fifteen Minute Tour – setting an alarm
clock, and typing PORN into Google – just to see what is available
on a screen at home, to a curious adolescent. Reader, I admit it: I
couldn't face it – not least because I have an irrational fear of trig-
gering some police-related invasion of my civil liberties. So I will
trust Flanagan's account that 'By minute three you are watching
events that have an obvious aspect of assault. What does a twelve- or
thirteen- or fourteen-year-old-girl make of those non-stop images?'[6]
Could it be, I want to ask Flanagan, that a girl's reaction, certainly
to the less violent forms of pornography, will depend on context?
For some, it may trigger a sense of upset or real trauma; for others
it might only ignite a form of horrified hilarity.

Either way, a growing worry about the extent and effect of sexual
and violent images is now uniting women (and I suppose a few men
– not that they enter the debate, or not in such a public way) across
the political spectrum. Traditionally, pornography has polarised liberals
and conservatives, with the former protecting freedom of expression
and the latter concerned to protect a more traditional vision of
individual and family life. Over the two years I have spent researching
and writing this book I have watched this division break down in
this country, a potential new consensus merge, through the medium
of a newly revived, cross-party, all age, feminism. Those of a more
traditional perspective – writers such as the *Mail*'s Bel Mooney,
Caitlin Flanagan (author of *Girl Land*) and Allison Pearson of the
*Daily Telegraph* are joined by strong voices from the feminist side,
writers like the *Guardian*'s Kira Cochrane, contributors to *Fifty Shades
of Feminism*, and Kat Banyard, author of *The Equality Illusion*.

Listen, then, to two very different voices, on this same theme.
Caitlin Flanagan first:

> As a parent, I am horrified by the changes that have taken place in
> the common culture over the past thirty years. I believe that we are
> raising children in a kind of post-apocalyptic landscape in which no

forces beyond individual households — individual mothers and fathers — are protecting children from pornography and violent entertainment. The 'it takes a village' philosophy is a joke, because the village is now so polluted and so desolate of commonly held, child-appropriate moral values that my job as a mother is not to rely on the village but to protect my children from it.[7]

And here is UK Feminista's Kat Banyard, interviewed in the *Guardian*:

Banyard points out that . . . the [porn] industry is now worth $97bn (£63bn) a year, 'more than the combined revenue of Microsoft, Google, Amazon, Yahoo!, eBay, Apple, Netflix and EarthLink'. She wonders how this massive expansion of pornography and prostitution will play out in terms of the lives of young women. 'We're currently experiencing a level of sexual exploitation which is industrialised', she says, 'the scale of which is unparalleled in human history. We don't know exactly what the effects are going to be — we just know that they will be big, and we need to deal with it urgently.'[8]

For the conservative commentators, not only is pornography morally and aesthetically repulsive, but, they believe, there are indisputable links between the rise of certain kinds of sexual behaviour and assaults on young women and the increasing circulation of such 'polluted' material. Writing in March 2013 about the case of a fourteen-year-old girl who was found bound, beaten, gagged and raped by boys of fourteen and fifteen obsessed with online pornography, *Mail* columnist Bel Mooney pointed to the terrifying consequences of a society where the biggest 'consumers of internet porn are the twelve to seventeen age groups, years when children are terrifyingly impressionable.'[9] Her worries seemed borne out by a disturbing report on growing levels of sexual violence, published by Britain's Deputy Children's Commissioner, Sue Berelowitz, in late 2012.

'Child Sexual Exploitation in Gangs and Groups' was initially rejected by the government on the grounds that its findings were 'hysterical', a claim it had soon to withdraw when faced with the evidence. The report found that crimes were taking place against girls from every kind of background and social class — and the problem was rising.

Writing, sympathetically, about Berelowitz's findings, liberal feminist Mariella Frostrup, argued,

> The most conservative estimate has 16,500 young people suffering or in danger. The true figure is believed to be much higher . . . one fact stands out: anal rape is now a more frequently experienced form of abuse than vaginal rape – apologies for spoiling your Sunday. These attacks aren't sex crimes but hate crimes, with the aim of humiliating, terrifying and blackmailing into submission girls (72 per cent of the victims, ranging in age from 11 to 18) who should be playing with friends and listening to boy-bands.[10]

Parental worries about the impact of pornography on young people's behaviour was forcefully borne out in a recent thoughtful piece by Chloe Combi in the *Times Educational Supplement*. Combi described how

> this is, thanks to the internet, the first generation with free, easy and mass exposure to hardcore pornography. These are the first teenagers to have grown up with 'sextin', sex tapes, making their own sex tapes on phones, saucy snaps of classmates on Facebook, MSN orgies and extensive insight into the sex lives of celebrities and politicians – hell even teachers.

Combi rightly notes the distinct step up in sexual knowledge the new pornography represents:

> As little as 10 years ago, experimenting with sex was considered to be something you gave a great deal of thought to. Pornography has made sex seem more casual, creating a generation of teenagers who are not only au fait with, but have in a way reclaimed as their own, the notion of friends with benefits, no strings attached, sexting, slutting, fishing and a million other acronyms and slang terms I'll never understand now I'm not a teenager.

The girls she teaches have crushes on James Deen – yes, seriously:

> [T]he new big breakout crush in the US . . . unusually pretty-boy porn star who appears in hardcore films, that go under the genres of Everything Butt (extreme anal sex), Bound Gangbangs (gang rape)

and Public Disgrace (the previous two combined, but also including women being smacked about).

But, says Combi, the biggest impact that pornography is having is on the way that teenagers see their own bodies and those of the opposite sex. It will affect boys — but girls seem the biggest victims. In a discussion in sex education:

Most of the boys stated that pubic hair on women was 'disgusting' and 'should be shaved off' and this of course led me to ask why. After much sniggering, they answered that women in porn don't have pubic hair. (When I asked them if their penises all looked like the ones on the men in porn films, there was of course a deathly silence.) So where does this leave the girls — the teenage girls who are represented in pornography as the holy grail, the ultimate fantasy? Nowhere good, that much is certain . . . I have lost count of the teenage girls who have told me about their desire to have their breasts surgically enlarged. While this is undoubtedly due in part to many female celebrities being cosmetically enhanced, it is also because boys vocally favour the two-doormen-in-a-headlock look over something more natural. And where are boys developing this preference? Porn, of course. If boys' pornography-prescribed aesthetic desires are influencing how girls see themselves and what they do with their bodies, what the hell is going to happen to the actual sex lives of teenagers? Boys and girls brought up on a diet of extreme and hardcore pornography are going to have a pretty distorted attitude to their own sexual boundaries, the pressure ever on to keep up with the stuff they see on the internet. Schools are having to deal with the new phenomenon of pornographic bullying on phones and social media. All too often, I hear of some inappropriately smutty or downright shocking pornographic picture or film of a schoolchild being passed around among students. Girls tell me they suffer enormous pressure from boyfriends/friends/peers to 'sext' (send a half or fully nude picture of themselves and/or a sexually explicit explanation of what they are going to do later).[11]

Combi's account is clearly an accurate representation of what happens in some schools, to some girls. However, it is hard to assess the evidence as to how many girls are directly affected by this behaviour. The UK Campaign group End Violence Against Women commissioned a You

Gov opinion poll in late 2010; their key findings suggested a teenage world of brimming, latent sexualised violence. They found that 71 per cent of sixteen-to-eighteen-year-olds say they have heard sexual name-calling such as 'slut' or 'slag' towards girls at school daily or a few times per week. Close to one in three (29 per cent) say they have experienced unwanted sexual touching at school, while 28 per cent of sixteen-to-eighteen-year-olds indicate that they have been sent sexual pictures on mobile phones at school a few times a month or more.

However, recently reported research from the London School of Economics indicates that the problem is less pressing: they found that 7 per cent of UK eleven-to-sixteen-year-olds have been sent a sexual message (not necessarily with an image), and 4 per cent have seen a sexual message posted online – the numbers at the age of twelve are very small, more like 2–3 per cent, going up to 14 per cent at sixteen. (As Zoe Williams of the *Guardian* wrote, 'I don't find this surprising. Did none of us have a conversation with sexual content by the age of sixteen?') Only 2–3 per cent have had experience of each of the following: seen others perform sexual acts in a message; been asked for a photo or video showing their private parts; or been asked to talk about sexual acts with someone online.[12]

Combi believes that 'Parental control locks on family computers are pointless: the kids have smart phones.' In July 2013, UK Prime Minister David Cameron announced plans for automatic internet 'porn filters' – soon admitting that his suggestion might be unworkable. The Icelandic government is the first of the western democracies to consider a ban on hardcore pornography, using filters similar to those used by China to block its citizens from access to the web. Ogmundur Jonasson, Iceland's interior minister, is reported to be (at the time of writing) drafting new laws to stop the access of online pornographic images and videos by young people through computers, games consoles and smartphones. 'We have to be able to discuss a ban on violent pornography, which we all agree has very harmful effects on young people and can have a clear link to incidences of violent crime,' he said. Methods under consideration include blocking access to pornographic website addresses and making it illegal to use Icelandic credit cards to access pay-per-view pornography which would of course prohibit adult access to this material. 'There is a strong consensus building in Iceland. We have so many experts, from educationalists to the police and those who work with children behind this, that this has become much broader than party politics.'

Halla Gunnarsdottir, a political adviser to Mr Jonasson, told the *Daily Telegraph*, 'At the moment, we are looking at the best technical ways to achieve this.' 'Iceland is taking a very progressive approach that no other democratic country has tried,' said Professor Gail Dines, an expert on pornography and speaker at a recent conference at Reykjavik University. 'It is looking at pornography from a new position — from the perspective of the harm it does to the women who appear in it and as a violation of their civil rights.'[13]

Grave doubts have already been expressed about how Iceland — or any other country, particularly with a boundary-less world-wide web — could police or enforce such a ban. According to Dr Brooke Magnanti, writing in the *Daily Telegraph*,

> Black markets inevitably arise, criminals inevitably profit, and activities which might otherwise be in public view are now by definition off the radar. Does that sound like a formula for a safer or healthier society to you? On the government's balance sheet it might look like something resembling success. In the real world, the unintended consequences would surely cause more problems than they solve.[14]

These unintended consequences would surely include sexual images produced, and transmitted, among consenting couples (or groups), as well as the kind of material produced by women like Cindy Gallop, an Oxford graduate, former advertising executive and founder of makelovenotporn.tv, a company with a mission to make 'real world sex videos' for those who enjoy images of sex, shorn of violence, misogyny or weird, unpalatable extremes.[15]

Is there not something bogus about some of the mainstream alarm about mass pornography? One does not have to be a cynic to understand that 'grave concern' about sexualisation permits the endless further circulation (with a pinch of added outrage) of a diluted version of the images being protested about. How, for instance, does the rising moral panic about pornography fit with the British national treasure status accorded to the bare-breasted model on Page 3 in the *Sun* – a long standing target of feminist ire – or the exploitative images of so many 'lads' magazines or the largely unfettered growth of lap-dancing clubs? Does the increasing 'pornification' of society merely wash up, and show up, long-enduring double standards?

Can we really ever act as a 'common culture' – I like this phrase of Flanagan's – on this issue? Was I the only reader of the UK *Guardian* newspaper to be a little surprised to find a thoughtful eight-minute interview with the Californian porn star James Deen, the very same one mentioned in Combi's piece, on the newspaper's *Comment is Free* video interview section? Maybe. Deen, filmed against a cool white-walled background, looking just a touch wan (demanding work, I have no doubt) discussed some of the technical aspects of his 'day job', his ethical and practical opposition to 'Measure B', a proposal that would enforce the use of condoms during the filming of pornography ('We've had zero HIV transmissions in the last ten years'), his enthusiastic female fan base ('I don't consider myself someone who objectified women') and his belief that the industry is about 'freedom of choice'. The interview was a reminder not just of the more sophisticated take on sexual imagery among free-speech liberals but even more complex questions about the consent – or not – of both participants and viewers of such material.

I am also struck by the way that the pornography, safety and violence-against-women-and-girls debate seems to be conducted entirely among and between women. When novelist Lucy Ellmann was asked about a character in her latest novel, a plastic surgeon who discovers his 'inner feminist', she said,

> I started making scrapbooks full of articles about women, about them being mutilated, raped, killed, and from there I had to write the book. I felt something had to be done about these issues . . . I'm fuming. It goes on and on and something has to be done. I've complained enough about it before, but now it's time to find a solution. I think I have done it. I liked the idea of making it the man's job to sort this out. *They caused the problem, and they can bloody well sort it out. I don't think it should be up to us – I'm tired of it.* I said it in five other novels, and nobody's listened, so I decided to say it from a man's perspective, and see if anyone listens this time.[16] [My emphasis.]

Most articles, books or polemics looking at these issues put responsibility for the issue on women. *Mothers* are to blame if girls get into
any kind of sexual or violent trouble. It is a *mother's* responsibility
to protect and police her daughters. Sons and their fathers do not
seem to figure in this conversation at all, even though pornography
is largely made by men, for men, and it is overwhelmingly men and
boys who assault women. Where, then, is the major debate about
keeping our teenage boys in line — or indoors? Where are the calls
for a sex-education programme that encourages boys to look at
pornography with a critical eye, or think about sexuality in more
rounded, tender ways?

Surely, as Mariella Frostrup recently argued,

> What's happening to our children is of concern to us all and fathers,
> husbands, sons and brothers should be marching alongside women,
> demanding the sexualisation of young girls and the objectification of
> women in advertising and pornography comes to an end. We need a
> Man Army determined to change cultural stereotypes, full of blokes
> that boys revere — footballers, musicians, actors and even Top Gear
> presenters (not normally short of opinions) — saying, loud and proud,
> that rape is for cowards, child abuse is despicable and treating girls like
> pieces of meat is simply unacceptable. Real Men Don't Rape, it said
> on a road sign I passed in the capital of Liberia in West Africa following
> the epidemic of sexual violence during the civil war. We need a similar
> campaign to enforce the message that there's nothing to be proud of
> in forcing someone of any age to have sex with you. Only a tiny
> minority of men are violent and abusive but the fact remains that the
> majority of perpetrators of these sorts of crimes are men and the
> majority of victims are female. It's time for men, not women, to do
> the talking.[17]

Kira Cochrane added her voice to this swelling chorus when she
declared:

> I'd love more men to get involved in this conversation, speaking out
> against the threat of male aggression we all live under, pushing the
> message that victims are not to blame, that issues surrounding consent
> must be taught in schools, that alleged perpetrators must be named
> — not to name and shame, but to name and PROTECT.[18]

But surely we need to do more than ask men to 'speak out', vital as that is. Does the talk not now have to come much closer to home? There is something disturbing, almost schizophrenic, about the daily public reminders, through a string of cases in the news, of the constant brutality, of man to woman, while so many find it hard to discuss the reality of sexual violence within our own families, with our own children. So argued Desmond Tutu, Jacob Lief and Sohalia Abdulali, three individuals 'from three generations (aged 81, 50 and 36), three faiths (Christian, Muslim, Jewish) and three continents (Africa, Asia, North America)'. In a recent article, they observed that:

> Until rape, and the structures – sexism, inequality, tradition – that make it possible, are part of our dinner-table conversation with the next generation, it will continue. Is it polite and comfortable to talk about it? No. Must we anyway? Yes. It seems daunting. But which is more painful: talking sensibly with young people about this issue, the same way we might talk with them about drugs, guns or bullying, or waiting for something terrible to happen so close to home that you have to address it in a time of turmoil?[19]

Frostrup's rousing call for a new Man Army smoothly elides the existence of violent pornography with the existence of sexual violence. It is an argument we are hearing more of these days: *this* stuff causes *that* stuff. I am not so sure. There is no doubt that many women who appear in pornographic films are cruelly used and exploited. But just as I found myself quizzing Caitlin Flanagan's assumption that merely to watch pornography online is to corrupt or traumatise a teenage girl, I find myself wondering which boys will move from watching porn to re-enacting it? In some sense, it is the mirror image of my question about what resources, personal, familial, intellectual or material, protect a girl from feeling humiliatingly objectified. What is the lack in those boys' homes, their families, their futures, that allow them to dehumanise a girl to that extent? There must – to use a current fashionable term – be quite a *backstory* there?

The same dilemmas – or complexities – apply to the generally acknowledged misogyny of some rap artists. Over the past few years, the lyrics of rap stars, Eminem, the French singer OrelSan ('You are only a sow who deserves her place at the slaughterhouse', 'We'll see how you suck [cock] after I box your jaw') and Plan B, among others, have triggered intense public debate, reaction from American presidents (according to George Bush junior, Eminem was 'the most dangerous threat to American children since polio') to female rap artists who have variously incorporated, or passionately protested at, woman-critical lyrics in their own music. Studies of the actual impact of hate-full lyrics on human behaviour are, as studies tend to be, less conclusive. So that while one academic paper found that 'rap music exposure has no statistically significant effect on the political efficacy of young black women, but it does have a positive effect on the political efficacy of young black men',[20] a 2011 study suggested that within an eighteen-to-twenty-four-year-old group, the older the students were the less they listened to rap and when they did, the more negatively they reacted to it.[21]

Is sexism rather than sexualisation the real unseen issue? Given that violence against women pre-dates the internet and mass-market pornography, and still exists, at far higher levels, in societies with far less commercialisation of sex, we should be careful about giving it such a central relevance in our analysis of our culture. The Delhi rape case — and the generally much higher levels of violence against women in India — is surely an indication of how deeply held attitudes towards women and their role, or lack of, in society precedes, exacerbates and excuses sexual violence. Novelist Sohaila Abdulali, who was gang-raped at the age of seventeen, sees clear connections between violence and more general attitudes in society: 'Isn't there something wrong if we go out and protest rape, and then we go home and men are always served first; are we not sending out a clear message about who is worth more?'

> 'Isn't there something wrong if we go out and protest rape, and then we go home and men are always served first; are we not sending out a clear message about who is worth more?'
> Sohaila Abdulali

I would not argue that women in the UK or the USA or many other western democracies face the same levels of prejudice, or violence, but is there such a big difference between public figures suggesting that girls should watch what they are wearing or how much alcohol they are drinking and those leading politicians in India who, in the wake of the Delhi rape case, warned of 'dented and painted' women? How do we decide what harms our daughters the most: the circulation of violent pornography among teenage boys or the fact that, according to a recent Edinburgh Napier study, an astonishing 80 per cent of eleven-year-olds think it's right to hit a woman who doesn't put your meal on the table on time?[22]

In this context it is pertinent to look in detail at a landmark piece of research conducted in the UK by the NSPCC and University of Bristol in 2009 on the growing problem of violence in relationships among young people (under eighteen) in the UK: a depth and kind of violence that is, understandably, bringing 'anxiety and unhappiness' into their young lives and particularly girls' lives. The report surveyed 1,377 young people, in both heterosexual and same-sex relationships, and undertook over ninety interviews to try and grasp the extent of inter-relationship violence between young people.

In answer to a question about how much they had been subject to physical force, a quarter of girls and 18 per cent of boys reported some form of physical violence – that is, 'pushing, slapping, hitting or holding you down from a partner'. However, girls were also much more likely to report that the physical violence had occurred more than once, indicating that for girls this may represent a more established pattern of victimisation than is experienced by boys.[23] When respondents were asked if partners had ever used more severe physical force such as 'punching, strangling, beating you up, hitting you with an object', worryingly, *one in nine* girls (11 per cent) and 4 per cent of boys claimed they had experienced this. In addition, girls were three times as likely as boys to have experienced repeated severe violence from their partners, with many reporting more detrimental impact on their well-being. Some form of sexual violence was reported by 31 per cent of girls and 16 per cent of boys, and three-quarters reported some form of emotional violence in their relationship. Just over a third of girls (36 per cent) reported that their partners had shouted at them, screamed in their face or called them hurtful names. A similar proportion of girls (35 per cent) also stated that their partners said negative things about their appearance, body, friends or family. Very few girls – or boys – felt able to talk to adults about what had happened to them. Overall, 12 per cent of girls and

4 per cent of boys said that their partners had used mobile phones or the internet to humiliate and threaten them; for those young people who were in a violent relationship, such technologies provided an extra mechanism by which partners could exert control.[24]

There was clearly a strong correlation between teenagers who had experienced family violence and went on to suffer peer violence, although not in any simple way. (Girls who had witnessed violence at home were particularly desirous of avoiding their own mother's experience and the researchers were honest about not being able to trace the reasons why they were often so unsuccessful in doing so.) Girls were at much greater threat from older partners, rather than their peers; all forms of aggression were more prevalent in same-sex partnerships: emotionally and sexually violent relationships were found across the sexual spectrum.

It was also clear that girls found it much harder to assert themselves more generally in terms of the relationship and sexual claims of boys (than boys did of girls, or boys of boys) but that they often blamed themselves for this behaviour. When interviewers asked young people if their partners ever told them whom they could see and where they could go, there was a 'more distinct gender divide'. A third of girls reported experiencing this, compared to just over one in eight boys (13 per cent). In the interviews the girls report a variety of reasons for the violence, including (unjustified) jealousy and the urge to control. Sexual coercion was most frequently exercised through five strategies: loss of partner, allusion to love, accusations of immaturity, manipulation of saying 'no' and fear tactics.[25]

It is painful to read of the girls' lack of confidence. One interviewee, Julie, perceived her refusal to have sexual intercourse as 'unfair' on her partner. This reflects a great many other accounts by participants who reported feeling guilty for not agreeing to have intercourse. Such feelings were intensified if they had an older partner due to perceptions about their increased sexual experience:

> Thus, sexual pressure, either overt or covert, was often intensified for girls due to their feelings of responsibility for their partner's sexual needs. Additionally, Julie reported that her partner repeatedly attempted to initiate sexual intercourse but she does not view this as sexual

coercion. This is an important definitional issue. If young people view certain actions as acceptable or 'normal' in relationships, they might also fail to recognise the extent of their impact. Julie recognised that his behaviour constituted a risk as it may have resulted in her undertaking something she would later regret. Other girls may not necessarily make the same assessment.[26]

The link in young women's minds between male desirability and aggression was another problem:

Worryingly, sometimes the attributes that characterise a high-status boyfriend . . . may actually be detrimental to girls' wellbeing. As demonstrated both in the survey and in interview findings, a 'hard' or 'overt masculinity' can be directed towards partners as well as wider peers. For example, in some of the interviews when girls identified partner violence, they also spoke about their boyfriends' routine use of violence and intimidation with male peers. Thus, paradoxically, the behaviour that some girls perceive as increasing the desirability of a boyfriend also places them at heightened risk of victimisation. This form of masculinity was often portrayed in interviews as providing them with care and protection, although in many cases the reality was quite different.[27]

> 'If a girl slept around and people found out then they will start calling her a slag, a ho', all that.' 'What do guys get called?' 'Nothing, a player.'

And no surprise here, double standards are found to be alive and well. As one boy, echoing several others said, 'Well, if a girl slept around and people found out then they will start calling her a slag, a ho', all that.' Interviewer: 'What do guys get called?' 'Nothing, a player.' Here, too, then, the theme of female obedience emerges, in more extreme form.

Whenever I think about this issue, I feel a bit like Lucy Ellmann: *I am tired of it*. Sitting with a group of friends not long ago I was astonished to find that each one had experienced, during their youth, an act of forced sex, completely against their will, but had never told anyone about it or tried to make any kind of complaint. I would not describe them as traumatised but their revulsion and resentment was visible, decades on. 'I just wanted to forget about it,' more than one of them said. But, of course, none of them had. We know how hard it is for women to pursue a claim of rape through the courts and the shockingly low rate of conviction. In the UK fewer than one victim in thirty can expect to see their attacker brought to justice.[28] A survey of 1,600 women, conducted by website Mumsnet, found one in ten had been raped, four-fifths of those who had been assaulted hadn't reported it, and 70 per cent felt the media were unsympathetic to women who report rape — considerably more than the 53 per cent who felt the legal system lacked sympathy. The NSPCC/Bristol report suggests it's just as difficult for a teenage girl to report violence against herself. Amy was assaulted by a boyfriend but like many of the girls sampled in the study, she 'didn't tell anyone and then I eventually told Libby [friend] and she told Mary [welfare officer] . . . And then I've been seeing . . . a counsellor since then. They wanted me to take him to court but I didn't want to because, I don't know, I just didn't want to.'

INTERVIEWER: Why did you feel you didn't want to?
AMY: *Because I thought it would kind of make things worse.*
INTERVIEWER: You thought he would become worse if that happened?
AMY: Yeah, well I don't know, if that happens again I've promised I will.[29] [My emphasis.]

Clare is a strong, outspoken girl in a co-educational urban comprehensive; smart, secure and always towards the top end of the class academically. A couple of years ago, she was assaulted by a classmate; he came up behind her and grabbed her breasts. He had done the same to several other girls in the class, and a couple of younger female members of staff. But no one, including their teachers, wanted to take the next step and report it; they felt to do so would not only expose themselves to possible criticism (i.e. 'What did you do to encourage his approach to you?') but also risk the wider concern that the boy's behaviour would be too harshly punished and possibly categorised as 'assault', which might have serious consequences for him.

Clare, however, felt that it was important to stop the boy doing it again. With the support of a female teacher, she decided she *would* make an official complaint, only to find that the consequences of her bravery were even more unpleasant than the original incident. The boy concerned began a concerted campaign against her within the school and on social media while several girls in her friendship group made it clear that they thought she was making 'too much' of the incident which was no 'big deal'. At times, she sensed that they were resentful of the positive attention she was getting from a couple of members of staff, who admired her for taking a stand. Thanks to this teacher's support, the boy's 'campaign' was halted within days and his parents called in. Clare and her mother made it clear that they did not want the boy to be permanently excluded for what he had done; they felt this was a disproportionate penalty. The boy therefore received a severe warning, and returned to class, where for the rest of the year he made clear his contempt for Clare for 'lying' about what had happened. For Clare, this inaugurated an unhappy period, with her sense of security and enjoyment within class severely damaged.

But Clare's courage had an impact. That boy never assaulted another girl again. With a strong sense of personal justice, the backing of a supportive parent and a female mentor within the school, she had the resources, emotional and other, to withstand the prolonged stress of pursuing her case. In her eyes, she had put down an important marker of protest at the way that 'boys think they can get away with things'. Many girls do not have the personal resources, bravery or endurance to do this. That should be the job of the adult world: of parents, schools, the police, law courts.

Clare's story – and so many like it – points up a difficulty we still have, individually and collectively, not just with believing girls' or women's testimony but in somehow granting their experience its due weight. In Clare's case, and several others of a similar nature, it was as if their sense of humiliation and hurt was continually being weighed, semi-publicly, against the possible damage that might be done to the boy who perpetrated their distress; it became clear that, in some people's eyes (and not just those of the boy's parents), it might be he, not she, who was most in need of protection. Why is this? Not only are there complex confusions, and conflations, in culture between sexual pleasure and sexual dominance but we seem to find it difficult to put ourselves in a woman's place in anything but the most horrendous cases of assault; our sympathy for female trauma is like an unused muscle that too easily results in a form of neglect and dismissiveness that has echoes of the original brutality. One rape victim told me that one of the most important factors in her being able to 'come to terms' with what had happened to her was 'that there was never any question about my not being believed. My parents, indeed my entire family, accepted my account of what happened, without question. There was absolutely no hint that I might have brought it upon myself. No one ever suggested that I should "put it behind me" or "get over it." My family also had the sense to know that it would take a very very long time for me to heal.'

John McCarthy, the journalist held hostage in Lebanon for five years from 1986 to 1991, made a similar point in a recent talk to school leaders. 'The most important thing that helped me to over-come my experience was my story being given credence. I was treated literally as a hero. Nobody ever doubted my word. I know children and women whose traumatic experiences didn't happen thousands of miles away but here at home, who are not treated as heroes. They haven't been encouraged to tell their story. If you give credence to people's story and give them the space to tell it – that has to be the way forward.'[30]

And please note: we have already travelled quite a long way from the problem of pornography. We are back to our 'common culture', our shared attitudes to women and men, and the failures of such key institutions as the police and judicial system that are supposed to protect those who are harmed, and punish those who transgress.

At its worst, a conservative narrative of 'sexualisation' not only fails to protect real girls from real violence, which should be our primary concern, but it risks encouraging a blanket condemnation of sexual activity, particularly for girls, in the teen years. For some, the encour-agement of abstinence for girls is now considered the right way through the 'pornified' sexual maze. In May 2011 Nadine Dorries, the Conservative MP for mid Bedfordshire, argued that girls between the ages of thirteen and sixteen should be given separate lessons in sex. 'The answer to ending our constant struggle with the incredibly high rate of teenage sexual activity and underage pregnancies lies in teaching our girls and boys about the option of abstinence, the ability to "just say no", as part of their compulsory sex education.'[31] This despite the UK having the lowest rate of teenage pregnancies since the early 1980s, according to the ONS.[32] Abstinence focused approaches have been a strong feature of US sex education over the past couple of decades – with no record of success.[33] A politician like Dorries believes that the answer to 'high street shops selling padded bikinis to seven-year-old girls' is to stop girls from engaging in consensual, as well as non-consensual acts, in the teen years. Once again, there seems no plan to talk to boys.

Alarmist stories about the rise of mass oral sex among teens – a particular feature of the US debate on the problem of sexualisation – risks obscuring the complex and delicate matter of girls' sexual desire.[34] No one quite says it, but the thinking is clearly along the following lines. Boys want it. Girls don't. Girls Give It Up because They Want to be Loved or They Don't Know How to Say No. That's certainly true in many cases – but it is clearly not so straightforward. This struck me when reading a typically worried account by journalist Allison Pearson who described how a 'friend's daughter recently started at a highly regarded boarding school. When her mother asked how she was enjoying the mixed-sex environment, the girl said quietly: "You have to give the boys oral sex or they get cross." Reeling with shock, the mum protested that her darling daughter did not have to do anything of the sort. "Oh yes you do," replied the girl. "And you have to shave down there or the boys don't like it."' Unsurprisingly, Pearson said the story had 'unleashed her inner Mary Whitehouse'.[35] I agree: fourteen seems alarmingly young for this kind of sexual pressure (but, dare I say it, co-educational boarding schools are bound to be a slightly risky proposition when it comes to the policing of teenager intimacy?) At the article's end, Pearson touches on the importance of teaching our children 'a healthy, emotionally connected view of sexuality' but, in general, we read little of girls' emerging sexual curiosity rather than of boys' presumed bodily barbarism. Surely we owe our daughters an ongoing understanding that they, too, may have sexual desires, and that we approve of these?

> Surely we owe our daughters an ongoing understanding that they, too, may have sexual desires, and that we approve of these?

Most commentators, including Pearson, believe that parents – sorry, mothers — should police their daughters. Check up on their internet. Ban computers from the bedroom. Scan Facebook, check Twitter. And if you can't do it yourself, get an 'aunt' to do it for you.[36] All this, of course, is an updated version of the mother who 'accidentally' finds her daughter's diary, and opens it — all for her own good, you understand.

Such secret surveillance seems unnecessary on two counts. No parent who is seriously worried about their daughter's — or son's — safety would hesitate to invade their privacy if they felt they were in real danger. The protective instinct *always* takes precedence over abstract conceptions of privacy. But where no real cause for concern exists, endless furtive checking and sweaty-browed surveillance will not just be time-consuming but counter-productive. Too many mothers are far too over-involved in their children's lives as it is. It is also a form of madness to try to enter into, and understand, another's mental space or social space — adult or child. One can so easily jump to entirely the wrong conclusion — misinterpreting a phrase, a photo, a joke. Too much interference is going to create genuine and long-lasting problems in trust and good relations just as in those good ol' days when girls had diaries with flimsy gold-plated locks and bored mothers pored over their jumbled contents.

Surely it is much more sensible to try and keep lines of communication open with our daughters in the broadest, daily sense: to get to know their friends; to take a lively and tolerant interest in their social world; to spend as much time with them as we can (and they can tolerate): in short, to stay alongside our daughters, rather than treat them with distrust and suspicion? It is more courteous, it is more practical and it's more helpful, to parent and child, in the long term. It just takes time, and thoughtfulness.

As I discuss in the next chapter, we would do far better to cultivate our children's trust in their own emotions and instincts, to help them to develop sound judgements about people and situations. The NSPCC/Bristol report revealed, rather sadly, how very few young people felt that they could turn to an adult in their lives, and how few parents spoke to young people about their relationships even generally: these were mostly mothers with a history of domestic violence, who specifically raised the issue of violence in relationships in order to prevent their daughters from suffering the same.[37] It is clearly our job to protect our daughters, in their teenage years; discussion, openness, willingness to listen are surely a better way through – however difficult – than mere – more? – prohibition and panic.

For those who cannot rely on parents, families or friends to guide them through the complex desires and demands of the teenage years, good sex – and sexuality – education is vital. Not only is the abstinence scenario unnecessarily punitive, it is, once again, supremely impractical. Helena Horton, now a student at York University in the UK, believed that her own sex education at school was inadequate, with 'videos about the "consequences" of sex, such as pregnant teens articulating their regret, or the patients in a genito-urinary sexual health clinic':

It was not told to us that these were consequences of unsafe or irresponsible sex, it was just implied that this happens if you dare to sleep with someone. We were told, truthfully but not realistically, multiple times that the best way to prevent pregnancy and STIs is celibacy. We weren't told where our nearest STI clinic was, or about LGB sex, or consent, or that sex is a completely natural and pleasurable thing. We were shown a quite graphic video of people's infected privates, but not what a clitoris does. We were taught about the dangers of taking heroin, but not that people having lesbian sex, for example, should probably use protection too. There seemed to be a fear, from the adults, of our sexuality.

According to the UK-based Campaign to End Violence Against Women, close to one in four (24 per cent) sixteen-to-eighteen-year-olds said that their teachers never told them unwanted sexual touching, sharing of sexual pictures or sexual name-calling are unacceptable; 40 per cent of sixteen-to-eighteen-year-olds said they didn't receive lessons or information on sexual consent, or didn't know whether they did.[38] This was a picture confirmed by the NSPCC/Bristol report where one girl reported the following, surely not uncommon, experience:

I only ever had probably about two lessons in this school about it and it wasn't good [laughs] . . . maybe they should get a professional to come in and put it on the timetable as a citizenship lesson and maybe from Year 9. But I think it is really important, well I think

there is not enough of it because kids don't know anything about
. . . They teach you about drugs . . . and everything and the cause
but when it comes to sex and things it's not there.[39]

American studies on oral sex have shown
that for those who have taken the abstinence
pledge, oral and anal sex become the substitute
sexual experience.[40]

> American studies on oral sex have shown that for those who have taken the abstinence pledge, oral and anal sex become the substitute sexual experience.

Once again, austerity plays a negative role.
In the UK there have been extensive cutbacks
to local authority and school budgets, with
more experienced sex educators losing their
jobs or funds to do important outreach work
and more emphasis on 'payment by results'
(the mind boggles.) As Libby Brooks, the author of *The Story of
Childhood: Growing up in Modern Britain*, has observed,

> It's an ongoing poverty of provision that is beyond baffling, when we
> know that evidence-based, relationship-focused, age-appropriate
> teaching, delivered by specialised staff, has been proven by decades
> of research to reduce teenage pregnancy and STI rates while devel-
> oping young people's confidence to say no as well as yes — and to
> access the services they need when they need them.[41]

In the UK, sex education was not made statutory by New Labour
when in government, and the Coalition government elected in 2010
has been inactive on the issue; in addition, academies and free schools,
which now make up over half of all the UK's secondary schools, can
opt out of statutory provision. On Valentine's Day 2013 a cross-party
group of women MPs, headed by Labour's Stella Creasy and
Conservative MP Amber Rudd, secured a debate, and a vote, in
Parliament on the question of making 'personal, social and health
education (PSHE) a requirement in schools, including a zero-tolerance
approach to violence and abuse in relationships'.

Talking about their campaign and the reasoning behind it, Creasy
said, 'The need to teach young people about consent and sex is
paramount.' Amber Rudd revealed that 'Young women [have told
us]: "Please give us some help here. We're taught about sex, but not

'Young women [have told us]: "Please give us some help here. We're taught about sex, but not about relationships."'
Amber Rudd

about relationships."' Rudd added, 'It's also so important to talk to boys – and to talk about questions of consent.' In short, modern sex education should be about just that: what sex is, what it might make you feel, its medical risks and consequences, legal matters, as well as questions around trust and consent and safety. It should not carry with it implicit moral lectures about the rights of wrong of sex itself. And teachers also need proper training in order to carry it out.

Leslie Bell, author of *Hard to Get: Twenty-Something Women and the Paradox of Sexual Freedom*, issues a wise warning: 'The kind of sex education the young women with whom I spoke need is not merely about birth control, STDs, or abstinence, but *sexuality education*' – a term coined by Michelle Fine to describe a curriculum that teaches students the physical and emotional aspects of sexual desire, discusses how to realise what they feel, and suggests ways to effectively communicate desire to achieve their wishes in sex. 'While sexuality education for women could go a long way towards helping them to get what they want, as long as their potential male partners are schooled in the acceptability of sexual violence against women, young women will continue to be thwarted in their efforts.'[42] These worries were underlined by a special report published in spring 2013 from the Office for Standards in Education (Ofsted) which found that many schools were failing to give pupils adequate sex and relationship education and so increasing pupils' vulnerability to inappropriate behaviour or sexual exploitation. In more than a third of schools, provision was simply not good enough.

How can we help our daughters negotiate the sometimes impossible ideals of modern visual culture when it comes to what a real woman looks like? And how do we teach girls about their right to, and the importance of, sexual pleasure?

It is still a parent's job to provide our daughters with useful information and endless reassurance: often, we need to state the obvious over and over again. (One gets used to doing this anyway, as a parent.)

It may not be so easy when it comes to discussing images of femininity in pornography given that our children may not wish to tell us what they have seen and we may not want to indicate to them that we, too, may occasionally have glimpsed sexual images or films. But should the subject arise — and it may well do, when daughters are older — we could follow the wise advice of Kate Figes on her excellent blog called 'Spots and Cellulite':

> The flesh displayed in pornography bears even less resemblance to real female bodies. Fact — women have pubic hair and good men like women that way. Fact — breasts come in all shapes and sizes, just like penises. Fact — very few women enjoy sex the way it is portrayed in porn. Fact — very few people have sex the way it is portrayed in porn and don't let anybody tell you otherwise, particularly teenage boys. How do they know? Fact — your body is yours and yours alone. Your vagina is yours alone too so if you want to shave your pubes or dye them purple then that is your choice. But if that is because of pressure from boys or other girls then remember that this fashion has been created by the porn industry.

Figes has sound advice on a less dramatic level too: 'You know . . . If you met this or that model in real life, you might well judge these women to be unhealthily and unattractively thin. It's just that that kind of unhealthy thinness looks better on the page.' Or: 'Don't forget that they use hundreds of pounds' worth of make-up. Wind machines. They wear expensive dresses.'

Even still, it can be hard to reassure. As Figes has written, 'My daughters are intelligent, capable, beautiful, ambitious and kind people and I couldn't be more proud of them. But I also see how they cannot help but internalise the message that they are not attractive, thin or sexy enough, and need regular, repeated reassurances that they are, in fact, utterly stunning.'[43] Most loving parents tell their daughters that they are lovely; our daughters need to hear it, they appreciate it, but they also understand that we are genetically biased in their favour, and want them to feel good about themselves. There may be no way round that. But, at the same time, it may be useful and interesting to start a (life-long) conversation about the complex realities of human attraction.

Ever since my daughters were little, I have talked to them directly about appearance, and tried to introduce them to the idea that there are few fixed truths, but a vast array of perspectives, on human beauty. It is important that the questions discussed should be authentic, arising out of genuine situations and impulses, not phoney plants, for the purposes of education or reassurance. It's more about developing a habit of thinking about these things. So I might often ruminate out loud on the question of whether we find someone less attractive if we don't like them? (That continues to provoke lively debate.) Are there hard or soft faces, and do these accord with experience, effort, kindness and so on? Why is it that 'personality' − or that even more elusive element, a 'sparkle' of some kind − is so much part of what draws us to others, and them to us? Why is it that those who are 'comfortable in their skin' are almost always more attractive, but that getting to feel like this may be a life-time quest, part of the slow building of self-confidence?

In a recent interview, the editor of *Vogue*, Alexandra Shulman highlighted the essential, if enjoyable, falsity of the glamorous world of fashion modelling. Shulman has audibly tried to use her position to bang the drum against some of the more extreme aspects of body consciousness. As one interviewer noted, 'She is a staunch defender of the fashion industry in general, but believes it needs to be seen as fantasy. How do you make young girls see it that way, I ask? She says she is excited by a current plan she has to put together "some kind of package for schoolgirls", about what actually goes into a fashion shoot, to inform them that magazines always . . . have 24 hours to get the image you want, and (there are) 32 people working on it, and (then there's) all the retouching and lighting and hair and make-up. Just to make it clear that this is not how anyone would expect to look when they get out of bed in the morning. It's a construct, like a movie is a construct. The harm is the idea they are reality.'[44]

No parent of a daughter can be unaware of the role that the internet and social media play in our daughters' upbringing. Rowenna Davis, twenty-eight, is a journalist and councillor in Southwark, south London. She says,

Girls . . . will go out wearing extra make-up − so they look better in the photos even though they know they are wearing too much.

The photos will last. There is this obsession with perfection, with how we are perceived . . . and I think that is stifling their personal development because all the girls are thinking is: what do I look like, what do other people think of me, rather than who am I? And who or what do I want to be?

She also thinks there is a greater division than ever along lines of class, with 'educated middle-class women having interesting and exciting debates about things. Whereas a lot of working-class women are aspiring to celebrity culture.'

Fashion journalist Caryn Franklin says of many of today's girls, 'Instead of asking, "What do I stand for, what do I want to say?", identity is condensed into a "physical veneer" . . . not about what you stood for/believed . . . the question becomes, "Is the veneer glossy enough, and if not, we must put more effort in" . . . all about getting the look, wearing the right dress.'

Davis is right about the importance of the picture; capturing a moment, a pose, a snap of our best self; the so-called 'selfie' circulating on Instagram, Twitter, Facebook and Tumblr-style blogs. There are numerous reasons why girls might be in particular thrall to the self-image — and not all of it concerns sexual display or even a need to prove oneself part of a group. After all, photography provides a continuous tool in the quest to find and capture the best image of one's imagined best self; it is also a way to hold time to account, keep it still; proof of a life and life well lived which is, ironically enough, as important to a thirteen-year-old as a sixty-five-year-old. I am much less worried, as a parent, by the risks of public sexual display on social media sites than by the cultivation of certain narcissistic habits, and an erosion of the very notion of privacy itself.

Here, too, there is an emerging consensus on some of the dangers of this Alice-down-the-rabbit-hole nature of the online world. *Girl Land* author Caitlin Flanagan echoes the concern of radical socialist philosopher Nina Power when she argues, 'There is no such thing as a private experience any more . . . I would contend that [this] is most punishing to girls.'[45] Flanagan mourns the vanishing of the dream space and its replacement by relentless communication as a real loss for girlhood, if not the very erosion of a precious period of life altogether. I am not so sure. Like so many technological developments, social media can be used in a number of ways, some positive, some negative. We cannot wish the world of the smart phone and lap top and iPod away; to some extent we have to trust our daughters to discover both its delights and dangers. Access to an extraordinary range of music, films and short videos are just some of the delights. Instant communication makes it easier for parents to keep track, keep in touch. Yes, there can be an annoying, obsessive quality to peer-to-peer communication: the empty eyes, lack of response, as fingers dance busily over the hand-held BlackBerry. Annoying to adults? Certainly. The creation of a new etiquette of social relations? Undoubtedly. The means by which our children, and particularly our daughters, are being corralled and corrupted? No. Those who are already emotionally fragile may be vulnerable to online 'bullying', but these kinds of pressures pre-date the internet. Those who are sexually at risk face new, albeit magnified, forms of very old dangers.

What about sex? Even young children realise, if only subliminally, that they owe their very existence to the act of sex; they are born from their mother's all-too-human body. *Eeeew. Disgusting.* Etc. It does not prohibit discussion of 'the facts of life' but it certainly throws up a barrier between mothers and daughters (and even more so between fathers and daughters). Talking recently about coming out to her mother, the actress and comedian Sue Perkins said that the really difficult thing about it was the introduction of the idea that she was actually having sex, regardless of who with. That is the mortifying, if utterly obvious, fact in play. Despite these embarrassments, it is vital to get across the simple message to our daughters that only they can decide what to do, and with whom, and that a young woman who values herself is more likely to be valued by others.

I asked four friends, all of whom are involved in 'communications' in some way, how they dealt with this delicate issue:

*Friend number 1:* I answered any questions directly put to me about sex but didn't talk about the act itself, or its effect on me, or sexual pleasure etc., and recently, a newspaper asked me to write a piece about my first sexual experience and I turned it down specifically because of my daughter. If I hadn't got her, I would probably have written the piece.

I told her about the commission and she said she'd be fine about me doing it, but I felt inhibited. I don't think it's part of the parent–child relationship, to talk about intimate experiences, UNLESS they come to you and ask. In which case, I would feel duty bound and indeed willing to discuss it. Something about boundaries here, I think.

*Friend number 2*: Despite having what I'd describe as a very open relationship with my children they were always very guarded about their private lives. And so as my two daughters were growing up I found myself wary of saying anything; since I grew up in a pretty sheltered environment and they didn't. There was an unspoken under-standing that in a way they knew MORE than me. Also they were both always 'sensible', late-ish developers, so no boyfriends till twenty-odd. They also read a lot, debated things like safe sex at school, and so I felt I had permission to have a very hands-off approach. I never felt I was ducking out. Instinctively I knew if I raised the subject of sex with them they would either shrug, laugh or scream. Oddly, I feel I can be more open with my teenage son on all these matters. He's not as embarrassed as they were.

*Friend number 3*: When they were little, I gave them the basic facts of life – and tried to be quite honest about it. By the time they got to the early teen years, I was passing them basic material – booklets and things – on 'what happens to your body in puberty' but in a slightly shifty manner. I would sometimes sit with them when certain programmes were on late at night – those entertaining but ghastly shows about sex and bodies. I found them almost shockingly frank. There was this one TV journalist called Anna who took a sex educa-tion show around schools – and she would put naked men and women, of different ages, up on a stage – and get the children to talk about it. It was great actually. My daughters and I sniggered a bit but it was very instructive and I felt a weight taken off my shoulders. Once my elder daughter got involved in a relationship, at seventeen, it was harder. More books, I'm afraid. So I ordered a copy of *Our Bodies Ourselves*, the American bible of self-help feminism of the second wave (one of the very few available from Amazon) and said, 'OK so I think this has important information which you need to know about.' More laughter – but I noticed that they would flick through it and I heard them talking to each other. 'Look at this chapter heading "What if I can't come?"' and 'Oh my god, there's a chapter on masturbation'. And I would say – 'Yes, very important theme', and then run out the room. That was the best I could do – I mean, what parent is going to show their child how to masturbate? Or even say those few magic words, 'Find your clitoris and make it work for you.' I guess, if I'm honest, that's the one message I would really like to get over.

> 'Looking back, I probably should have talked more about sex when [my daughters] were younger. To tell them they have a right to sexual pleasure, a right to say no, that you're not a slut if you sleep with a boy.'

*Friend number 4*: Looking back, I probably should have talked more about sex when they were younger. To tell them they have a right to sexual pleasure, a right to say no, that you're not a slut if you sleep with a boy. They should learn how their bodies work. They should not be ashamed to 'get to know their bodies'. I suppose one of the most important lessons is that there are different kinds of sex. And while I would say, 'learn to masturbate', because then you will know how to show others how to give you pleasure, it's also OK to have sex, and not to come. Maybe you can only come fairly intermittently. The point is, there are different kinds of sex. I feel it is my duty as a parent, if I want to promote real happiness for my daughters, to be more honest about this stuff.

Have we somehow come full circle, I wonder? Perhaps we should be grateful to 'pornified culture' which provides more information than we dare? Mainstream comedies like *Friends* or *Love Actually* or *Sex and the City*, for all their unreality, pass on a lot of useful messages. In many ways, they are mild in content and deeply conventional as far as their story lines go (true love being the end game in almost all cases) but they are also strewn with references to breasts, blow jobs and orgasms; the stuff of real sex between real people. Yes, the female stars are mostly stick thin, and always sexy in a particular mould. Yes, the men want sex – and usually only heterosexual sex – but they want love. These programmes are important because, through sharp scripts and engaging story lines, they introduce young people to the idea (but not, on the whole, the representation) of women enjoying sex, even as they largely perpetuate stale myths about how women's bodies work in relation to sex and pleasure. *Sex and the City* contains frequent references to the clitoris and the pleasures of oral sex, even if there is only one scene, as far as I can recall, that features a man actually touching a woman's clitoris, and this during the act of penetration.

Inevitably, adolescent girls will be curious, moving towards, or having, sexual encounters, and possibly trying out all sorts of sexual identities in this period. In order to do this successfully, they need both space and separation from the adult world, but a sense of the continuing safety and approval of the family, like a safety net, under a high wire. Too many young women have felt the chill and confusing disapproval of parents — or their neglect — when they first embarked on sexual experimentation. Surely we can do better. We need not only provide information on the practicalities of sex, contraception, the risks of infection and disease but we can, watching quietly from the sidelines, help our daughters negotiate a new emotional phase. As Hilary, the main character in April De Angelis's play *Jumpy* — a comic exploration of the parallel biological breakpoints of puberty and menopause — says, 'Sex means Big Emotions.'

Experimentation, after all, means just that, a coming to terms with the new language of physical intimacy, its extraordinary power, and the ever unstable balance that will occur and reoccur throughout life, the constant push and pull for girls and boys between sex as romance, sex as intimacy, sex as power, and sex as pleasure and play. We should also, as adults, try, if only occasionally, to drop our own jaded suspicions and try to recall the mix of uncertainty and euphoria of these early years, the sense of complete secrecy and transform-ation of first encounters. I have never found it better described than in Curtis Sittenfeld's brilliant coming of age novel *Prep*, in which the main character, Lee Fiora, a scholarship student at a prestigious co-educational boarding school, becomes infatuated with star athlete, Cross Sugarman, who pursues her for reasons neither we, nor Lee, ever quite grasp. Lee fiercely desires, and desires to be desired, while feeling perpetually unsure of her privileged lover's true motives. She craves intimacy and approval, recoils from her ultimate and inevitable rejection, but is surprised by the sudden force of her own erotic pleasure. It is a moving, authentic account of a young woman's sexual awakening. And I'm pretty sure there's a blow job or two in there too.

# 3

# The Myth of Perfection

*In which we discover that perhaps the greatest gifts we can give
our daughters are emotional freedom, broad intellectual encouragement and the courage to fail (but that we need to face up to our
own stories in the process . . .)*

A few years ago, my daughters, then on the cusp of puberty, were
walking, with friends, through the streets of a city far from home,
when they were approached by a group of boys. Something happened
– an exchange of words, an intimation of violence – that made the
girls feel deeply threatened, frightened enough to come racing back
through the streets to find the adults, breathless with anxiety. Seeing
how upset they were – and remembering vividly the profound impact
of such incidents on me, when I was a child – I was ready to hear
the entire story then and there, to absorb the various fractured story
lines that were only now emerging and to show interest, and trust,
in the account the children were giving us. Almost immediately, one
of the other adults in our group cut the entire conversation short
with a disparaging comment along the lines of 'Don't be silly . . . it
couldn't have been as bad as all that.' The children were now demoralised, twice over: first, to have felt themselves in danger, then to
have had their sense of danger dismissed out of hand, and without
a fair hearing. They were being asked to deny their own experience
in order to fit in with an adult's view of what was appropriate. Out
of politeness, surprise, embarrassment or a muddled combination of
all three, neither I nor my husband insisted that our children be
allowed to tell the story, particularly not as the other children had,
in effect, been enjoined to stoic silence. For the moment, then, a
hug and brief statements of reassurance had to do. It was only later

that we asked our daughters to tell us what had happened, and showed ourselves more than happy to 'go over it', however many times they wanted or needed to do so, in order to come to terms with the disturbing scenario.

It would be easy to dismiss this as a minor incident. But this, and several like it, made me wonder about the cumulative effect of exactly this ordinary, brisk, so-called 'common-sense' kind of dismissal on a child's emerging self-belief, and whether it was something that happened more commonly to girls. Clearly, temperament, social class and mere chance play their part, but why is one girl able to deal with the pressures of the peer group, a first relationship or sexualised culture while another is uniquely vulnerable to these messages? Why are some girls able to stand up to boys who harass them or put them down while others crumble? What makes one girl decide to study physics rather than psychology or hair and beauty? And what about the kind of inner confidence that allows a girl to recognise, and handle, a range of emotions, and use those feelings in the service of the self, without straining for outer-directed perfection: the rare young woman who can, in Carol Gilligan's words, say, 'If you don't like me the way I am, fine!'?

Girls (and adult women) often read situations acutely and accurately but they are also frequently dismissed as 'neurotic' or 'exaggerating'.[1] (Indeed, the two truths may be related.) To be always obliged to deny, as I believe girls are under greater pressure to do, the complex, overlapping layers of reality that they so often perceive – particularly if it runs counter to received wisdom – or to 'make things nice' at the price of their own sense of personal truth or justice, risks fatally undermining the trust they place in their own observations and feelings: with predictable long-term consequences. It diminishes the reach of authenticity, which the American psychotherapist Mary Pipher has sensibly defined as an 'owning' of all experience, including emotions and thoughts that are not socially acceptable. And it renders girls more vulnerable to further diminishment of their self-confidence.

> Girls (and adult women) often read situations acutely and accurately but they are also frequently dismissed as 'neurotic' or 'exaggerating'.

★

> Up to puberty, most girls are not overly aware, nor bothered, by the presumed judgements of the outside world.

Up to puberty, most girls are not overly aware, nor bothered, by the presumed judgements of the outside world or by the complexity of desire or the strange, refracted world it sets up: a visual, emotional and sexual 'hall of mirrors', in which it becomes easy for girls to become (acutely) preoccupied with how they appear through others' eyes. I was reminded of the clarity and boldness of these early years recently when, walking through an exhibition, I noticed myself being stared at by a young girl, not much more than seven, wearing a red woollen hat, and a red coat. Her gaze was straight, as she studied me for thirty seconds, perhaps longer, without undue friendliness or hostility; with no predetermined attitude at all. She just *was*. And, under her calm, fair gaze, I, too, felt as if I just *was*. When I smiled, briefly, as if to grant her (unnecessary) permission to look, without explanation, at a stranger, she inclined her head a fraction, and continued to stare, before suddenly looking down and carrying on reading her book. How different an approach this is to the teenage years when, so often, any kind of human exchange is burdened with undue self-consciousness: the endless refracted judgement of self and others. And what a loss it can be, to girls, to lose this cool, other-and-outer-directed neutrality so young in their lives, even if it returns, in later life, and with full and added force post menopause.

Suppression of self is a clear theme running through the more thoughtful commentaries on what happens to girls in adolescence – that first, crucial biological 'breakpoint' in their lives. Over the past half-century a number of writers have looked at the variety of ways that girls' emotional or intellectual needs are diverted, played down or punishingly disregarded, despite radically changing social and economic circumstances. It's fascinating to read the magisterial Simone de Beauvoir on the struggles of the 'young girl' in *The Second Sex* – her monumental tome on women, written in the mid twentieth century – and so to grasp quite what has changed and what remains the same. De Beauvoir's central thesis is that woman is born, and shaped into, a second-class existential subject, dependent upon, and inferior, to man. Within her existential schema, adolescence for boys is the beginning of the finding of freedom, and while for girls adolescence is the surrendering of pre-pubertal freedom and boldness, a period of extended preparation for sexualised domestic serfdom – the time when a girl comes to terms with what she cannot do, the limitations of her future:

> While the adolescent boy makes his way actively towards adulthood, the young girl awaits the opening of this new, unforeseeable period, the plot of which henceforth is woven and towards which time is bearing her . . . her youth is consumed in waiting, more or less disguised. She is awaiting Man.[2]

Giving up the outward-directed energy and unselfconsciousness of youth, the adolescent girl takes refuge in narcissistic and unrealistic fantasies and crushes. Physical pursuits are discouraged, while violence – as a way of settling disputes or asserting sovereignty – is denied her. Even the girl who finds some satisfaction in educational or intellectual pursuits is stymied by the burden of housework imposed on her, and not on her brothers. 'And just here is to be found the reasons why adolescence is for a woman so difficult and decisive a moment. Up to this time she has been an autonomous individual: now she must renounce her sovereignty . . . she is thus doomed to insincerity and all its subterfuges.'[3]

Towards the end of her extended digression on the helplessness and self-deceptions of the adolescent female, de Beauvoir sees a glimmer of hope. She sketches out a vision of a potentially different future for women:

> Today it is becoming possible for her to take her future into her own hands instead of entrusting it to a man. If she is absorbed in studies, sport, professional training, or some social or political activity, she is released from obsession with the male, she is much less concerned with sentimental and sexual conflict. Still, she has much more difficulty than a young man in finding self-realisation as an independent indi-vidual . . . [for] if she devotes herself completely to some undertaking, she [is likely to fear that she] will miss her womanly destiny.[4]

In some ways, de Beauvoir's analysis has been superseded, if rendered irrelevant, by economic and social developments, massive cultural shifts and by feminism itself. Our culture no longer explicitly or enthusias-tically endorses the idea that a girl's *main* job is to marry, although one might argue that to 'partner up' (gay or straight) is considered one of her key economic/emotional *tasks*. As I argue later, the contemporary romantic or sexual narrative is more diffuse and ambiguous: and as we have seen in the previous chapter, the widespread educational achievements of young women now render de Beauvoir's comments on girls and intellectual freedom apparently obsolete. With a new generation of young women potentially able to outstrip their male peers at work, social change has countermanded her assumptions. In some ways, one of the most interesting aspects of her account is to read a description of girlhood that is not shaped or tainted by commercial sexualisation. In de Beauvoir's world, the restrictions on women's freedoms stemmed from unthinking convention, patriarchal family and social norms; of course, in many ways, it still does, but not in the unthinking, deeply authoritarian ways which to my mind look as inhibiting as popular culture's exploitation and cheapening of femaleness as a tool to market goods and services.

In other ways, de Beauvoir pinpoints continuing truths, as in her observation, made almost in passing, that a girl is more 'attentive to her feelings and so they become more subtly diversified; she has more psychologic insight than boys have, with their outward interests. She can give weight to the revolts that set her against the world. She avoids the snares of over-seriousness and conformism.'[5] She, too, perceives a direct connection between, or mirroring of, the autonomy and confidence of the pre-pubertal girl and the post-menopausal woman. One stands at the portal of the elaborate imperatives of adult womanhood, the other has exited from its often tiresome obligations, including the need to please or create connection – through relationships or motherhood; the post-menopausal woman returns, once again, to the outgoing autonomy sketched in the young girl, but this time cultivating her interests and activities with the benefit of experience, now enjoying an unfettered, more courageous yet enriched individualism. In other words, adolescence is a preparation for the job of caring, still allotted to women; menopause signals, biologically speaking, that the work of caring is largely done (although in the real world, many women are still caring for both children and elderly relatives, long past menopause).

Jump forward half a century – to the early 1990s – and, somewhat improbably, the messages on girls and adolescence had become distinctly more dramatic. Despite massive social and economic changes, for all the challenges of second-wave feminism, there was a sense – particularly in the USA – that adolescent girls were in some kind of crisis.[6] Journalist Peggy Orenstein was spurred to write her book *Schoolgirls: Young Women, Self Esteem and the Confidence Gap* following a survey by the American Association of University Women that confirmed that girls were not feeling good about themselves, either intellectually or physically. Orenstein spent a sustained period of time in two schools, one in a suburban affluent area, the other in the inner city, trying to get to the roots of this sense of 'personal inadequacy'. It was possible to read her analysis as a statement of how far we had come – and not yet come – from de Beauvoir's era, in which girls were only being socialised to marry. By the close of the twentieth century, this was no longer the case: girls in the relatively wealthy western democracies were being socialised to learn and earn but also to seduce and settle down.

Girls were taking this intensified pressure on themselves; they were taking it personally. Orenstein wrote:

> We live in a culture that is ambivalent towards female achievement, proficiency, independence, and right to a full and equal life. Our culture devalues both women and the qualities which it projects onto us, such as nurturance, cooperation and intuition. It has taught us to undervalue ourselves. We denigrate our successes: blow up our failures.[7]

Orenstein could even see this double vision within her own life story: on the one hand the 'perfect daughter, who always obeyed her parents, was a leader' and went to a good college:

> But there is another book I could write . . . it would be about how, in spite of all our success, in spite of the fact we have attained the superficial ideal of womanhood held out to our generation, we feel unsure, insecure, inadequate . . . it was not until I began this project that I truly confronted my own conflicts and recognised their depths. It was not until I saw how these vibrant young women were beginning to suppress themselves that *I realised how thoroughly I, too, had learned the lessons of silence, how I come to censor my own ideas and doubt the efficacy of my actions.*' [My emphasis.]

Orenstein noticed clear cultural differences among various ethnic groups; Afro-Caribbean girls had high self-esteem and stronger body confidence, she observed, but were not more confident at school. Latino girls had the lowest level of self-esteem, across the board.

At around the same time, psychologist Mary Pipher was exploring similar themes. A therapist, who had seen many girls in her consulting room, she was unequivocal and angry, 'Girls today are much more oppressed. They are coming of age in a more dangerous, sexualised and media-saturated culture. They face incredible pressures to be beautiful and sophisticated.' We have created, she said, a 'girl poisoning culture' in which adolescence signals the beginning of a struggle by girls to stay whole, emotionally intact; authentic. 'Something dramatic happens to girls in adolescence. Just as planes and ships disappear mysteriously into the Bermuda Triangle, so do the selves of girls go down in droves. They crash and burn in a social and developmental Bermuda Triangle . . . their voices have gone underground – their speech is more tentative and less articulate.'[8] Adolescent girls, she claimed, had been ignored by psychologists and had long 'baffled' therapists. Because they are secretive with adults and full of contradictions, they are difficult to study. So much is happening internally, that is not communicated on the surface.

> 'Something dramatic happens to girls in adolescence. Just as planes and ships disappear mysteriously into the Bermuda Triangle, so do the selves of girls go down in droves . . .' Mary Pipher

Carrying on this enduring theme of self-suppression, Pipher argued that 'adolescent girls experience . . . a pressure to split into true and false selves, but . . . the pressure comes not from parents [but] from the culture.' She believes that 'Girls are supposed to smile. If I'm having a bad day, teachers and kids tell me to smile. I've never heard them say that to a guy.' She adds, 'Often bright girls look more vulnerable than their peers who have picked up less or who have chosen to deal with all the complexity by blocking it out. Later, bright girls may be more interesting, adaptive and authentic, but in early adolescence they just look shelled.'[9] (So true.) Pipher's anger is palpable, her advocacy of girls and their needs important. Girls who speak frankly are considered 'bitches'; girls who are not attractive are 'scorned'. By the time girls become teenagers they look around and see that they exist in a largely male culture; their mothers are struggling with the same issues. Girls attribute their failings to lack of ability and their success to good luck and hard work; 'all this stops girls from wanting to be astronauts and brain surgeons. Girls can't say why they ditch their dreams, they just "mysteriously" lose interest.'

> Girls attribute their failings to lack of ability and their success to good luck and hard work.

Part of this comes from a shift girls make from 'a focus on achievement to a focus on affiliation'. Like de Beauvoir, Pipher too saw a parallel between the pre-adolescent self and the post-menopausal woman; a return to self, and the best kind of self-interest, after a long, often agonising, self-questioning, gap of thirty plus years. The trouble is, that's a very very long time to wait.

One of the most interesting writers to explore the theme of what happens to girls at adolescence, the exact ways in which they 'become tentative and inarticulate', and ideas for liberating them from this psychic prison, is psychologist and feminist Carol Gilligan. Gilligan is associated with a form of 'difference feminism' that has raised women's concerns to a higher moral plane.[10] Her 1982 book *In a Different Voice* laid down a direct challenge to male-defined, developmental psychology. Gilligan argued that traditional psychology laid down norms of justice that best fitted male models; girls thought in different ways about human situations and how to resolve them, and that these involved a greater sense of awareness and care for all the actors involved in any given situation. While *In A Different Voice* is considered a seminal – if contested – work, Gilligan has continued to write about adolescent girls – and their emerging voice, in particular exploring the idea of suppression and self-censorship.

She picks up these themes in her most recent book *Joining the Resistance* in which she explores the interesting idea that girls have a 'knowledge that often runs counter to what they are told by those in authority. So they are left, in effect, with at least two truths, two versions of a story, two voices revealing different points of view.'[11] We have come a long way from the slightly condescending tone of de Beauvoir and her belief that girls take refuge in 'insincerity' rather than authentic feeling and expression. Gilligan takes us to a potentially more gloomy cul-de-sac. She says that girls know – or intuit – things but then suppress them rather than clash with outside authorities. Her interpretation of adolescence is that girls embark on a conscious struggle between two parts of themselves:

> The tendency in girls' lives at adolescence [is] for a resistance that is inherently political – an insistence on knowing what one knows and a willingness to be outspoken – to turn into a psychological resistance, a reluctance to know what one knows and a fear that one's knowledge, if spoken, will endanger relationships and threaten survival . . . [this] leaves them with a knowledge that often runs counter to what they are told by those in authority.[12]

As a parent this makes sense to me, watching a cohort of robust, outer directed girls suddenly wrestling with complex feelings and impulses that too easily drive them underground, in an unhelpful way. I am often struck by how boys are permitted or positively encouraged to speak their minds, on whatever subject exercises them, while girls, who have plenty to say, sit by, apparently unwilling or unable to project an opinion or view. What is going on? Are they too self-critical? Do they not believe they will get a fair hearing? Do they struggle to find the right language in which, with which, to express themselves? Gilligan trusts that girls have plenty to say. She compares the depth and breadth of girls' emotional knowledge to 'a naturalist's rendering of the human world . . . [but] often dismissed as trivial or seen as transgressive, with the result that girls are repeatedly told not to speak, not to say anything, or at least not to talk in public of what they know.'[13] She gives numerous examples of girls seeing to the truth of a situation – one girl's awareness of the conflict between a Pollyanna-ish version of niceness that she is expected to adopt and her direct experience of a violent father and brothers; another's perception of teachers at schools who like to present themselves 'as nice and compassionate' but give away their true 'colour' – but being unable to speak it, for risk of punishment or ostracism.

In one particularly fascinating case study, Gilligan analyses one of the most famous and public documents of modern girlhood as an example of the way that girls are encouraged to silence an honest voice: Anne Frank's diary. Anne Frank hid herself twice over, 'I hid myself within myself . . . and quietly wrote down all my joys, sorrows and contempt in my diary.' That much is known – and celebrated; but Gilligan argues that Frank, who edited her own diary in the hope that it might appear post war, cut out certain (further) sections in order to present a certain version of herself to the world. Some of the passages edited included those that revealed she had looked at her naked body; sections which showed that she, her mother and sister were 'thick as thieves' after periods of falling out; her observations of how culture treats women as inferior and her subtle understanding of the way her mother was unhappy in her marriage to Anne's father, Otto. (Anne's father, Otto Frank, had been in love with someone else but had married Anne's mother, leaving the latter only too painfully aware that her husband didn't love her.) Thus, Anne, who well understood the truth in the adult relationships around her, presents herself as 'assuming a mark of innocence, a kind of psychological virginity, she – who knew so much – presents herself as knowing less than she knew.'[14] As a result the published, public version of Anne's diary presents, says Gilligan, an unmodulated anger towards her mother, rather than the more chaotic and complex truth of their ambivalent but loving relationship. After Anne died, Otto Frank added his own edits to his daughter's diary.

Gilligan believes girls can lose an honest emotional and intellectual voice in early adolescence, around the time that some boys lose their capacity for empathy. '"I don't know," girls will say as they bury an honest voice inside them; "I don't care," boys say as their relational desires become deep secrets.'[15] Paying close attention to the content and style of adolescent girls' speech, she notices the way that at a certain point it often becomes peppered with a series of verbal tics, that suggest a struggle between what the girls want or need to say and what they sense is acceptable. 'I don't know . . . I know . . . you know . . . do you know?' or the ubiquitous 'like', with its varying intonations, Gilligan describes: 'Voices from the underground, speaking under the sign of repressions, marking disassociations that are still

> Carol Gilligan believes girls can lose an honest emotional and intellectual voice in early adolescence, around the time that some boys lose their capacity for empathy.

tenuous, knowledge that is fragile, reaching out for connections that sustain in the hope that a secret underground will become a public resistance.'[16] (Referring to her transcription of an interview with one young woman, Gilligan observes with clinical efficiency, 'The "I don't knows" have doubled again but alternate now with the phrase, "You know".') This kind of wordplay, reflecting a rich and fascinating mix of the covertly certain lying beneath a top soil of apparent public uncertainty, will be familiar to many parents of adolescent girls.

One answer to the problem of clashing inner and outer selves is to aim for perfection, to subscribe to, and occasionally try to embody, the myth of the so-called 'perfect girl', an 'incredible construct [Gilligan's term] who is always nice, always generous, who has only good feelings and is good at everything.'[17] (A construct that sounds remarkably like the supposed ideal adult woman.) And just as with adult women, perfectionism is such a pressure for teenage girls not because it involves unrealistic striving but because it means suppression of a true self. The desire to do or be it all has an odd effect on girls; it makes them go inward, deny what they really feel. Carol Gilligan dissects the 'incredible' myth of the 'perfect girl' as meaning girls are in danger of losing their world . . . 'What once seemed ordinary to girls – speaking, difference, anger, conflict, love and fighting, bad as well as good thoughts and feelings are now seen as treacherous, laced with danger, a mark of imperfection, a harbinger of being left out, not chosen . . .'[18] Anger becomes taboo, but with the repression of anger comes the risk of depression.

It is interesting to revisit the 'girls on top' education narrative, with this more complex external/internal perspective in mind. Around the time that Pipher and Orenstein were dissecting the industrial-scale sense of inadequacy among teenage girls in the USA, and particularly at school, similar kinds of work were being done here in the UK. In 1989, as part of her work on girls, social class and mathematics, Valerie Walkerdine argued that girls' talent for mathematics was often dismissed on the grounds that 'the discursive production of femininity is equated to poor performance, even when the girl or woman is performing well.' And in a large-scale study into *Gender and Classroom Interaction* published in 1997 (by which time girls were already steadily outperforming boys in

GCSEs) Christine Howe concluded that girls were still routinely disadvantaged in the classroom situation. Boys dominated the physical context by controlling the use of limited resources; during whole-class interaction, boys contributed more and received more feedback from teachers. The research also discovered that the role of girls in the classroom is 'to do the listening and to some extent the responding' and that 'when girls' voices are heard, it is in a more private context'.[19]

Does this still hold? Most public concern today is directed at marginalised or demoralised boys, pushed out the way by a generation of high-achieving, determined girls. But this may not paint the full picture either. Emma Brent, an assistant head, and experienced teacher, is one of many educators who believes that Howe's analysis still holds, and that one can see 'boy bias' in the education system; and this relates to the ways that girls change around puberty:

> Girls appear to seek approval even from about 9 years old and limit themselves to how they engage in class. In the best classrooms, girls are engaged, put their hands up, volunteer, work with various partners, sit in mixed or single-sex pairings out of choice, offer up their answers, work and opinions, have confidence to challenge the teacher, enter into competitive games and laugh openly.

'Girls appear to seek approval even from about 9 years old and limit themselves to how they engage in class.' Emma Brent

According to Brent, in these classrooms, a positive relationships is seen between the teacher and both boys and girls. 'This is not about favouring girls. Behaviour is often of a very high standard in these classrooms which allows all students to be themselves and included.' However, 'in the worse classrooms, boys dominate the girls . . . because they also dominate the teacher. If a class is disruptive, the teacher will often not see the withdrawn, disengaged girl as an issue to be addressed. Often in poor classrooms, questioning and teaching and learning activities will rely heavily on question and answers led by the teacher and this is not effective for any classroom but allows some students to disappear.'

Some believe the answer to girls' lack of robustness in relation to boys at puberty is single-sex schooling. This particular debate has been running since the end of the nineteenth century. In the 1920s it was argued that co-education could help overcome 'sex antagonisms' and even improve the quality of marriage. In the 1960s and 1970s, studies found that boys, girls and teachers were happier in co-educational secondary schools, but that boys did better academically in them. In more recent times, some religious groups have encouraged single-sex schools, partly as a way to control girls' sexual behaviour, while in the 1970s and 1980s feminists advocated a girls-only environment in the belief that it would provide girls with more attention from teachers and a fairer share of resources; it would also stimulate girls' ambitions. In recent periods, it would be fair to say that single-sex schooling has been the preserve of two distinct groups: the better off, where the often unspoken subtext in parents' decisions concerns social class or ethnic difference, and the religious.

Some teachers and parents today put up a strong case in the media for the benefits of a girl-only environment, suggesting it provides refuge from the chaotic world of adolescent boys and the pressures they put on girls. Here is how one parent with three daughters at a single-sex school (but a co-educational sixth form, an increasingly common arrangement) in north-west Manchester describes the reasons behind her choice:

> Without the possible distraction of boys in the classroom they have become confident in their own skills, abilities and judgement; they question and enquire and seek to develop a thorough understanding of their subject. They are eloquent and thoughtful young ladies. I have watched them and their friends excel in courses and extra-curricular activities which in mixed-sex settings might tend to be considered to be the preserve of boys. These activities, including outward-bound trips, working in the local community, participating in workshop, focus days and a variety of foreign travel opportunities, have seen them develop their leadership and team-working skills and create a positive approach to their own individual potential.[20]

But closer examination of the benefits of single-sex schooling give a much more mixed picture of the outcomes associated with segregating the sexes during the teen years. In 2007, in what is probably the most in-depth survey of the long-term effects of single-sex versus co-education schooling in Britain, feminist researcher Diana Leonard collated a mass of information on the school experience, life outcomes and attitudes of the 1958 and 1970 birth cohorts – with 17,000 newborns in each (although there was some attrition) – in the light of their single-sex or co-educational experiences. Among the many results she unearthed, it appeared that there was within each school sector – private, grammar or comprehensive – 'a slight tendency for both boys and girls at co-ed schools to be more positive about school'. In terms of academic 'self concepts' (i.e. how highly a girl or boy rated their own academic abilities), they found girls in single-sex schools were more likely to rate themselves highly for maths and science (and to pass more public examinations in these subjects) while girls in co-educational schools had a higher perception of their abilities in terms of English. In terms of raw results, at first sight, it looked as if 'single-sex schools provided an enormous advantage to both boys and girls, but particularly girls'. However, as the researchers quickly note, 'these raw differences are extremely misleading, given the concentration of single-sex schools within the private and selective sector'. Taking these into account, 'the difference in exam results between single-sex and co-educational schools appears generally more modest'. In terms of the impact of single-sex schooling on post-school qualifications,

> Single-sex schooling was not significantly associated with either the chance of having no qualifications or of having gained a degree by the age of 33, once school sector had been controlled. So, having been to a single-sex school was not linked, except through selective schooling, to the chances of an individual getting a degree or other post-school qualification, but it did influence the subject area of that qualification.

In terms of wages, 'women were paid substantially less than men; but across school sectors, women who had attended single-sex schools gained higher wages' (although the researchers were not able to establish the link between this and qualifications/subject area or work experience).

How do these debates impact on the growth of single-sex teaching within co-educational schools? Co-education is still the norm in the vast majority of our schools and attention needs to be paid to ways to raise girls' intellectual potential and personal confidence in mixed school environments. While the number of girls taking maths has risen, science remains a stumbling block. Athene Donald, professor of experimental physics at Cambridge, recently pointed out the few numbers of girls who study science at A level; nearly half of English maintained (state) co-educational schools (49 per cent) don't enter a single girl for physics A level. The parallel figure for boys is only 14 per cent.

In her book Orenstein reported on innovative attempts by teachers in co-educational schools to take male and female students on a 'gender journey' as part of the attempt to break down negative or limited self-perception by either boys or girls. Nowadays, single-sex teaching is the more likely institutional response. On the face of it, it might seem a positive development. In the words of one headmaster, who separated the sexes between the ages of eleven and fourteen years, this

> shift from total to partial separation to full integration reflects children's learning styles. Children are at their most different when they are youngest; there has been a great deal of evidence to suggest boys and girls have different behaviours and respond to different learning styles. Boys tend to need more direction, while girls work better in groups, and we are able to tailor our classes accordingly.[21]

But feminist researchers believe that gender, and the negative impacts of gender stereotypes, can be exaggerated further in single-sex classes. According to Dr Gabrielle Ivinson, co-author of *Re-thinking Single Sex Teaching*,

> When we create single-sex classes e.g. for technology or languages – teachers often approach boys and girls by using examples that they think boys (or girls) will identify with. Teachers are usually wrong and they usually end up reinforcing gender stereotypes and compounding the problem. This is what we demonstrate in the book. Teachers teaching boys tend to use macho example that they think engage boys, but they only engage SOME boys. Others can feel patronised. And the same goes for girls.

Rather depressingly, some of the so-called new thinking about girls and science in 2013 seems to take us back, rather than away from, entrenched gender stereotypes and ignores the wider social context of girls' choices. In a recent blog aiming to rectify the low participation of girls in science subjects, Emma G. Keller suggested:

> Teachers at a science conference in New York a couple of years ago said that while girls are increasingly resistant to the idea of 'science' as a stand-alone subject when they reach middle school, they are invariably receptive and energetic students when the same scientific principles are presented to them as 'social studies' . . . The weather forecast, climate change, what we eat, illnesses and allergies, methods of transportation, the electronics that fill your house – are all areas of science that surround your daughter. *Scientific theory fires her imagination when connected to current or domestic affairs, or when she can empathise.*[22] [My emphasis.]

Girls, said Keller, learn with different parts of the brain, use language differently and need to be coaxed into more rational subjects through the use of cooking, recipes and references to shopping. 'Shopping is filled with math problems, particularly if your daughter wants something that is too expensive.'

In a furious riposte to the Keller piece, Kate Clancy and Chris Chambers argued:

> Central to many of the tips offered to encourage girls to take an interest in maths are purported facts about gender differences in behaviour and the developing brain . . . What about the claim that 'girls generally begin processing information on the brain's left, or language, side' and therefore that girls 'deconstruct math concepts verbally'? Existing studies do indicate a slight advantage for girls in acquiring language at a very young age (1–2 years), but – crucially – this difference has been shown to disappear by the age of six. A recent review even concluded that overall sex differences in language ability and language-related brain functions are 'not ready identifiable'.

As Clancy and Chambers point out, such assumed neuro-scientific 'sex differences' are now rigorously contested.[23]

Athene Donald has also highlighted the problems that might occur when teachers take a girl-friendly approach to a subject like science:

> Superficially, of course it is good to do things that will encourage more girls to stick with science, but then I began to wonder at what cost. If

my 14-year-old self had been presented with teaching about lasers in the context of cosmetic surgery as was being proposed, I would have been completely uninterested by the case studies presented and simply seen it as pandering to the readers of *Hello*, had such a magazine existed. Moreover, it could have backfired and caused me to lose interest.

Moving on to look at the idea that 'doing' science threatened a girl's self-perception and that therefore scientific topics needed to be presented in a more feminine manner, Donald observed:

> In my idealistic view, a much better solution to the problem identified here would be to reduce the early socialization of children in which young girls are encouraged to play with Barbie dolls (the dolls who presumably would be clear targets for cosmetic surgery at a later stage of 'life') whereas boys get to build rockets from Lego: I use stereotypes deliberately here. It is known that the disparity in interest in different sorts of scientific issues between adolescent boys and girls is much less in the developing world where, I would posit, this socialization into stereotypes is less. So patching up the science teaching at 14 to correct a set of problems generated earlier, probably at the expense of losing other children's interests . . . may not be the optimum solution.[24]

But there's a wider benefit to co-education, surely? According to the findings of the 2007 survey of the long-term effects of single-sex schooling, there was, despite the fears of religious opponents of co-education, 'no significant deterrent effect' of single-sex schooling on teenage parenthood for either girls or boys;

> however, the chief emotional impact of single-sex schooling seems to have been on men, as the study found that 'men who had attended boys' schools in the private and grammar sectors suffered from slight but statistically higher levels of malaise in mid-life than their peers from comprehensive schools – and were somewhat more likely to have divorced or separated by the age of 42.'[25]

According to Anthony Seldon, a leading educator in the British private sector, 'there is simply no overwhelming evidence that single-sex education is better academically for young people':

It is not enough to just be part of a co-ed school that teaches girls and boys separately in class, because the really valuable interaction in co-ed schools occurs in lessons. For much of the rest of the time, boys and girls are separate, socially and at games. So what happens in lesson time in terms of learning about each other is crucial. In English lessons, it is invaluable to have both female and male perspectives on texts. Girls learn about how boys see poems, plays and novels, and boys understand the very different readings girls often give. They learn to understand and respect different views and opinions. In science and even maths girls and boys respond differently, with boys being quicker to express themselves, and girls being more thoughtful and considered.

Seldon adds,

The word 'education' means 'to lead out'. What is it that is being 'led out'? It is all the different intelligences or aptitudes that go to make up each child. Even if there was a clear argument that children do better with their logistical and linguistic intelligence if educated in single-sex schools – and there is no clear case – what of the other aptitudes that schools desperately need to draw out if they are to educate the whole child? The development of the creative intelligence critically needs male and female perspectives; so does the personal and the social, the spiritual and the moral.[26]

So in what other ways might girls be productively 'led out' in their learning? Teachers at one London school attribute their recent success in encouraging a number of girls into science to a concerted effort on their part to counteract any negative stereotypes about what physicists might do, or be like, in the real world: 'We realised there was a dearth of girls, so we tried to get more speakers and role models to come into the school and talk to the pupils. Also it helps to get girls to do it together.' The importance of a supportive network of friends taking the same subject is key. According to one student, it is often 'a question of seeing more positive role models on television and in schools'. Although there are prominent male presenters in popular science in the UK – Brian Cox, David Attenborough – they have hardly any female counterparts. And when female scientists do make it on to the pages of newspapers, or into television studios, the way they are presented can be extremely patronising. A 2010 paper

A 2010 paper by academics at the University of Cardiff examined fifty-one interviews with scientists, eight of whom were women, pulled from a sample of twelve UK national papers in 2006. Half of the profiles of the women referred to their clothing, physique or hairstyle, compared with 21 per cent of the profiles of men.

by academics at the University of Cardiff examined fifty-one interviews with scientists, eight of whom were women, pulled from a sample of twelve UK national papers in 2006. Half of the profiles of the women referred to their clothing, physique or hairstyle, compared with 21 per cent of the profiles of men. The male scientists interviewed were often used to signal gravitas, while women were more likely to be said to make science 'accessible' or 'sexy'.

Donald also notes:

Some very simple interventions have been shown to have dramatic effects to overcome what is known as stereotype threat, a phenomenon in which individuals perform badly because they belong to a group (such as girls in physics and maths classes) who stereotypically are expected to do badly. A couple of years ago a study showed that a brief 'self-affirmation' exercise had a remarkable effect on the grades of women doing physics at US colleges. Perhaps something like that should be introduced in UK schools to counter the negative messages that girls appear to be receiving.

She has also argued that 'Messages, cues [discouraging girls] will be being picked up all the time around the school from peers and other teachers. That is why the ethos in the school is so important and gender stereotyping, of any sort and anywhere within the school, must be actively challenged.' Donald perceptively notes that it only takes 'one unguarded remark' to a teenager to discourage a girl from taking or pursuing a scientific subject, often with long-term effects. 'Teachers and parents alike should consider what implicit subtexts are being conveyed to the girls around them.'[27]

It is important to encourage girls in ways that are realistic but not regressive. For example: a school may have noticed that only boys come forward for the school debating society, and take part in public competitions. In a bid to encourage girls, it invites any students who are interested to come along at 4 p.m. on a Wednesday afternoon in order to create a girl's debating club. This may encourage a few interested girls – but it may not – and the idea dies. Perhaps a particularly persistent teacher decides to craft her own class, and hand-picks a couple of eloquent or enthusiastic girls from every class and introduces them to the somewhat arcane rules of formal debating with its proposer, seconder, protected time, and all the rest of it. The girls are told to go away and research a subject – and an attitude towards a subject – and then debate it in this particular format. A couple of the girls prove competent at it; two or three more dissolve into giggles and/or nerves when asked to perform before a group, and plead with the teacher to be excused from participating – particularly when a 'friendly' competition is proposed between them and the apparently more assertive boys. Another complains that she doesn't like having to argue a position that she doesn't really believe in; it feels false. So, over the course of a few weeks or a term, the idea of the girls' debating sessions dies; the persistent teacher feels somewhat demoralised but can reassure herself that she tried. Meanwhile, the girls breathe a sigh of relief at not having to take part in such a formal and possibly alienating or even terrifying process.

Such a problem is not unfamiliar to teachers, at every level of education. Anna Rowlands taught young women training for ordination at Cambridge University and now teaches young women at King's College London, and finds that

> There's a huge contradiction there . . . fiercely intelligent women who have come through the education system already, who have a zero tolerance approach to patriarchy, and sexism, but are still ambivalent about speaking in public. They are held back by a combination of the 'norm of niceness' – that women should listen first – and a sense that they are less sure that what they want to say is valuable. So you will notice that often women in the room are the last to speak, which leaves space for their male colleagues to dominate.

Rowlands also believes that 'the oral rhetorical culture represents the vestige of a public-school model and that only a minority of women thrive in that kind of environment'. As an experienced teacher, she makes the considered decision not to 'construct a classroom as a rhetorical debating society':

> You level the playing field. You make sure that you use a variety of teaching methods to ensure that everyone speaks. I use small groups, I ask each member to 'prepare a precis' of a passage for the following week, to ensure everyone's participation and I create a conversational rather than adversarial speaking culture. And I try to be very aware of who is and isn't speaking in a session. When there is someone – a man who has already spoken – I will say, 'I can see that you want to say something, is there anyone who hasn't yet had a chance to speak and would like to say something.' On the whole, I find that women will speak more often when such conditions are laid down.

What she – and many education experts – understands is that the job of creating confidence – for girls and boys – goes far beyond the formal skills of debating. Robin Alexander, the architect of progressive reform for a UK primary curriculum (that has been largely rejected by the current Coalition government) stresses the vital importance of oral skills throughout schooling, so that learning to know what one thinks or feels, in any field or subject area, becomes a kind of second nature. Reflecting on the 'deep concern in many quarters . . . about what is seen as a severe weakening of the profile of spoken language in government thinking about the curriculum', Alexander refers to the strong evidence that has already been presented to the Education Department:

> That evidence makes talk that is cognitively challenging and rigorously orchestrated absolutely essential to children's thinking, learning and understanding both within each subject and across the curriculum as a whole. It is also a vital tool for effective communication and a life-line for those children who are disadvantaged socially and linguistically. And we now have a critical mass of international evidence demonstrating that high quality talk raises tested standards in the core subjects.[28]

Anne-Marie Slaughter, professor of politics and international affairs at Princeton University, and former director of policy planning at the State Department, also makes a conscious attempt to 'push the young women in my classes to speak more':

'They must gain the confidence to value their own insights and questions, and to present them readily. My husband agrees, but he actually tries to get the young men in his classes to act more like the women – to speak less and listen more. If women are ever to achieve real equality as leaders, then we have to stop accepting male behavior and male choices as the default and the ideal. We must insist on changing social policies and bending career tracks to accommodate *our* choices, too. We have the power to do it if we decide to, and we have many men standing beside us.'[29] [My emphasis.]

> 'If women are ever to achieve real equality as leaders, then we have to stop accepting male behavior and male choices as the default and the ideal.' Anne-Marie Slaughter

Anna Rowlands talks about 'listening for the silences' and 'trying to draw the voices (of women students) out', while Dr Gabrielle Ivinson believes that

We live complex varied social contexts and girls along with any minority group need to learn to function creatively and well in all kinds of social contexts. So, we need to work to make classrooms, spaces where girls can express themselves confidently even when boys are present. This is definitely challenging for teachers who need to be very aware of how gender influences enter and work within the dynamics of co-educational settings – but we should strive towards this understanding – not give up and retreat into old structures.

Carol Gilligan also sees the problem in a wider context, including the lack of confidence of female teachers. 'Girls' voices, recorded in private and amplified in the public space . . . resonated with women teachers, encouraging them to ask themselves what they were teaching girls about relationships, about speaking, about conflict, about disagreement, about psychological and political resistance.'[30] Put more baldly, a female teacher who can't speak her mind to a male colleague or superior, is unlikely to offer genuine inspiration, or be a positive role model, to a female student.

Emma Brent puts it this way:

Teachers need to ask themselves the key questions: Where do I stand in relation to the tradition which I am practising and teaching in my classroom? Where do I stand in relation to girls as the next generation of women and what version of society do I want to project in my classroom? Like that student, you have to disentangle your own voice from every other voice you are hearing in the classroom, from the boys, from a male teacher. It takes more time to do that. And it is hard work.

But the process of discovering who one is, in all its fullness, inevitably begins (and, of course never actually ends) within one's first family. In the introduction to his monumental tome of collected academic papers on *The Role of the Father in Child Development*, Michael E. Lamb observes, with resounding common sense, that 'many of the behaviour patterns acquired in childhood are the result of lessons derived from observing others and adjusting one's behaviour accordingly'.[31] And no one who has raised children can fail to see the degree to which so many girls become uncannily similar to their mothers in speech, tone, attitudes to others, kinds of friendship created, expression of opinion and so on. This goes way beyond 'learning lessons'; it is more akin to a process of submergence, over decades, in one particular way of being (a way of being that it can take decades for a daughter herself to be aware of, moderate or indeed reject).

Surely, then, a mother who can appropriately display a full range of emotions – happiness, anger, joy, sadness – and who enjoys using her intellect, speaks out on matters that concern her, is going to offer her daughter something truly valuable. (Try to remember this when your children start shouting at you – it helps.) It is striking how many of the public women I interviewed for this book spoke warmly of both their parents in this regard. Miriam O'Reilly, who won a protracted sex-discrimination case against the BBC, talked of her father in this way:

> Everyone was treated equally in our house; we knew what it was like, as an Irish immigrant family, to be treated negatively . . . My mother would always ask me, when something was unjust, 'What are you going to do about it?' Even when she was dying, I knew she wasn't going to let me off the hook in terms of acting to prevent injustice. She did not believe in turning away, turning a blind eye to such injustices. She believes that she – I – we – had a responsibility to do something about it.

Similarly, a mother who significantly suppresses her anger or her discontent or her point of view or who places little value on enjoyment in life is passing on key messages that will influence or shape her daughter's behaviour for years to come. The trouble is, these are not simple polarities: the human qualities at issue are not shared out like sweets at the end of a party. Many women embody, and display, a complex mish-mash of strength and outspokenness, passivity and pretending.

This is hardly surprising. Most grown women wrestle with the spoken and unspoken imperatives of femaleness throughout their lives; and these can be re-ignited by having teenage daughters, with their fresh-minted hopes and raw angers, that seem both familiar and yet ghostly reminders of who they once were but may be no longer. Mary Pipher writes of adult women who come to her consulting rooms and finds that 'they struggle with adolescent questions still unresolved. How important are looks and popularity? How do I care for myself and not be selfish? How can I be honest and still be loved? How can I achieve and not threaten others? How can I be sexual and not a sex-object? How can I be responsive but not responsible for everyone?' If a mother has not begun to address these questions (for the answers take a longer time to emerge – if they ever do) then a daughter will struggle also.

One of the key ways in which women model and pass on attitudes to their daughters is in relation to food. Sally, who became an anorexic in her teens, says, 'Since I was eleven my mother would say, "You're getting a bit fat." I was a rather chubby adolescent, so I began to put my lunch in the bin.' Susie Orbach believes that the modelling of women begins even earlier – and that the message is therefore unconscious, deeply rooted: if a woman is trying to keep her weight down when pregnant or starving herself when breast feeding that the daughter will inherit a deeply 'unstable body' – and that this passing down of the codes of thinness from generation to generation is part of the reason that the weight epidemic has spread throughout the female population.

I recently conducted a little experiment. Sitting with a group of women, most of them mothers, I asked them what did they think were their *real* messages to their daughters? What – without thinking about it overly much – were they modelling in their uncensored Sunday morning, dressing-gown, behaviour? What attitudes pointed up or summed up the real them (attitudes that their daughters would recognise) as opposed to the image that they wished to convey, or tried to pass on, when out and about, with faces prepared for the faces they meet? Everyone smiled; this seemed fun. Out came some fascinating answers. 'Be nice. Make things nice. Do what is expected of you,' said one. 'Curb your eating if necessary, don't stuff yourself, don't let things hang out,' said another. 'It's not worth going to university if it isn't a top university,' said a third. It wasn't long before the conversation ground to an uncomfortable halt, the participants involved in a general shuffle of embarrassment at the reality of self-disclosure, the gap between who we wanted to be and who we really were, behind closed doors. (Only later it occurred to me that it is these gaps that often provide the fodder for human-interest columns, usually by women).

Do mothers treat their sons differently to their daughters? A number of women I interviewed made particular comment on the new girlification of childhood and the effects this is having on a new generation. Writer Rebecca Asher thought that 'girls are having a very gendered upbringing – think back to my childhood, we ran about in our dungarees. There was much more of a sense of androgyny about the whole process . . . it's regressive.' But what I am trying to get at is something slightly different and more subtle. Surely, the most warping form of treatment for a girl within a family is to feel herself not taken seriously – and not taken as seriously as her brother? In certain societies, the pride of place for a male is still accepted – and we see it clearly as such. Radikha is a twenty-one year-old student at the University in Cumbria. She described to me the long, fraught process by which she cut off relations with her grandparents because they refused to treat her two sisters and herself as full human beings 'simply because we weren't boys. In the end we went to them and we said, "We want nothing more to do with you, because you treat us so badly." Amazingly, our Dad supported us.'

But less extreme examples also abound. Surveys of the distribution of housework among teenage children indicate that in two-parent families, where 'there is a male breadwinner, strong gender divisions remain, with girls doing more housework; when a mother goes to work, or is a lone parent, then the contribution to the home rises markedly, particularly for boys.'[32] A 2010 survey of 2,500 parents, by the parenting website Netmums, found that

> Although almost one half of mothers say they know it is wrong to treat boys and girls differently, almost 90% admit they do exactly that . . . While they praise particular characteristics in their sons – seeing them as being 'funny', 'cheeky', and 'playful' – mothers admit that they are likely to denigrate their daughters for showing similar attributes, referring to them instead as 'stroppy', or 'argumentative'.

A newspaper report on the survey quoted psychotherapeutic counsellor, Chrissy Duff, arguing – logically – that 'this combination of a more critical upbringing and attributed negative personality types can have a long-lasting and serious effect on daughters. Women in particular seem to carry the feelings of parental disapproval and negative typing into their adulthood. The experience of receiving more negative reinforcements for stepping out of line than their male counterparts can lead women to view themselves as more needing of censure. This could be why women are far more self-critical than men, who have a more happy-go-lucky attitude when it comes to making mistakes and moving past them,' she added. Almost half of the mothers questioned also admitted that they regarded their sons as 'mummy's boys'. Over one in four confessed to loving their boys 'differently' to their girls.

Inevitably teenage daughters will be the first to spot, and decry, that sometimes yawning ravine between what a mother says and what she does, in whatever form it expresses itself – including in relation to male partners or husband. 'When my daughter got to about fifteen she used to say, "Oh, you're just a fifties housewife,"' says Nina, a highly-regarded professional, 'When she first said it, I giggled. It seemed so *ridiculous*.' (Other women, often in similar high-profile or senior jobs, reported being told the same thing by their daughters.) 'But when I thought about it, I could see what she meant':

> Since the children were little, I had begun to give way on small things in order to make family life work well. I would 'let things go' that irritated me or make an extra effort to be nice if someone else was unable to be. I began to hear myself saying 'Oh, it's just *easier* to do it myself' – the classic line of the put-upon housewife. And at some

point that become a habit and I split into two people; this out-there-speak-my-mind woman, which is what is expected of professional women these days, and then this other me, who dwelled in a kind of shadow state, an almost-but-not-quite now-you-see-it now-you-don't domestic martyrdom. My daughters see all that, of course they do – and what kind of message is it sending to them? That you can have work and a family as long as you capitulate on small – or large – stuff? And of course no one talks about this kind of capitulation any more; it officially no longer exists.

Kate Figes, author of several books of teenage life, partnership and infidelity, thinks that greater honesty, particularly between mothers and daughters, is essential:

> And I suppose it starts with self-awareness for a mother – the more self-aware you are as a woman in your own life – recognising the compromises you have made, the way you may have put yourself last – in previous relationships, at work or even now – just vocalise it. Your daughter will see it anyway. All you are doing is explaining the way you are. It doesn't mean she has to do the same thing.

In fact, it will help her not to do so.

Urging adult women to greater honesty as a way of urging their daughters to free themselves from unhelpful constraints is an important message. But it may not be as easy as all that, given the power balance of many families. Who didn't gawp in surprise during the recent UK court case at the claim that talented senior economist and authoritative civil servant Vicky Pryce felt bullied by her husband Chris Huhne into taking his speeding points or aborting a much longed-for baby? And yet, unlike many commentators, who were cynical at the marital coercion claim, it seems quite feasible to me that a woman who appears strong in public life might feel herself to be both dependent and disadvantaged at home.

Often, it is literature that most skilfully captures the distortions and dependency of modern marriage and motherhood. Emma, the main character in Margaret Drabble's *The Millstone*, published in 1964, says of her husband David, 'Our tempers are evenly matched, and we usually conduct our discussions with equal virulence, but one is at a hopeless disadvantage with a baby on one's knee, with milk dripping all over, and the prospect of a sleepless night if one loses one's temper.'[33] Nearly thirty-five years later, Dorrie, the much put upon protagonist of Helen Simpson's comi-tragic tale of modern domestic life, *Hey Yeah Right Get a Life*, reflects:

> It was for her to adapt, accommodate, modify in order to allow the familial organism to flourish. Here she was weeping over her own egotism like a novice nun, for goodness sake, except it was the family instead of God . . . She wanted to smash the kitchen window. She wanted to hurt herself. Her ghost was out there in the garden, the ghost from her freestanding self. If she were to let herself be angry about this obliteration, of her particular mind, of her own relish for things, then it would devour the family.[34]

Sally is in her twenties. She grew up watching her father abuse her mother, out of a twisted sort of jealousy at her mother's greater social and career success. 'I love and admire her now, but I really hated her so much when I was a teenager. She was one of the youngest female executives in her company – aloof, clear, competent. Then she got married and my Dad couldn't cope with her success.' Sally remembers horrendous rows:

> My Dad threw her clothes out – and I remember them hanging there in the tree. She'd sit in the car because he'd be busy smashing things up. I was eight years old – and I'd be the one who had to help her. As I got older, my anger was misdirected – I felt it was her fault and weakness that she didn't leave him, not properly. I became anorexic. I wanted to hurt her and show him how much damage he had done us.

Nina began to be franker within the domestic setting as the children got older – in part, because she wanted to set an example to her daughters:

> Slowly, I started to become less tolerant or not so keen to smooth things over. To speak my mind a little more. It seems crazy that these things are so hard to do in a domestic setting – but I think silence can easily settle over people in routine or intimate situations. Men, too, although they may talk less about it to others whereas women would rather sit

and complain to their friends or simmer in silence, with all sorts of consequences for the quality of their lives and relationships, than say, 'Enough, I'm not having it.' I suppose, too, there is a fear of the whole thing – the family thing – blowing up in their face. But then I used to wonder: 'If that is really going to happen, then perhaps it should?'

> **Girls can also challenge mothers to think about things differently.**

But girls can also challenge mothers to think about things differently. As a young woman, I was incensed by the unquestioned assumption that women were primarily responsible for the private tasks that make up domestic life. But I could also see that it wasn't such a simple question; I loved all the rituals of family life, from family meals and birthday events to holidays; at the same time I could see that their very weightlessness was largely created and sustained by my mother's herculean efforts. I must have wondered if, at some point in the future I, too, would be expected to labour long, unseen hours in order to produce, over and over again, the illusion of spontaneous, collective enjoyment: and if so, how would I ever get to do the things I loved to do, such as read, write, walk, daydream, talk, go dancing or fall in love? And what did the ability to give birth have to do with the ability to hoover a house? Why were men's tasks – speaking, meeting, plotting – more valued than the cherishing, cooking, cleaning jobs allotted to women?

One year, snowed in at Christmas, I sketched, on some pieces of A4 paper, a series of crude caricatures: stick figures acting out a variety of domestically enslaved postures, from a mop-haired woman wielding a blunt-fronted hoover to a wild-haired creature stirring a pot on the hob. Beneath these, I wrote some deliberately inflammatory slogans about fair sharing of household jobs and then pinned my home-made posters round the common parts of the house, along with some explanatory material as to why I was waging this particular domestic war. What was interesting was the response. My father loved the argument – and responded with his own home-made leaflets, rightly pointing out that as I seemed to do so little housework myself, what, exactly, was the basis of my complaint? A few days later, he even did a sudden blitz of housework – to show he could. But my mother was just too busy – fitting her own work into the narrow margins of time left to her after keeping all the domestic side afloat – to take my agitations all that seriously, beyond an approving giggle or an exhalation of loving exasperation. (I can still hear, as if within my head, the exact timbre of that sigh.) It was years later that I met a woman who had passed a long train journey in conversation with my mother, who had told her that my fierceness and my feminism had completely changed the way she viewed her own life. That memory – of a dialogue that I never witnessed, except at a sort of ghostly third hand – still touches me deeply.[35]

In conventional wisdom, it is fathers who draw out a child's interest and intellect, mothers who provide the bedrock of emotional security and create a sense of safety. Parenting guru Steve Biddulph puts it like this:

> For a girl, Dad is her personal ambassador from the Planet Male. He teaches her what to expect from men. A girl can practise joking, arguing and talking over deep things with Dad and these skills can carry into her friendships with boys later on . . . Pyschologists have found that mothers and fathers play complementary roles with daughters. Put very simply, mothers make girls SECURE, but dads give them SELF ESTEEM. Mum supports her daughter like a rock, steady and solid. Dad lifts her up, like a helicopter.[36]

This traditional pattern certainly holds true for successful women of a certain generation. Margaret Thatcher, Britain's first woman prime minister, was famously close to her father, Alfred Roberts, an alderman in Grantham, who stimulated and encouraged her political interest and involvement. Eva Tutchell and John Edmonds have interviewed well over a hundred successful women as part of their research into the question of why so few women hold positions of power in Britain. They told me:

> Most of the successful women who told us about their upbringing mentioned at least one aspirational parent. However, we noticed a significant difference between the way women described the support they received from their mothers and the support given by their fathers. Backing from mothers was welcomed and quietly acknowledged but support from their fathers was specially valued and

celebrated. 'He told me that I could achieve anything I wanted,' said one interviewee. 'He always expected me to do well,' said another with a great big smile. It was almost as if a father's active support gave these women permission to be ambitious and even to do that very unfeminine thing, to admit to their ambition.

Of course parental encouragement is not essential for success. During the interviews we met a number of talented women who have succeeded in the face of parental indifference and a few who have even overcome tough parental opposition. We were told by one very eminent interviewee that 'My grandfather had to persuade my Mum and Dad to let me go to university. They thought it was just a waste of time.' But these are the noble exceptions. Overall there is little doubt that supportive parents, and particularly supportive fathers, play an important part in building the confidence of women at the beginning of their careers.

For Ellie Mae O'Hagan, writer and activist, twenty-seven years old, it was both her parents who spurred her on, intellectually:

When we were growing up, we didn't have much money – but my mother was very aspirational. My dad is very intellectual. From an early age, I was very clever and able to argue beyond my years. He would treat me as an equal – even at a young age, when I was eight or nine. My mum read to me every night until I was thirteen. She was convinced that I was a genius and would go on to do great things. She really pushed me.

For O'Hagan, 'My parents were my privilege.'

Anna Rowlands's father laid the foundations for her self-confidence. Now an academic and teacher, and mother, Rowlands was raised in a second-generation Irish immigrant family in Manchester:

Both my parents came from working-class families, but both benefited from aspirational Catholic schooling that enabled them to become teachers, and my father became a head of a comprehensive. There was a great emphasis on excellence in the family. If you were going to do something you were expected to do it well – yet, this was not at all about being 'pushy'. It was also an incredibly oral household. We were expected to talk over meals, to have views and to be ready to talk to others. I always felt that my father would talk to me as an adult.

When Rowlands won a part scholarship to a private school, aged eleven, her parents talked to her in a 'grown-up' fashion about what was involved in the decision:

They genuinely felt divided because they wanted the best for me but also knew what the wider ramifications would be. What they did was to lay the entire picture out before me and we talked it through. On the one hand, there were the opportunities that I would have. On the other hand, because I would be on only a partial scholarship, it meant there would be no money to give all three siblings the same opportunity so that if I went to the school, we might not be able to afford family holidays and so on. In the end, I chose freely and happily to go to the comprehensive school. There were consequences to this: I did not have such a broad education. I did not, for instance, come across classical music or learn about wider cultural history but I had an education in, and for, life and was still expected to do well.

Rowlands won a place at Cambridge and went on to become an academic. She believes, 'What matters is that one has an environment – or some encouragement – at some point in life, a place where the fullness of who you are can be explored and expressed. For some it will be through school or a teacher, an extra-curricular activity. For some it will be home. For me it was home, extended family and the Church community.'
Novelist Kate Mosse says of her father,

He believed people should use the advantages life had dealt them to do good for other people. He and my mother thought we should work hard and do what we said we were going to do. Not let people down. There was none of the pushiness that you see in some modern parenting, nothing like that at all. He and my mother supported whatever we said we wanted to do. My sisters and I were allowed to be who we wanted to be, rather than conform to their idea of the children they wanted.

But do fathers still play this particular role in family life, as more and more women gain an education and go on to have more fulfilling work lives? The old image of the father coming in through the door in the early evening, briefcase in hand, abrim with news from the outside world feels like a deeply old-fashioned model. Surely working women provide as much of a window to the world as their male partners? Are they not also, to use Steve Biddulph's words, 'joking, arguing and talking over deep things' with their daughters?

Jill Armstrong is doing a doctorate on the influence of successful mothers on their twenty-something daughters and is 'quite excited about the evidence I'm getting that the daughters have clear and specific reasons for thinking it was *better* for them to have a career mum who was more of an occasional maternal presence – as long as they knew that they were well loved and their mum was really interested in them'. Such a mother allows girls to see the satisfaction that a mother experiences gaining validation out in the world and how – going against decades of clichés – this is completely consistent with her being a hands-on, encouraging and emotionally involved parent. She quotes one young woman who says,

> I think the main advantage is if you know someone who's done it [combined career and motherhood], you know it's concretely possible. It's not just 'all women can, women have the right' if you can see that they've done it and how they've done it. Aside from the obvious advantage of being brought up and not having felt the absence of a mother, and knowing that that's possible. my mum has taught me to be ambitious, to know what I want from work or life, and know that I can get it. I guess it's encouraged me to know I could be successful if I wanted to in whatever career I wanted to but then equally to think that I can do that and be a successful mother, to have both.

At the same time, studies on modern fatherhood indicate a deep shift in what fathers can, and do, offer their children. *In The Role of the Father in Child Development*, Michael E. Lamb traces the changing approach to fatherhood from a developmental psychology dominated by 'theoretical analysis' through to a more empirical approach. He traces the way in which fatherhood has changed over eras and cultures: thus, Euro-American fathers at a time of colonial power were 'mainly moral teachers' while fathers during the industrial revolution had a 'breadwinning role' and during the Great Depression they were 'role models'. Changes from the mid twentieth century onwards have seen fathers become more 'involved' and 'nurturant'. Researchers now recognise that fathers 'play a number of significant roles – companions, care providers, spouse, protectors, models, moral guides, teachers and breadwinners – whose relative importance varies across historical epochs and subcultural groups'.[37]

Many modern fathers concur with these findings. Tom Schuller has not lived full time with either of his daughters, but even so believes that 'doing things with [my daughters] is a really nice way to spend time. Collusive activities. Telling stories together. Cooking with. My elder daughter will take the sous-chef role while cooking [although] it can be hard to get the balance right between showing an interest and intruding.' Schuller believes that 'Demonstrating that you care about them as a person is the single most important thing. Indifferent permissiveness is a form of not caring. If you only care about them if they achieve then they're not really a person.' He also believes it is the job of a parent to 'model' certain kinds of behaviour. 'What are you concerned about? How do you treat people? If someone's put themselves out, you should thank them. These are all important lessons.' But he adds that 'men find it harder to love someone when they're going through a grumpy, aggressive phase. Women are more likely to tolerate it.'

Stewart Park, a father of two daughters in their late teens, says, 'Childhood is about enjoyment – we are, as a society, far too focused on stages, on having things happen.' As a father, he has tried to instil confidence in his daughters' 'selves, their abilities and who they are as people':

> We always took them seriously, we never belittled them. When they were sad we took it seriously. When they were happy, we enjoyed that. Also we were both around a lot, so that they had time and real attention. I think you need to help them to trust their instincts, their intuition, their perceptions, follow their interests. I never tried to hide from them when I was upset. It might be done casually but I would express my anxiety about something that might be quite small, like a work meeting or being in a social occasion. I always felt it was important that they didn't see me pretending.

According to Lamb, 'Sensitive fathering – responding to, talking to, scaffolding, teaching and encouraging their children to learn – predicts children's socio-emotional, cognitive and linguistic achievements just as sensitive mothering does.' Lamb particularly rejects the idea that it is a father's masculinity that shapes a daughter or son rather than 'paternal warmth and closeness . . . the characteristics of the father as a parent rather than the characteristics of the father as a male appear to be more significant.'[38]

> Children with highly involved fathers were characterised by increased cognitive competence, increased empathy, fewer sex-stereotyped beliefs, and a more internal locus of control . . . there is no evidence that children do better psychologically when they have more masculine fathers, or that gender differences between mothers and fathers are of great psychological significance to children.

Put another way, the characteristics of individual fathers are much less important than the quality of their day to day relationships with children, and 'the amount of time spent with children, much less important than what they do with that time'.[39]

# PART II

## Promises, Promises

# 4

## Lean In – Or Lose Out?

*In which we discover that the new wave of highly qualified women graduates are not doing quite as well in the pay stakes as the media would have us believe and look at why the majority of young women are being left out of the 'lean in' discussion altogether.*

It is the only job she has ever wanted to do. As a child, Dawn Cowley wanted to be firefighter so much that she would go down to her local fire station, 'just to hang about. I would go to open days, clean some of the equipment, go and sit and have toast with some of the men. Try out the breathing apparatus. I was even allowed to go into a smoke-filled basement! And I would watch them do drills.' Cowley, now twenty-seven, was born nearly two decades after the beginning of second-wave feminism and at the height of Thatcherite Britain, both developments that changed our ideas about women, daring and ambition for ever. Or did they? For it has not proved that easy, in various ways, for young Dawn to pursue and fulfil her – marginally – unconventional dream.

Born in Liverpool but brought up in the East Midlands, Cowley had one advantage in that she was

> a bit of a tomboy at school. I never really listened to what people said. So people would tell me, being a firefighter, 'It's a bloke's job.' Female teachers would joke around and say I had a penchant for men in uniform. Even career advisers would tell me to 'aim higher' or people would say, 'No, you'll be wasted in such a job.' Still, I couldn't get it out of my head.

Cowley was initially rejected from the fire brigade because she was colour blind. 'Basically I saw the Chief Medical Examiner and he said, "You'll never get in." I was devastated, I tried to get into the army instead.' After a brief stint in the army she decided to go back and study, and did a psychology and criminology degree; she was rejected again by the London Fire Brigade and then starting working with young offenders. Only after an amendment was passed to the disability act was she able to apply to the fire service and finally got through.

When I ask her if the job is all that she dreamed it would be, there is only a momentary hesitation. 'The image of the fire service that is portrayed by film and television can be quite unrealistic. There is a lot more preventative work – doing training, lecturing, safety talks and installing fire alarms and so on. So fighting fires is not all of it.' As for tackling the blazes themselves:

> I wouldn't say I have never felt scared; you certainly have a healthy respect for the incidents you attend but your training equips you with the skills to deal with the situations you encounter. Also, working in such a close team, you work together, supporting each other and as a relatively new firefighter I am always learning from the more experienced firefighters. I do still get that surge of adrenalin though when attending bigger incidents.

Anna Coles is also forging new paths, of a different kind. Now thirty, she is a successful UK TV documentary maker who is considering her next move in life. As a younger woman, she had less clarity of ambition but equal amounts of determination. State and Oxbridge educated,

> There was never any question that I wouldn't work. I knew that I would have a career – and that it would be in something creative. I drifted a little at the beginning . . . I wouldn't have considered training in law, to become a barrister – which may have been a class thing – also I didn't fancy it! It wasn't creative enough for me [she comes from what she describes as an 'ordinary' middle-class family]. So I did some short-term contract jobs, some teaching abroad, which showed me I didn't want to be a teacher – it's such bloody hard work and also not creative. Then there was a bit of moping at home. I got a little bit melodramatic for a short period before going back to London to work again – as a researcher in documentaries.

After some work experience, she told the company she couldn't

afford to work for free, so they said, 'OK we will pay you . . . thirteen grand . . . I talked to my mother — and she said — 'Think of it like an apprenticeship.' I think this whole period of my life was characterised by wanting to find a job I was passionate about. Something that didn't seem 'boring', which to me then meant working in an office. TV seemed exciting, diverse and played on my desire for 'adventures' and meeting people who had lived different lives to my own. I really had no thought about where I would end up, but that at that time, day to day, I would be kept interested. This was more important to me than being challenged, or having an obvious career trajectory. I love my job and I made a good career choice at the time — my early twenties — but as my priorities change, it may turn out to be a poor choice . . .

To an outsider, the pattern of her work life seems both absorbing and nail-bitingly insecure, although she appears sanguine about it. 'You do a job — and you work really hard and then the contract ends. And you think you won't work again — and when the contract ends you start to question the whole direction of your life — and then another contract comes along.' Early on Anna realised that she was going to have to negotiate her own pay rates if she wasn't going to fall behind in a highly competitive industry:

I could see from the figures that women often earn up to 25 per cent less than men. And because in this industry you set your own rate, I realised that I would have to negotiate. I *had* to talk about money. And I had to ask colleagues, what are you earning? I was on £500 a week as a researcher. There was a guy I knew, in the same office, and he was about to go for a new job. He told me he was going to ask for £625 a week — I couldn't believe it — his reaction was that he thought he was worth it. But I've tried to take this attitude myself.

One of the things that she realised early on was that pay was connected to a person's skill sets in her industry: a lot of women 'don't like shooting — using the camera themselves — this can mean they get lower rates of pay. Whereas I've rarely met a man who's afraid of the technical side of the job.' Over the years, she has watched less confident women earning less and less as a result of their failure to determine, and demand, their worth.

> Three years ago, I was an experienced assistant producer. I knew one of my female friends was earning up to £200 pounds a week less than me. Why? Because I had done that 'push hard for the top weekly rate' thing from the beginning. But I would say, 'You know you can ask for more.' On the whole men come across better than women, and seem more confident in interviews. As the apparently stronger candidates, employers want to pay them more.

On the face of it, Cowley and Coles, in their different ways, represent a new generation, busting old stereotypes and forging ahead in their chosen area of work. They are also the lucky ones: in work, and good work, with definite prospects. To an older generation, these kinds of young women seem to possess not just a greater freshness but a sort of in-bred confidence, as if their very DNA has been altered by the political struggles of those who have gone before them. Maybe it has. Frances O'Grady, the first woman to be elected head of the Trades' Union Congress, a single mother at twenty-six, speaks of her own daughter, who is now in her mid-twenties, with both a mother's fondness but a keen, professional eye:

> She may be grappling with a similar set of problems as I once did – but she's very clear that she won't put up with any shit. I admire her – she goes out and grabs life. There isn't that degree of self-doubt that I grappled with. But the question is – ultimately will she – and her generation – close that equality gap? Will her financial independence end if she has a baby? Will she pay a big penalty? Will she have a satisfying work life and get the judgement she deserves?

O'Grady is not sure. 'The promises of a property-owning democracy are dead. Generations of children are at the mercy of private landlords – with dead-end jobs – working far below their qualifications, and there is a lot of general exploitation.' Blogger and editor Jessica Bateman sums up the current mood even more succinctly: 'Your early twenties are awful: no money, [you're on] the bottom rung of the career ladder and full of uncertainty.'[1]
Certainly, I came away from all my interviews with young women

with the same hard-to-figure-out mixture: tales of extraordinary competence and boldness mixed with an amused realism, and a brewing, sometimes burning, resentment. There is a new-minted anger among young women at sexist treatment: in part, a reflection, I would guess, of the recent revival of a more public feminism. 'I used to think that things were happening to me at work because I was young. Now I realise it's because I was a woman.' Susan works in publishing and she describes herself feeling

> 'I used to think that things were happening to me at work because I was young. Now I realise it's because I was a woman.'

a profound lack of confidence. The arena in which I work is male dominated. They speak in a particular discourse. And it's hard [for me] to express things in that particular language. I have this sense of not being correct − not using the right words. But also, they − the men I work with − seem to be so ordered − and therefore the connections that I see between things − make my speech messy and proliferating, rather than crystallising things. As one male colleague said to me, 'Sometimes you're really hard to follow.'

Another young woman, six months into her first job at a multinational bank, told me:

It's an incredibly macho culture. Every single success that the men around me have, they let *everyone* know about it. But it somehow doesn't work if I do the same. It's seen as bragging. I have to find other ways to let my bosses know that I have done well.

For her, it is clear that successful women are almost always seen as less likable. 'They have to proceed very carefully, with co-workers and bosses, if they want to progress in their careers.'

> Successful women are almost always seen as less likable . . .

A lot of the difficulties, particularly in the private sector (although increasingly in the public sector) are about conditions of work; long hours worked, lack of time not just for a significant relationship but for friends, family, leisure or pleasure. According to Laura, a lawyer, who, until recently, worked for a top law firm,

The hours were absolutely punishing. It was normal to finish at 8.30–9 p.m. And that was an easy day. For six months I would be working until nearly eleven every night. Often I would arrange to meet friends for a meal near to work at about 9 p.m. and someone would come in at say 6 p.m. and say, 'This needs to be done.' And there was no question, I would have to stay on at work until it was done, maybe until two or three in the morning. That sort of works when you're single. You can meet friends for lunch and dinner on your one day off.

Laura hesitates.

I guess what I found harder was the environment, I just couldn't get used to it. I would go into a partner's office and he would be cold, abrupt and critical. I was used to people smiling at me! To me, that was the scary part of the job and the profession. I was walking around super super tense. My friend A, well, now she doesn't get stressed, she's just much thicker skinned. So maybe it was me? I know I was getting ridiculously overtired. At one point, I had a senior associate shouting at me at 6 a.m. in the morning. That kind of low-level bullying was incredibly commonplace – to find people crying in the toilets.

In 2010, newspaper headlines in the UK announced an epoch-defining shift in the relations between men and women's earnings. 'British women in their twenties have smashed the glass ceiling and are now being paid more than their male counterparts – reversing the traditional "gender gap" in pay for the first time.'[2] The Office for National Statistics reported that 'women aged 22 to 29 now earn 1.7% more than men in full-time work. Last year men in their twenties earned slightly more – 0.7%.'[3] Meanwhile figures released by the Chartered Management Institute in August 2011 indicated that

Female executives are earning as much as their male counterparts for the first time since its records began, albeit only at junior executive level. Earning an average salary of £21,969, female junior executives in the UK were, the CMI declared, being paid marginally more (£602) than male executives at the same level, whose average salary is £21,367.[4]

The ONS figures for 2010 (released in 2011) on full-time pay for men and women were again encouraging for young women: women in their twenties in full-time work were still earning more (a solid 3.6 per cent — a rise of nearly 2 per cent) than men.

It was clear what social and economic shifts had made this possible: the long-term decline in manufacturing, the rise in women's educational achievements, the sharp increase in ethnic minority women's achievement. According to employment experts Jacqueline Scott, Shirley Dex, Heather Joshi, Kate Purcell and Peter Elias, 'We are now able to see that an enormous increase has taken place in the percentage of middle-class women of all groups in Britain, gaining degrees from the early 1990s to the early 2000s.'[5] This group has particularly benefited from the growth of the knowledge economy, which expanded so dramatically from the late 1980s onwards, from 8 million jobs in the late 1980s to 12 million in 2005.

Scott, Dex, Joshi, Purcell and Elias assert that

Recent and ongoing research on graduate employment enables us to reassess the prospects for equality for women who have acquired the credentials to compete for opportunities in the knowledge economy. It is here that we see the rapid growth in employment opportunities in general, with the growth of female full-time employment exceeding that for males.[6]

Not all women were in corporate hi-tech occupations; many were making their way in older professions such as advertising, banking, law, medicine, media. And according to the Office of National Statistics,

The social revolution taking place among the nation's twenty somethings [is] being driven by a rise in the number of women attending university and their subsequent entry into the better paid professions, notably the law; around 63% of solicitors under the age of 30 are female.[7]

Looking at these 2010 figures, journalist Gaby Hinsliff, keen watcher of the modern economy, suggested that we were seeing the beginning of something culturally significant in the UK:

It is not often, in these dark times, that one stumbles across a snippet of good economic news. So it's strange that one such shaft of sunlight in the gloom has gone mostly unsung. According to official statistics released last week, the pay gap between men and women – that barometer of shifting power between the sexes – has quietly shrunk to a record low and among younger women has shot clearly into reverse. Women in their 20s now earn a solid 3.6% more on average than men their age, after narrowly overtaking them for the first time last year. The rise of the female breadwinner, it seems, was no blip, but the beginning perhaps of a social and sexual sea change.[8]

It was a sea change that also appeared to be happening across the Atlantic. In 2011 *Time* magazine reported that unequal pay had been something of a 'festering sore for at least half the population for decades . . . But now there's evidence that the ship may finally be turning around.'[9] *Time* reported on an analysis of 2,000 communities by a market research company, in 147 out of 150 of the biggest cities in the US. This survey found that the 'median full-time salaries of young women are 8% higher than those of the guys in their peer group. In two cities, Atlanta and Memphis, those women are making about 20% more.' This squares with earlier research from Queens College, New York, that had suggested that this was happening in major metropolises. But the new study suggests that the gap is bigger than previously thought, with young women in New York City, Los Angeles and San Diego making 17 per cent, 12 per cent and 15 per cent more than their male peers, respectively. And it also holds true even in reasonably small areas like the Raleigh–Durham region and Charlotte in North Carolina (both 14 per cent more), and Jacksonville, Florida (6 per cent).[10] Again, the usual qualifier: this trend, the reverse gender gap, only 'applies to unmarried, childless women under 30 who live in cities'. Interestingly, the cities where women earned more had at least one of three characteristics: they had local industries that were knowledge based; these were manufacturing towns whose industries had shrunk; or it had a majority minority population.

Significant findings? Certainly. Yet only two years later, it appears that things are not so simple after all. According to the major Futuretrack survey, a detailed analysis of a cohort of UK graduates from 2006 and 2009 and their employment patterns and opportunities post graduation, the evidence was pretty clear: 'male graduates earn £24,000 to £26,999 on average, while female graduates' earnings are much lower at between £21,000 and £23,999.'[11] According to the report's co-author, Peter Elias,

> One of the more continuing and disturbing find-ings, which underlies all of the salary analyses, is the gender pay gap in graduate earnings that we found in a study 10 years ago has persisted and shows no sign of diminishing. Male graduates with similar qualifications, experience and in similar jobs earn more than females at the outset of their careers.[12]

> 'Male graduates with similar qualifications, experience and in similar jobs earn more than females at the outset of their careers.'
> Peter Elias

Once again, statistics from America show exactly the same pattern. According to a report from the American Association of University Women, a professional body that has an impressive track record of advocating the rights of women in education and employment, just a year out of college, 'the average woman makes $7,600 less a year than her average male peer. Among graduates from private universities, the difference swells to a staggering $12,600.' In a special AAUW report on the pay gap it states:

> After we control for hours, occupation, college major, employment sector, and other factors associated with pay, the pay gap shrinks but does not disappear. About one-third of the gap cannot be explained by any of the factors commonly understood to affect earnings, indi-cating that other factors that are more difficult to identify — and likely more difficult to measure — contribute to the pay gap.[13]

One part of the answer to the conundrum depends on how you choose to figure out pay — and therefore how you work out the pay gap. Take for instance the weekly pay of men and women in all occupations in the UK in the twenty-two to twenty-nine age group. In 2011, the median wages of a full-time male worker was £413.7 a week, in contrast to that of a female, £393.4. This is a fairly substantial gap by anyone's reckoning and reflects, if in narrowed form, the gap that has existed since 1998, the first date in the current series of figures from the Office of National Statistics (ONS) on annual national pay (then an average man working full time earned £308 a week compared to £263 for an average woman). Strip overtime out of this equation, and the gap shrinks considerably. A full-time male worker will earn only £396 compared to £385 for a woman. But it is only when you begin to analyse hourly pay – the basic building block of an individual's pay – that you begin to glimpse a female advantage: here suddenly women begin to creep up and overtake their male peers. Gross average hourly pay for men in 2011 was £10.19 an hour, while women were on £10.32. Strip that hourly pay of overtime and women begin to streak ahead, relatively speaking, in the pay stakes, with the average woman earning £10.32 an hour, and men only on £10.08.[14] (The same figures in 1998 were £7.72 for men and £6.91 for women: a far larger gap, but still far smaller than the gap in gross weekly earnings.)

So who earns more? In the real world – where individuals can boost their pay by working more overtime – it still appears to be men.

There are other reasons for the continuing pay gap, including the gendered nature of job choice. Kate Purcell argues that as long as you have

> gendered skill development (where girls make 'traditionally female' subject choices at school and go on to do traditional women's jobs) generally avoiding occupations in which men have predominated in the past, the gender pay gap is likely to persist. Girls tend to close off more options at a younger age, on the whole. Numeracy is incredibly important to access many career opportunities – and girls have recognised that. Significantly fewer girls than boys do maths or physics at A level, let alone to a higher stage.

A recent major EHRC report on 'How Fair is Britain?' spelled out the extent of the problem. 'Boys are more likely than girls to expect to work in engineering, ICT, skilled trades, construction, architecture or as mechanics. Girls are more likely to expect to work in teaching, hairdressing, beauty therapy, childcare, nursing and midwifery. These career choices have major implications for employment trajectories and income levels.'[15]

In 2011, school inspectors visited sixteen primary schools, twenty-five secondary schools and ten further education colleges to conduct a survey on the choices of courses and careers made by girls and young women at various stages in their education and training. They found a far from progressive picture:

> From an early age, the girls surveyed had held conventionally stereotypical views about jobs for men and women. They retained those views throughout their schooling despite being taught about equality of opportunity and knowing their right to access any kind of future career. A narrow range of gender-stereotypical work placements dominated choices in almost all the settings seen. It also found that from almost all of those interviewed the careers advice offered at school had little impact on their choice of career and failed to identify jobs that were 'unusual' or traditionally undertaken by men. Girls predominantly selected subjects such as dance, art, textiles, sociology, health and social care, biology, English and psychology and of the 1,725 examples of work placements for young women, collected from records, only 164 represented 'non stereotypical' experiences.[16]

Evidence given to the Parliamentary Select Committee on women and employment in the UK by the Royal Aeronautical Society (just to take one example of an area of work that does not customarily attract high numbers of women) also highlighted what it called the 'leaking pipe', which, in their words, 'begins from an early age with the different toys given to girls and boys and continues throughout education and into careers. Exam and university figures show conclusively that the number of young women taking science-based subjects declines from GCSE to A levels through to engineering degrees.' More disturbing still is that the UK Resource Centre for Women in Science, Engineering and Technology (UKRC) reported in 2010 that 'only 29.8 per cent (185,000) of all female STEM graduates of working age in the UK are employed in [science, engineering or technology] occupations compared to half (782,000) of all male graduates of working age. Nearly 100,000 female STEM graduates are either unemployed or economically inactive.'[17]

In her book, *What Women Want from Work: Gender and Occupational Choice in the 21st Century*, Ruth Woodfield suggests that young women, and their parents, are seduced by the illusion of greater choice of, and diversity in, potential work opportunities for females than actually exist; a significant amount of children's occupational information is based on television, magazines and advertisements. The gap between image and reality tends to further straitjacket girls and their choices, and contradict the narrative of unending change and progress. Woodfield argues that 'against a backdrop of female educational successes, the service-shift within the economy, and the spectre of discrimination being confined to anachronistic pockets, parents and daughters perceive a world of unfettered employment options.' Instead, she argues, they need to look realistically at what is on offer and think outside the girl box.[18]

> Genuine progress in employment and pay is confined to a particular cohort of girls: the 'decoy generation' in the making.

Thus, genuine progress in employment and pay is confined to a particular cohort of girls: the 'decoy generation' in the making. These young women often come from more affluent, highly educated families, with a strong educational background, have attended an elite university and establish themselves in work very young. Add to this, or include in this, the daughters of certain (but not all) ethnic minority backgrounds, families that place a huge importance on education and work, skill and qualifications. Many of these young women far outperform white working-class boys or even middle-class boys but tend to be outstripped by their own brothers. Anecdotal evidence suggests that within an ambitious ethnic-minority family a girl will be encouraged into the less prestigious profession while her brother is encouraged and supported to go for top jobs and top salaries.

Gaps in pay rates also very much depend on the sector a young woman enters. The ONS figures, quoted above, assess the median pay for all jobs in the UK, private and the public sector. But it is well established that the private sector, with its more individual pay scales and rates of negotiation, as Anna Coles discovered, has a larger gender gap in annual earnings than public or not-for-profit jobs, with the banking, finance and insurance industry showing one of the biggest pay gaps. Women in traditional industries such as agriculture, engineering, mining and quarrying, also fall far behind in terms of pay rates. This might well be due to direct, actual discrimination (as opposed to subtle, structural differences that can be put down to an individual's preference concerning type of job or hours worked and so on). Kate Purcell says,

> Life for a woman who works in engineering can be quite difficult. It is still very much a man's world. Women who go into these industries often describe how they are set up to do difficult tasks that they are likely to fail at, or put on smaller projects. In areas like this, you have clear examples of direct, actual discrimination.

In the public sector and some not-for-profit employment, routes of progression and transparency of pay are more established, which benefits women, although the pay overall is less, which does not. The smallest salary gap is in education. According to Kate Purcell,

> Women often choose the public sector not only because one can make clearer progression there but also because they know that some point along the line, they will be able to have a child, and not suffer unduly for it. That in itself is not a bad deal.

The private-sector gender pay gap — with women earning around 18 per cent less — is double that of the public sector, where the gap is only just above 9 per cent.[19]

As a public-sector worker, firefighter Dawn Cowley is on a clearly established, and transparent, pay 'spine'. Nurses, like teachers, progress through a number of well-established, and known, levels — although this may be changing with the extension of performance-related pay. A young female junior doctor is able, depending on her specialism, to plan her children at a certain period of her work life, and then go part time for a period, retaining and sustaining professional status and skills.

But another key difference, established from the start, is that young men tend to work longer hours than women. This is what is known as an 'attitudinal difference' — and considered beyond the reach of legislators and pay negotiators, part of what is euphemistically described as 'a complex balance of preference and constraint'. Of course, once women have children we can understand more directly what elements of preference and constraint are at work (children, in short). But what stops younger women from working round the clock when they are in their twenties and early thirties?

What stops them, in Sheryl Sandberg's words, from really 'leaning in'?

A couple of years ago I received an email from a young friend. Let's call her Ruth. Could she come over and talk to me about a problem she was having, that she couldn't sort out on her own? Of course, I emailed back to say I would be happy to help, if I could. Then in her mid twenties, an exceptionally lively and creative young woman, my friend had recently won a prestigious internship at a leading law firm. She loved her work, even though she found it difficult. The conditions were great: plush offices, good food, classes to help with stress, pods to sleep overnight in, great pay. But the hours were *crazy*. It was not uncommon to work overnight and snatch a few hours' sleep in the office. However, it wasn't really the now that was worrying her: it was the future-as-revealed-in-the-now. 'I look around the offices and wonder where are the older women, where are the mothers? And if there are mothers there, then when do they see their children?' She had hoped that one day she would have children and that when she did, she could have what her parents had; a life where they both worked but were both there for her and her siblings when she was growing up, and where there would be time, just to be, to enjoy life. 'And I can't see any way that I will be able to do what I do now – work in this environment – and be that kind of parent – even if I found the time to meet someone, which looks equally unlikely.'

The choice seemed stark to her: drop out – and waste all the hard work so far. Or, should she ever have children, 'contract out – childcare – and see my children at nine at night which will even then restrict my working hours to such an extent it will mean I am not taken seriously as a senior partner or whatever.' She hesitated. 'At home, when I was a kid, we always ate together at night.' She hesitated again. 'I guess what I've come to realise is, I don't just want to have children. I want to have a family.'

It is these questions that Sheryl Sandberg raises in her recent global best-seller *Lean In*, in which she urges young women to show greater personal ambition. Sandberg recalls:

When I worked at Google . . . what I noticed over the years was that for the most part, the men reached for opportunities much more quickly than the women. When we announced the opening of a new office or the launch of a new project, the men were banging down my door to explain why they should lead the charge . . . the women, however, were more cautious about changing roles and seeking out new challenges. I often found myself trying to persuade them to work in new areas.[20]

Young women, she says, do not 'come to the table' but instead — hang back — waiting to be beckoned over. They do not know how to negotiate on their own behalf.

In her view, women like my friend Ruth tend to withdraw from the workforce mentally, far too early, long before they even consider having babies. Indeed, it is the *prospect* of motherhood, concern about how they will manage it, perception of those who haven't managed it; all of this makes them pull back before they need to. 'The moment a woman starts thinking about having a child, she doesn't raise her hand anymore.' But, she believes, young women will be in a better position to barter for acceptable terms, post maternity, if they have risen as high as they can go. They will better be able to afford high-quality childcare, bargain for appropriate and flexible working conditions. This means that they will not disappear from view, after motherhood; or, like so many women, return to a junior position working for a less-experienced man.

> 'The moment a woman starts thinking about having a child, she doesn't raise her hand anymore.'
> Sheryl Sandberg

Sandberg's book is engaging and emotionally honest, but hers is a realist's position. She accepts the long working-hours culture, particularly predominant in the States, and the intense demands of high-status professional employment. Like the good den mother she so clearly is, *Lean In* attempts to find ways for younger women to work around what is a given. At the heart of her appeal is the same message, over and over, issued with drumbeat determination: don't give up, don't give up.

The young women I spoke to were not so sure. 'The main issue,' says Anna Coles with her typical directness, is that

It's almost impossible to be a director and a mother. Because you have to hang out with the people you're filming — and be available.

You've got to get up to Scotland or whatever and it all changes at the last minute. So the only people I know who can do it are those who have very wealthy husbands or they have a stay-at-home husband. But [not having either] I don't know how on earth I could manage. In my mind, I can't be an observational documentary director – filming real people – and be a mother.

Her tone is firm, totally unselfpitying. 'But at the same time, I do think this is a huge failing in the industry. Thousands of women are leaving TV in their thirties, due to parenthood, all the time – and the only advice we seem to be given is to "toughen up".' She has little truck with older women who have 'made it' in the industry telling younger women they need to face hard realities:

> I went to a 'women in the industry' panel and there was a woman there who had decided TV was not for her. She wanted a family – and she wanted a balanced lifestyle – so she had re-trained as a counsellor and therapist. And the other women on the panel had absolutely no time for her. They suggested she had wimped out. My friends and I in the audience were so alienated. We felt as if these 'having it all' monsters were devouring this woman before our eyes. I do worry about the future. It is a big unknown for me – and it saddens me that I love this job, and I'm getting better at it year on year, but that at some point, I will have a difficult decision on my hands.

Doubts about Sandberg's thesis come from two principal directions. On the one hand, policy analysts like British economist and writer Alison Wolf believe that there is an inevitable component of nature in play and that women are always more likely to fit the demands of work around family life than men are. Thus, in Wolf's briskly realist world view, utopian quasi-feminist demands for radical change are largely impractical. 'The likelihood of an economy structured for the convenience of mothers with children is vanishingly small whether at the pinnacle of the job pyramid or below.'[21] Companies are unlikely to introduce more flexible working if it means that they will lose that vital competitive edge; younger women, considering the shape of their careers, should, in effect, shape up or ship out. This makes it all the more interesting that some of the louder, more forceful demands for corporate change are coming from the US; but perhaps it is logical given that country's more punishing work culture, and reported lower levels of female happiness at the 'top'.[22] Anne-Marie Slaughter, a Princeton academic, and formerly director of policy planning at the State department from 2009 to 2011, has doubts of a different kind about the *Lean In* model. She resigned from her high-level government job when she couldn't reconcile the demands of her teenage sons with her work and subsequently published a blistering piece on women and work in *Atlantic* magazine, about the real conflicts that so many women have to face. Reflecting on her decision to step down from her State department job, she says:

> Suddenly the penny dropped. All my life, I'd been on the other side of this exchange. I'd been the woman smiling the faintly superior smile while another woman told me she had decided to take some time out or pursue a less competitive career track so that she could spend more time with her family . . . Which means I'd been part, albeit unwittingly, of making millions of women feel that *they* are to blame if they cannot manage to rise up the ladder as fast as men and also have a family and an active home life (and be thin and beautiful to boot).[23]

For Slaughter, what was particularly important about this epiphany was her understanding of what it meant for younger women and men. She felt a sense of responsibility to tell the truth about how hard the road was ahead. Going to give a lecture to a group of Rhodes Scholars students at Oxford University, she described her decision to leave her job and the fact that

> Further government service would be very unlikely while my sons were still at home. The audience was rapt, and asked many thoughtful questions. One of the first was from a young woman who began by thanking me for 'not giving just one more fatuous "You can have it all" talk'. Just about all of the women in that room planned to combine careers and family in some way. But almost all assumed and accepted that they would have to make compromises that the men in their lives were far less likely to have to make. The striking gap between the responses I heard from those young women (and others like them) and the responses I heard from my peers and associates prompted me to write this article. Women of my generation have clung to the feminist credo we were raised with, even as our ranks have been

steadily thinned by unresolvable tensions between family and career, because we are determined not to drop the flag for the next generation. But when many members of the younger generation have stopped listening, on the grounds that glibly repeating 'you can have it all' is simply airbrushing reality, it is time to talk.

Slaughter believes that Sandberg's *Lean In* style advice is part of the way

in which many young professional women feel under assault by women my age and older . . . Although couched in terms of encouragement, Sandberg's exhortation contains more than a note of reproach. We who have made it to the top, or are striving to get there, are essentially saying to the women in the generation behind us: 'What's the matter with you?'[24]

It is easy to write off these glossy, highly paid American women, with their unreal and privileged lifestyles, as irrelevant. That I can't – quite – do so is nothing to do with political beliefs but everything to do with being a mother and my understanding of the damage that might be done collectively to our daughters as a result of a life-long obedience to certain crippling norms. There is no question, as Sandberg argues, that while an ambitious, go-getting young (or old) man is deemed not just likable but admirable, a dedicated, talented, successful woman usually has to face a variety of responses through her working life from a hurtful neglect of her achievements to continuous diminishment (often from both men and women) to far more aggressive put-downs of her skills and successes. As in so many other areas of a woman's life, the cumulative effects of stepping out of the 'obedient woman's line' is exhausting and demoralising, and requires exceptional personal stamina and support (from others) to deal with.

None of these self-evident truths should put a woman off and I would not want our daughters of the future to be put off by them either. Should the next generation of young women continue to enter the employment/career 'race' – probably the right metaphor in these highly competitive times – then it is important – no, it is only just – that they demand, and receive, fairness in treatment and pay. Put it this way: it is outrageous that any young woman starting out as a lawyer or architect or engineer be appointed on a lower rate of starting pay, simply on account of her gender, and there is no reason why she should not demand equal pay. It is equally dispiriting that young women with creative ideas should hold back from approaching those in power. And why should the prospect of having a family act as 'ankle weights' on a female's work life, but not on a male's?

> Why should the prospect of having a family act as 'ankle weights' on a female's work life, but not on a male's?

Yes, *Lean In* is directed at a significant privileged minority: well-educated women, entering a profession, and anticipating preferment sooner rather than later. But on both a rhetorical and practical level, its optimistic arguments could just as well apply to women who are in non-professional areas of work or working at a more junior rank, or even those simply bringing in a wage. The ambitions of women across class and sector are often remarkably similar: to enjoy their work, to be appreciated, to be allowed to 'progress', to be justly rewarded. Firefighter Dawn Cowley might one day want to be a station manager. A young history or geography teacher may want to apply to be head of the Humanities department. A woman who starts out as a junior in a hair-dressing salon may well dream about running her own business. In other words, if all women, whatever their class or level of responsibility, want to enjoy the fruits of their hard work, the next generation need to develop greater personal confidence, and learn how to think strategically about their own work life in order to receive their rightful recognition, responsibility and reward.

But Sandberg's approach also begs many questions. It reflects and reinforces a broader argument that we are hearing in the UK increasingly, that we need to get more women at the top, to improve chances for those coming through the 'pipeline'. The argument in the UK seems mainly to be between those who favour a voluntary approach, a position represented by the Thirty Percent club, started by asset manager Helena Morrissey, and those who support the legal imposition of quotas, as recently proposed by the European Commission. But voluntary or compulsory, the campaign to improve women's representation on the boards of companies is probably the single most discussed issue in current debates about gender equality in the twenty-first century. It had a prominent place even in the terms of reference for the British government's 2012 Select Committee into Women and the Workplace, and took up large parts of the hundreds of pages of written evidence presented to that same Committee. According to Helena Morrissey, 'Quotas are not just controversial but they don't work either, *if we want better gender balance at all levels and better business outcomes*. Business culture needs a revolution to avoid the problems of the recent past. Better balanced boardrooms are one aspect of that revolution.'[25] [My emphasis.] But, as I argue below, getting more women at the top does not guarantee organisational change; even if it does, it may not be enough.

Similarly, general appeals to women just to *be* more confident may be useful but limited. They risk making some young women feel worse rather than better about themselves. ('What's wrong with me that I can't lean in to the table, but want instead to flee the bloody room?') I have already looked at some of the deeper reasons why girls may not be raised to be as confident as boys, and how we can, as parents, and as a society, start to redress that (enduring) imbalance. But this is clearly long-term work, as Sandberg herself acknowledges. For her part, she now recommends *Lean In* circles, which seem to merge elements of early feminist consciousness-raising groups and Women's Institute-type voluntary action with (one part of) the job of a trade union. According to one observer, her aim is to create a 'fully fledged social movement'. 'In small groups reminiscent of feminism's pre-corporate days, they'll gather after work to share success stories, view webinars and learn how they can rise to the top of their careers without forsaking "self-fulfillment"' – Sandberg-speak for marriage and childbearing. Sandberg has set a rigorous schedule for each group – '"three minutes for personal updates" at each monthly meeting, followed by 90 minutes of instruction – to be supported by videos and inspirational quotes on her "Lean In Foundation" website. Buy the book, lean in, and share – or click it.'[26]

Three minutes apiece sounds a bit short. Thirty minutes, if not three hours, might be more appropriate. But there is no doubt, sharing information is an important tool for women, whether it be through emotional support or swapping and sharing information on contacts, work opportunities or tricky situations. Among the young

– and older – women that I talked to, informal sharing of woes and ideas, at an informal level, was a crucial part of advancing their employment skills and confidence. 'My friends and I talk all the time,' said Anna Coles. Elizabeth Baines, a freelance writer, found her opportunities transformed when she developed a professional friendship with a woman working inside the newspaper to which she contributed occasional articles. It proved to be an invaluable contact. Elizabeth was able to find out what the going rate was for particular kinds of features, for particular kind of writers. 'It was all about knowing the ball park figure – and then sticking to my guns. It's no good demanding something that only a high-profile columnist is getting and you are a woman who has only contributed two features. If you do that, you are writing yourself out of a job. But it's also not a good idea to sell yourself short.'

Sandberg also offers some shrewd advice on mentoring which, she argues, can be too easily used by women merely to seek yet *another* authority figure to tell them what to do rather than seize initiative and power for themselves. Instead, she suggests: excel first, *then* look for someone who can help you; only seek a mentor whose work excites you: do your homework first before asking for help. If a young woman takes responsibility for her own advancement and enrichment, then older women in the same field will be pleased to help her. Estelle Morris, former Secretary of State for Education, and one of the few senior women in politics in the UK, now offers herself as a mentor to young women who are working in politics and the arts, two fields in which Morris takes a particular interest. She finds it tremendously rewarding because she is able to check the self-defeating voices in young women's heads that say, 'I can't do it. I am not good enough.' Even better is when companies introduce mentoring schemes that allow talented young women to progress, with company support, up through the ranks.

But is enough attention paid to the role of the organisation, the company, the outside world? As Sylvia-Ann Hewlett recently argued in *Time* magazine,

What accounts for women's career stall is not a lack of push, we've discovered, but rather a lack of pull. After surveying some 12,000 white-collar workers, interviewing nearly 60 executives and conducting some 20 focus groups, we [at the Center for Talent Innovation] can say with authority that what women lack is *sponsorship*. They don't have, as men do, someone in the C suite who will put their name forward and go to bat for them. When they do, our data shows, they punch through: women with sponsors are 27% more likely than their unsponsored female peers to ask for a raise. They're 22% more likely to ask for those all-important stretch assignments, the projects that put them on the radar of the higher-ups. The more progress they make, the more satisfied they are, and the likelier they are to lean in . . . In short what women lack is someone 'to go and bat for them' . . . without sponsors, our research shows, women lose their ambition to the steady undertow that home, children and community exert.[27]

> 'What women lack is someone 'to go and bat for them' . . . without sponsors, our research shows, women lose their ambition to the steady undertow that home, children and community exert.'
> Sylvia-Ann Hewlett

In the absence of sufficient sponsor-style programmes within the UK, many young women – and men – try to get foot on the ladder and valuable work experience through unpaid work experience and internships. These are often controversial as they favour those with families who can back them up through a period of unpaid work and can lead to shocking exploitation, unique forms of personal misery as well as unparalleled opportunities. (Just watch *The Devil Wears Prada* to grasp the full impact of this new aspect of working life.)

According to Frances O'Grady, internships can also lead to a particular form of sex-based exploitation. 'It's so shocking when you come across it in a particular field – such as politics. Younger women are asked to do these demeaning things, like change the bed sheets of the person they are working for – which they are only asked to do because they female. Or getting young women to "serve" at meetings.'

In 1982 I co-wrote with Ann Sedley, then Women's Rights Officer at the National Council for Civil Liberties, the first ever booklet on *Sexual Harassment in the Workplace*. At the time, our argument was widely ridiculed by many who argued that not only was an element of sexual tension at work inevitable, and beyond the realm of law and policy, but that, in general, approaches of a sexual nature were not that serious. Thirty years later, as a result of long-term feminist campaigning and action, attitudes have shifted substantially not just in legal terms — the 2010 Equality Act prohibits harassment of a sexual nature — but in terms of public understanding of the deeply damaging effects of certain kinds of sexual pressure.

Yet in many ways — and this is part of the contradictory nature of our times — the problem has got worse. Frances O'Grady puts it like this:

> While young women have benefited from more general job equality, they face a bigger attack in terms of how they are sexualised and how they are seen. There's this whole pressure and problem of body image. Sexual harassment needs to be kept alive as an issue. We [the TUC] believe there are things that could be done on a very practical level. For instance, we give guidance to employers on the issue of employees downloading pornography, and how that should be handled within the workplace.

Every employer or company should have a figure to whom a young woman — or man — can report threatening or difficult behaviour, and find it dealt with seriously. Whether that actually happens or not, even in a climate that now recognises a widespread problem for women, is another matter.

One of the best guarantees of equal pay is to keep pay levels relatively clear and transparent. Now, however, in the UK even the public sector is under pressure to dismantle its own protections. From September 2013, performance-related pay will be introduced in England's schools, giving head teachers greater freedom in determining what any member of their staff is worth. According to the British Secretary of State for Education, Michael Gove, 'These recommendations will make teaching a more attractive career and a more rewarding job. They will give schools greater flexibility to respond to specific conditions and reward their best teachers.'[28] In the spring of 2013, David Cameron also announced that nurses would be financially rewarded for demonstrating certain personal qualities: 'There are some simple but profound things that need to happen. Nurses should be hired and promoted on the basis of having compassion as a vocation and not just academic qualifications.'[29]

We do not know – yet – how these proposals will work out in practice, but they raise some important and worrying questions both in general, and particularly for women. It is rather odd, for instance, to find that members of the nursing profession are to be judged on the highly subjective and highly gendered quality of demonstrating 'compassion'. Surely, this could have regressive implications for other aspects of a nurse's tasks, such as taking the initiative or making medical decisions? It could leave them at the mercy of hostile managers or co-workers. And if teachers, most of whom are female, are to be judged according to the 'performance' – that is, the exam results of their pupils – it is possible that staff in schools with a higher percentage of deprived students will lose out. And will women find it harder to impress their public-sector bosses just as women in private enterprises seem to find it harder to win equal pay based on their presumed performance, or will they lose out merely on the basis of their lack of confidence in relation to their own performance? The introduction of market competition into public service bodes particularly ill for women.

We owe our daughters more than this. Playing the corporate game, albeit with a new sophistication and authenticity, is surely not the only option. At the very least, we owe them a reminder of other, more substantive debates about the organisation of work and different means of campaigning for improvements. Most of the advances won by women from the nineteenth century onwards were not secured by any individual woman's chutzpah and determination or even by the actions of the few who made it to the top, not least because, as Sandberg points out at some length, too often women who reach the top do not prove particularly helpful to those of their own sex in less powerful positions. Change within employment came about through collectively devised, and demanded, reforms, at both the professional and non-professional ends of the labour force.

The 'corporate feminist' approach does not address a number of pressing problems. Firstly, it has nothing to say, by definition, about the current state of the economy and in particular the rise of unemployment. Between a fifth and a quarter of all UK graduates are unemployed — and forced to take bits and pieces of work, at often appallingly low wages. In the USA, the Bureau of Labor Statistics reported in January 2013 that 7.3 per cent of all women older than twenty are unemployed, and that percentage almost doubles among black women.[30] At the end of 2011, 18.9 per cent of those graduating in the previous two years were unemployed, down from the high of 20.7 per cent at the beginning of 2010 but more than four times the rate for those graduating between four and six years ago. More and more graduates are also having to settle for low-skilled jobs. In the last quarter of 2011 more than one in three of those graduating in the last six years could only find work in low-skilled roles. In 2001 this figure was almost 10 per cent lower.[31]

It is a problem reproduced throughout Europe. A special report by *The Economist* on the jobless young who are being 'left behind' by economic decline found that, as early as 2011,

> In much of the OECD youth-unemployment rates are about twice those for the population as a whole. Britain, Italy, Norway and New Zealand all exceed ratios of three to one; in Sweden the unemployment rate among 15-to-24-year-olds is 4.1 times higher than that of workers aged between 25 and 54. Not only is the number of under-employed 15-to-24-year-olds in the OECD higher than at any time since the organisation began collecting data in 1976. The number of young people in the rich world who have given up looking for work is at a record high too. Poor growth, widespread austerity programmes and the winding up of job-creating stimulus measures threaten further unemployment overall.[32]

Secondly, 'corporate feminism' fails to address the growing gap in opportunities between women. Today's UK graduate who finds employment, earns, on average, £15.8 per hour while the typical non-graduate (still a majority — and a majority of women) earns just £8.92. Over a typical forty-hour week, this works out as a difference of £250.[33] Over a lifetime this works out as a considerable advantage for middle-class, graduate women. A recent report from the Institute of Public Policy Research (IPPR) estimated that professional women in their thirties and forties earn nearly three times as much as their unskilled counterparts. According to one newspaper report, 'while it is unsurprising that women who gain a university degree or professional qualification earn more than those who are low or unskilled, the scale of the gap – 198% – will be seen as shocking.' Interestingly, while having a degree still makes a difference in the earnings of men, the gap between 'unskilled and university educated male workers is significantly smaller, at 45%.'[34]

What does 'Lean In' mean for the thousands of young women who work in areas that pay below the living wage, or even the minimum wage, as cleaners or carers, for example? Many of these are now existing at near poverty levels, given the de facto depression of wages since 2010 and the parallel rise in the cost of living, and have no hope of individually negotiating a higher wage, or improved conditions. It is only through collective action that those who work in these roles in companies or institutions can ever hope to persuade employers to pay them a fair rate for the job. Hence the importance of the Living Wage campaign that has supported a number of groups of workers seeking fair pay, and measure of respect, for their jobs.

Thirdly, for all Sandberg's honesty about her own emotional struggles, corporate feminism does not address what we can only call the alienation of so much modern work. For this, we need to turn to other strands of feminist thought, which have important things to say about redefining the terms on which we live and work. One important starting place here is the second wave of women's liberation which emerged from a loose alliance of young, educated left-leaning women and a new industrial militancy among working-class women. As feminist historian Sheila Rowbotham observed, 'The emphasis on class and the need for connection with the labour movement was an important feature of the emerging women's movement.' But it also meant that for the 'young middle-class members of women's liberation . . . equal pay and equal rights at work were rather remote concerns. These were the demands made with a dutiful nod in the direction of *other women's problems* . . . in contrast to their passionate "personal" concerns about images in advertising, childcare, the response of left-wing men to women's liberation.'[35] [My emphasis.]

True, second-wave feminism had little to say about the dilemmas of professional women, in part because there were so few and partly out of a profound discomfort or uncertainty about whether to fight from outside, or inside, the system. This 'inside or outside' uncertainty only intensified with the rise of neo-liberal individualism and a language of self-seeking aspiration for women, in terms of work and money, that had, by this time, moved far from the original concerns of second-wave feminism with its strong connections to the labour movement. Dissecting her own disillusionment with the conditions of contemporary work, Anne-Marie Slaughter claims: 'Women have contributed to the fetish of the one-dimensional life, albeit by necessity. The pioneer generation of feminists *walled off their personal lives from their professional personas* to ensure that they could never be discriminated against for a lack of commitment to their work.' [My emphasis.]

I take issue with the claim that women's liberation courted or celebrated the 'walling off of personal life' from work personas. On the contrary, it was corporate neo-liberal feminism that shaped the agenda of 'women at the top' and that now faces the full implications of its own contradictions that it so long ignored. It is why for so many young women, like Susan, in her late twenties, working in public relations, 'feminism is not relevant . . . it's about more shoes, or getting a high paid job. It is part of the patriarchy. Participating and enabling the system to continue. Too many liberal feminists, they get into this idea that work is the best thing.'

In the meantime, important work has been done within feminism, the trade unions and the voluntary sector concerning ways to re-design work for all, including a shorter working week, more widely available childcare, and a less ruthless and self-seeking approach to work itself. Frances O'Grady believes that

> there are enduring themes in this arena, such as the importance of humanising work. It's particularly important because of the jobs that women tend to do. One of my first jobs – that awakened my own awareness – was serving at table at an Oxbridge college. I remember feeling like this invisible person, who was treated as if I didn't exist.

Such personal encounters sharpen O'Grady's sympathy for campaigners for the living wage for jobs like cleaning. They are not just asking for better wages but for some human respect, for their employers to say good morning to them, to look them in the eye. But the humanising agenda is also important in quite well paid jobs, such as the increasing use of zero hour contracts (contracts where the employee undertakes to be available for work but the employer does not undertake to provide work, and only pays for hours worked).[36] The dehumanising of labour has just got worse in every area of the economy.

Tess Lanning believes that, in the modern economy, 'We are all asked to put our role as economic agents before that of parent, partner, friend or activist, and our ability to participate in wider, political and civil life is sharply curtailed as a result.'[37] It is this curtailment, combined with ever longer working hours, that has encouraged what Slaughter calls 'The fetish of the one-dimensional life'. It's an interesting phrase. It speaks to a striking note of loneliness and alienation that I sensed in my conversations with younger women, often struggling to stay afloat in a world where worth is measured by one's competitiveness, tenacity and ability to withstand setbacks, and the need to suppress gentler or more thoughtful selves. It is a particularly gendered problem because when children come along (as we shall see in Chapter 6) many men rely on the women in their lives to set up and sustain human relationships outside work. But women can't always rely on the men in their lives to do that in return, and they sense that early on. If the 'race' is to be set in traditional corporate terms, they will almost always lose out, unless they have the extraordinary tenacity and luck of a Sheryl Sandberg.

For Tess Lanning, 'The political and economic crisis facing us require deep thinking and radical change . . . feminists need to re-engage with a critique of the nature of political and economic power.'[38] She has become interested in some earlier socialist feminist ideas, encouraging more employee and worker involvement in production and design, more mutuals and collectives, including communal living. (Lanning herself was brought up in a communal household, and speaks very positively of her childhood.) Several women I spoke to were enthused by the idea of the Living Wage, not just in terms of its aims but of the communal activism, and sense of solidarity, that it engenders.

Everyone from right to left agrees that we have reached a crisis point, and many on the political right believe our economy to be not just stagnant but unproductively and even dangerously unequal.[39] Economic emergency has engendered a moment of collective re-thinking that would, I think, appeal to some of those I talked to. It certainly wouldn't take much to connect these bigger picture ideas to the ambivalence I caught in the voices of so many younger women. 'Sometimes I think I just don't care enough,' said Anna Coles after we had been talking for over an hour. 'I really like my work. But I don't think I like it more than other things — my friendships, seeing my family, having a good walk or reading a book. I really like my time off.' Like so many young women today, she can do the bargaining thing, the working all hours thing, the staying late at the office thing. But there's another voice, strong within her, that thinks: is this all? For Susan, 'Sure it's good to work and I'm economically independent. But I'm working too hard . . . I don't know. It's empty. We can't live by ourselves. We just can't continue with the traditional models.'

# 5

## Love in a Cold Climate

*In which we learn that although today's young women enjoy greater sexual freedom than ever before, it comes with strings attached, and look at how we can help them tread the fine line between regressive puritanism and the exploitative commercialisation of their bodies and feelings.*

A few years ago, the Australian writer Nikki Gemmell started work on a novel about an innocent young bride who discovers a shocking secret that leads her to uncover her own, deepest, sexual passions. 'You've never been in control, until now; you've never, before, had exactly what you want . . . The lights turned off. A touch that's gentle, slow, provocative, that builds you up, that makes you want it too much . . .' So raw and explicit was the sex in the book, that Gemmell tried, at first, to publish it anonymously. Within months, the author of *The Bride Stripped Bare* was herself stripped bare, and both novel and writer became an overnight sensation.

In the decade since, Gemmell has become something of a global spokeswoman and eloquent enthusiast for the exponential growth of erotic literature and female sexual awareness. She tells me, 'There is a new era in women's reading. It is really exciting because it is a revolution. We've always read this stuff. Of course we have. Anais Nin. *The Story of O.* And we have been excited by it. But it was clandestine and embarrassing and shameful. It didn't occur to us to *talk* about it. Even ten years ago. And now – there's been this explosion of erotica. Regardless of the quality of the writing, this is an exciting and vivid era.' As a result of these cultural changes, Gemmell believes:

My daughter will have an empowered erotic life. I think it's wonderful. She will have the ability to say no, to articulate what she doesn't like. And (the chances are) that she will find a partner who will listen to her, who won't try and coerce her into anything she doesn't want to do. It's an exciting prospect.


It is hard, then, not to nod along in agreement with, and celebration of, author Hanna Rosin's sweeping statement that 'Young women are more in control of their sexual destinies now than probably ever before'. The sexual revolution of the 1960s and 1970s transformed women's behaviour, but in some ways the changes of the last thirty or so years have been just as profound. When I hear women, only ten years older than me, talk about their own coming-of-age in families and societies where 'a blank was drawn over the female body', where to fall pregnant was to bring shame upon yourself and your unborn child, when sex was furtive and full of danger, when to be gay was to risk a prison sentence or become a social outcast, I am relieved, and rejoice, for young women today, glad that they do not have to live or love like that. There may be the usual nervous embarrassment or worry between parents and children, some residual deep prejudice and the standard English throat-clearing silence about all the really important things in life. But in general, the wider culture is far more tolerant. Of course, there is an infinite variety of experiences within every generation; we can never generalise about the body, sex, women – or men. But we can certainly mark huge shifts in the culture, the expansion of opportunity, if not its realisation.

We live today in an era of easily available contraception, legal and safe abortion and now of mass-market erotic writing for and about women. Over the past year or so, I have sat opposite any number of young, middle-aged and elderly women deeply absorbed in the charcoal-covered delights of *Fifty Shades of Grey*. We are deluged with frank sexual memoirs; female entrepreneurs have set up their own TV stations to show erotic, not pornographic, material or opened 'no-strings attached' sex clubs for young women with disposable capital who want to enjoy themselves in a safe environment. Our grandmothers' and mothers' generation might have talked about 'career women' or had or helped friends who were desperately in need of an abortion, but they would never, ever, in a million years, have said the word 'vagina' in mixed company let alone participated enthusiastically in a stage show (as some older women do) in the now famous *Vagina Monologues*, in which the word 'cunt' is shouted from a public stage, to a room full of passionate participants.

This new frankness, a sense of a possible dialogue about sex and the profound and complex feelings it can arouse, is obvious from talking to younger women from very diverse backgrounds. Connie is a twenty-eight-year-old south-east Asian living in London. She is beautiful, clever and speaks very, very fast. Work, politics, love, friendship, sex: all subjects are dispatched with the same breathless articulacy.

> Sex? Oh God, yeah, there's a *lot* of enjoyment there, although it's less about something physical – I mean – it's not just about that time in bed – it's embedded in the context of life. It's a tool, it's about power. It's about how much you feel in charge. Whether you feel you're going to be objectified – whether you feel you're the person who is going to get what she wants. No one wants to be the person who is rejected but, actually, I am happy to pursue. I mean, if you get rejected, well at least you had a bash.

Connie has had two serious long-term relationships, but

> After the last relationship ended I really felt I needed not to be in a relationship, to incubate the new me. But recently, I jumped a man – I haven't done that before. And I'm thinking of pursuing this lesbian relationship with a woman I find very attractive. She's older than me. I think it took time for me – as a teenager and later – to enjoy sex. I can't quite put a word to it – but it's the radical otherness of sex, I didn't understand – back then – about inhabiting my body – there was a bit of a mind-body disconnect. I was tense and brittle. Now I guess I'm much less serious. I see erotic love as a form of play.

Radikha is a twenty-one-year-old student, living in Cumbria. Brought up within a traditional family, she says:

> I love my mother a great deal but I wanted to do things very differently to her. When I was fourteen and fifteen I started to ask her about dating boys and the answer that came back was that this was a taboo subject. The message was: sex is always sacredly bonded by

marriage and marriage is something I was not to think about until I had finished university.

Radikha was unhappy with the lack of consideration her parents gave to the subject of a possible partnership, but

> When I was sixteen, I met my now fiancé, who also happens to be white. And I made it clear to my parents that this was what I wanted. Actually, they didn't take it too badly because he came from a good family and had upstanding morals. It allowed them to accept that he was going to be my partner. These trying moments with my parents made me realise that though they [had] tried to avoid exactly these situations occurring, they were amazing to have accepted mine and my sisters' decisions and as a result have brought us up to be open-minded and given us the strength and ability to trust the decisions that we make for ourselves.

Add to this a third voice, from Leslie Bell's recent book *Hard to Get*, on the emotional dilemmas of the twenty-something generation:

> Between her first and second relationships, Phoebe had a series of encounters . . . having sex relatively quickly, after dating someone for two weeks or so, because sex was important to her and she wanted to know whether it was going to be a deal-breaker. For a time she serially dated, but relationships would last for less than a month, so she had several sex partners over a one-year period. Phoebe felt good about having lived 'like a guy' during part of her twenties. She felt pleasure in pursuing her desires, being comfortable in her body, and enjoying sex. She felt in charge, in control, and 'like a man' . . . not in a disparaging way, but as a value neutral description.[1]

But let me, straightaway, raise a nagging worry about this 'new world for women' – about the constraints and alarms that surround the new freedom. On the one hand, one can see there lingers, always, a risk of regressive puritanism, itself based on a fear that if women make themselves too sexually available, they will lose the care, respect and protection of men. Allied to this is a worry that if they enjoy a series of disconnected affairs – or mere sexual encounters – when they are young, they will fail to learn the lessons of commitment necessary for the rigours of raising children. There are, too, dismissive voices, even among progressives, who would claim that the question of women's sexuality is marginal to the weighty matters of economic or legal freedom. On the other hand, the market feasts upon the possibility of hordes of eager new consumers. Erotic books sell in their millions. Films, TV shows, all kinds of music, celebrating varieties of 'unhooked' culture are popular, profitable staples. Sex sells. We know that. And women are the new, relatively untapped market: we know that too.

Both these positions – a disapproving puritanism, a beckoning values-free marketisation – run the risk of denying women the full-ness of their experience, the specificity of their need. In all my reading about sex, erotica, the sexual revolution, there lingered in my mind, months later, some wise words of caution, written in the late 1980s by three American feminists, Barbara Ehrenreich, Elizabeth Hess and Gloria Jacobs, in their ground-breaking assessment of what the post-war sexual revolution brought and meant for women. In the final chapter of the excellent *Re-Making Love: The Feminization of Sex* they try to shape some key principles for women in relation to the ever-unfolding sexual revolution. They feel it important to assert the principle that women's sexual pleasure matters (in the face of excessive political sternness, I guess). They are right. On the other hand, they feel the need to rescue this relatively new (historically speaking) emphasis on sexual pleasure for women from mere consumption or exploitation. They fear that sex might 'become trivialised as a product of the consumer culture, the counterculture, the pharmaceutical industry – anything rather than being the product of our own desires and efforts. The consumer culture offers the ultimately meaningless version of sexual revolution.'[2]

But they also broach a further, difficult question, the kind of question that dovetails with the worries of a mother at that dead moment of the night, just before the dawn chorus, when she tries to match the apparently sparkling, seductive sexual freedoms on offer to her daughter with her anxious awareness of that same daughter as a loving, vulnerable, complex human being. Here is how Ehrenreich, Hess and Jacobs approach the problem:

Women have grounds to fear sexual liberation, even their own. The fear is not irrational or neurotic, for if sex is disconnected from marriage, childbearing and family commitments, women stand to lose their traditional claims on male support . . . women are more vulnerable than men to the hurts and dislocations of a society that is sexually more free than it is just or caring. Women still bear the risks and costs associated with contraception and abortion. If they become mothers they undertake a disproportionate responsibility for their children – in most cases, all the responsibility if their marriage dissolves . . . The fears are real; so, too, is the desire for a freer, sexually happier life. If there is a way out of the ambivalence, or at least a way to resolve it into alternatives and choices, it has to be a *feminist* way.[3]

This imperative is as important today as it was when Ehrenreich, Hess and Jacobs wrote those words. Few young women expect to pursue the kinds of lives that their mothers and grandmothers had: settling down, probably too young, often into unsatisfying, unequal relationships, at the cost of their own dreams and desires. Yet nor do they – yet – inhabit a world genuinely at ease with women as sexual beings, with dreams of a creative or work nature, and a wish to find a close relationship with a mate or two. As we have seen, external double standards, and internal conflicts, haunt young women from adolescence through to maturity. And a new set of conventions has taken the place of the old. In today's world, young women are entitled, even expected, to enjoy a period of 'no strings attached' sexual freedom from, roughly, the age of seventeen (the age when most girls lose their virginity) to their mid to late twenties, after which, there seems to be a bit of a scramble for partnership or marriage, conceived on fairly traditional lines.

But fail at one hurdle or the other, and you are sunk. Too much freedom and you are a slut – or have a 'heart of steel'. Too little freedom and you are no fun, lacking the right kind of sexual ambition or enthusiasm. Miss the partnership boat and you may well fear that you will become, and be judged as, the modern version of a sad old spinster: washed up, on the shelf. Unsatisfying love life with your partner? There are plenty of advice columns to read or even appeal to, but I was struck by how many young women said their

> Too much freedom and you are a slut – or have a 'heart of steel'. Too little freedom and you are no fun, lacking the right kind of sexual ambition or enthusiasm.

partnered or married friends 'closed the door' in relation to information on their sex lives. Ah, so some things never change.

It is no surprise then that an older kind of writer, invariably female, approaches modern sexual culture with a pronounced air of maternal concern. This is not quite the same tone as is used in the sexualisation and pornography debate; here, the voice is both more tender and chiding, a little bit more directive. Here, the worry has shifted from what is 'done to' girls to what young women apparently 'do to' themselves, although such chicken-and-egg considerations inevitably collapse in a confused jumble of cause and effect. But the underlying argument goes something like: *Come on, girls! Aren't you worth more than this?* It's not hard to see why. Even as one can spy the invisible ink of conservative assumptions beneath the hard and worrying 'facts' about modern sexual mores, one can share in the worry and the impatience. Even if one believes that young girls' lives are warped by misogyny and consumerism, it is still hard to understand why *anyone* would want to rotate their butts in front of a bunch of slobbering teen boys; I, too, want to shout: *Come on, girls! Aren't you worth more than this? Back to the library please!*

One of the best examples of the 'conservative maternal concern' genre is *Unhooked* by a *Washington Post* journalist called Laura Sessions Stepp. Stepp, echoing the concerns of English writers like Allison Pearson, sincerely believes that our sexual culture has undergone a seismic shift and that young women throughout the West are being corrupted by it. She was first alerted to this profound change, she tells us, as long ago as 1998, when she stumbled across an informal sex ring in a Washington middle school. A group of parents were called in to be told that 'as many as a dozen girls had been performing oral sex on two or three boys for most of the school year. The thirteen- and fourteen-year-old students were getting it on at parties, in parks and even in a couple of neighbourhood parking lots.'[4] Stung with horror, Stepp here offers one of several comparisons between her younger self and the young women she is describing:

> In 1964 my eighth grade girlfriends and I were no prissies; we had
> secure places around town where we went to kiss and neck with our

boyfriends. But when did teenage girls — everyday girls, not just the 'fast' and the 'loose' girls — start skipping the smooching and go straight to giving head? How did they come to believe that offering their services to guys they barely knew was 'no big deal'?[5]

Stepp asks a similar question when she comes upon another, equally disturbing, scene — by now we are in 2005 — during which hundreds of male students take part in a bidding war for young college girls. Once again, she makes a comparison with the good old days of 1968:

> Sure we used to leave our college dorm windows cracked so our boyfriends could sneak in. But we were terrified of being found out and wouldn't think of taking off our clothes until the guys were inside and the lights were off. Now girls were stripping in the student centre in front of dozens of boys they didn't know, pantomiming sex onstage and later doing the real thing without saying much, if anything, to their partners. When did conversation and negotiation drop completely out of the picture?[6]

Leaving aside the question of whether Stepp really knows about how much talking or 'negotiation' is — or isn't — going on between teenagers or consenting young adults, her unfolding tableaux gives any parent pause for thought. Reading the book in the silence of the British Library, I hear suddenly the quizzical, slightly anxious voice of a father I interviewed who said:

> I have absolutely no idea what is going on in my daughter's love or sex life. Young men arrive. Young men disappear. They sit for hours in my daughter's room. Occasionally one stays over. They seem very relaxed with each other. Are they friends, are they lovers? My daughter — the girls in general — seem completely in charge, the boys don't seem to be putting any pressure on them. But I've no idea what's really happening. Terms like 'going out' seem to belong to another era.

Another mother put it like this:

> They have this new phrase 'doing a thing' So what does that mean? I think it means you are having sex but you're not actually going out. My daughter explained it to me in great detail the other day.

There are several gradations of 'doing a thing'. Really casual sex: casual sex but you are sort of 'hooked up': then sex within a committed relationship. My daughter seems to be absolutely fine with it – and when I ask any questions – like – 'Doesn't it feel weird to be doing a thing but not be considered the partner of the boy?' she brushes me away, affectionately. As if *I am* the problem. As if the complexities of the dynamic are beyond poor, old me.

She begins to laugh, a little helplessly.

Stepp, who is very far from laughing, could be describing the exact dilemma (or delights?) of that same daughter, when she seeks to pinpoint 'a large culture shift' that, to some extent,

all girls are caught up in . . . Young people have virtually abandoned dating and replaced it with group get togethers and sexual behaviours that are detached from love and commitment – and sometimes even from liking . . . High school and college teachers I've talked to, as well as researchers, remark on this. Relationships have been replaced by the casual, sexual encounter known as hookups. Love, while desired by some, is being put on hold or seen as impossible; sex is becoming the primary currency of social interaction.[7]

Stepp adds, 'Many girls struggle largely outside the awareness of parents who either don't know what is going on or are vaguely aware but don't know what to do.'[8] None of this, she claims, is good for girls. And then we are back, in her own personal history:

Of particular interest to me, having come of age during the women's movement of the late 1960s and early 1970s is that the new sexual landscape has been designed in part by girls, to the delight of guys who no longer have to work very hard for girls' attention or their bodies . . . but who is helping them to think seriously about their goals for happiness beyond the law degree . . . who was helping them see that loving relationships are uniquely satisfying and manageable – and need not tie them down for the rest of their lives?[9]

And again, 'hooking up regularly puts girls at risk both physically and emotionally'.[10] And again,

Sex in fact is a Rorschach test for how we treat all people – casually or with care. Skin to skin, we are at our most vulnerable, and so is our partner. We learn to trust or distrust, to give and receive in the most basic way possible, and we take those lessons with us into the wide world.[11]

Stepp speaks the truth about the unique vulnerability in the sexual act; the visceral bond that is created when two humans touch 'skin to skin' and the powerful feelings that are inevitably unleashed. In my late teens an adult sought to advise me 'that young people have to be careful as sex arouses very powerful emotions that you might not be aware of'. At the time, I thought the comment both absurdly obvious and curiously irrelevant. Anyway, I believed myself to be exempt from the laws governing sexual relations for previous generations. At eighteen, twenty-one, twenty-three, I felt myself perfectly capable of handling my own intimate relationships and whatever 'powerful feelings' were unleashed. Wasn't sex supposed to be fun as well as meaningful? It felt inappropriate to freight every encounter with deep meaning; sometimes an encounter was just a nice enough mistake. But now as a mother, at one remove (inevitably), out of control (inevitably), I feel a nagging anxiety for young women who may believe, as I once did, that they are in charge of their emotions. I am now the well-meaning adult who wants to warn them about how powerful feelings can be triggered by sexual contact – and how difficult it can be to make good judgements of, and for, oneself when so viscerally connected to another human being.

Lynne Segal is a leading feminist voice in this country, and the author of *Straight Sex: The Politics of Pleasure*, which charts the development of the feminist sexual revolution in the UK and the many debates it engendered. For her, the ongoing sexual revolution is a largely 'positive development':

> There's much more of an acceptance of young women's sexuality today. When I was young, there just wasn't any. When I got pregnant at twenty-three, it was a catastrophe. You couldn't easily be pregnant and not marry. You would be called a slut, a whore, a 'fallen woman'.

For Segal, feminism changed the landscape completely:

> So now there is so much less shame about what's 'down there'. God, women even have genital jewellery, I hear! The idea that women have sexual agency, that just wasn't around in the 1960s. You waited for men to make a move. There's been a huge amount of sexual empowerment. Some say it's problematic, that girls are sexualised earlier and earlier. I don't dismiss that worry. Some women are more empowered than others sexually. But I suspect some of the critique is about older people disliking younger women's sexuality. But young women are just so much more confident about how to deal with things – about contraception, pregnancies – including unwanted pregnancies. There's just so much more sexual knowledge around.

At the same time, Segal recognises that

> There is still tension between girls and boys, which boys also share, a stand-off about how to approach each other. We all know how difficult romance and desire is. The situation is far more complex these days. There's a kind of 'male' braggadocio that some girls now have. I'm not saying that sexism has disappeared. It hasn't. Girls still have to look right and feel judged all the time, but boys are feeling that more as well. However, the increased knowledge. Well, it has to be a wonderful thing.

Segal is right. Feminism has always trodden a brave, and largely honest, path through the minefield of female sexuality, both in terms of challenging the accepted terms of heterosexuality and trail-blazing the rights, and pleasures, of lesbianism and homosexuality in general. (Indeed, Segal herself has argued that, at points, feminism seemed to be derailed by reducing sex to a form of politics, rather than trying to grapple with the often complex and contradictory pleasures of sexuality.) But, in the broadest terms, feminism helped women think of sex in terms of their own pleasure rather than as a way to conform to social norms and expectations.

True, the ground had been laid by a number of interconnected factors, including the rise of women's economic and political power throughout the twentieth century and an array of dynamic researchers determined to uncover the real truth of women's sexual response. Seminal works in this genre included Marie Stopes's *Married Love* (written in 1918) which suggested that a man might stimulate his wife to orgasm without penetration. In 1947, Dr Helena Wright's *More About the Sex Factor in Marriage* argued that the idea of an 'answering [vaginal orgasm] to match penetration amounted to a "penis–vagina" fixation'. Wright's dismissal of the centrality of the penetrative act to women's sexual experience was echoed in Alfred Kinsey's massive tome of research, *Sexual Behaviour in the Human Female*, and echoed, once more, Masters and Johnson's *Human Sexual Response* which asserted that 'the primary focus for sexual response in the human female's pelvis is the clitoral body.' Ann Koedt's self-explanatory 1970 paper, 'The Myth of the Vaginal Orgasm', had a profound influence on the emerging UK women's liberation movement.

Slowly but surely women were being handed the means to challenge an idea of conventional sex as a physical act, conducted largely on men's terms, bartered in return for commitment and protection. However, it was not until the ground-breaking *Hite Report* in 1976 that, in the words of Barbara Ehrenreich, Elizabeth Hess and Gloria Jacobs,

> For the first time, a volume of female voices statistically turned women's right to good sex into a political issue. The question of how to have sex could not be reduced to technique. 'If we make it easy and pleasurable for men to have an orgasm, and don't have one ourselves, aren't we just "servicing" men?' Hite asked her readers. She demonstrated statistically that more women were able to have an orgasm on their own than with men, who mostly encouraged them to be passive and obedient in bed. 'If we know how to have orgasms, but are unable to make this a part of the sexual relationship with another person, then we are not in control of choosing whether or not we have an orgasm.' Hite's analysis concluded that women, when it came to sex, were 'powerless'.[12]
>
> Hite's study was a call to action for women to openly demand orgasmic sex. Many of the women in her book clearly articulated what was wrong with sex down to the last anatomical detail. Women, it seemed, could speak about sex, and now it was time for them to speak to men. Hite stripped the orgasm of its layers of patriarchal illusions, and powerfully enhanced a woman's ability to negotiate in bed.[13]

In a way Hite took the mystery and emotion out of the erotic encounter, calmly returning – or reducing? – it to a question of sensation. *Women's* sensation. Shere Hite herself, a surreally beautiful blonde, was a most unexpected messenger for feminism's possibly most radical, and certainly most intimate, message. In interviews she sat, rock still, a Botticelli beauty reciting statistics, reeling off facts and challenging generations of accepted male behaviour. Her work, and the enormous publicity it engendered, widened the appeal of a message that had already exploded out of women's liberation consciousness-raising groups. As Anna Coote and Bea Campbell recorded in *Sweet Freedom*, the story of the UK feminist movement:

> In the safe space of small groups, women started to share their secrets – and what emerged, among much else, was an epidemic of sexual failure. Women were bored with their husbands in bed; or their husbands were bored with them; or they only had orgasms when they masturbated; or they felt awkward and humiliated; or they hated their own bodies; or they feared they were frigid. There they were, at the height of the Permissive Era, when everybody was supposed to be having such a terrific time, and yet . . .[14]

Suddenly 'the old romantic model of sex as an experience of abandonment and self loss would not work' any longer:

> Sex was now something that a woman went into with her eyes open – figuratively at least – her intellect alert, and her skills honed. There was no reason a determined heterosexual woman should not find as much pleasure as she was capable of experiencing. But she had to negotiate, to bargain, and if necessary, to shop around.[15]

Feminism, in all its various forms, has continued to transform the sexual culture, and in increasingly public ways. Eve Ensler's *Vagina Monologues*, a play that seeks to tell the history, and speak the truth, of the female organ, sparked a world-wide response. As Laura Flanders, a long-time friend of Ensler, albeit an early sceptic of Ensler's almost obsessive enthusiasm for all things vaginal, confesses,

> Then, in 1999, I found myself participating in *The Vagina Monologues* at Madison Square Garden. The whole event was wildly improbable. Part ringmaster, part mistress of ceremonies, Eve stood in bare feet in the gaping hugeness of that 18,000-seat stadium. Jane Fonda

performed giving birth; Glenn Close exploded the word 'Cunt!' loud enough to rock the very highest bleacher. I helped to hold a piece of glass for one of Elizabeth Streb's dancers to fly through, after which Queen Latifah stormed past us and into the spotlight, bellowing, 'This is a Rape Free Zone!'

Flanders went on:

Eve had stopped asking me about my vagina, but she hadn't stopped asking. She had kept on, asking more than 200 women everywhere she went. What she tapped into wasn't the clinical truth of individual bodies but rather a broad body of evidence of an invisible, silenced epidemic of rape, assault, brutalization and hate that scarred women of every age, every race, every class, on every continent.[16]

Ensler's link of the personal and political was hugely ambitious. In one bound, it tore the shroud of shame and secrecy from the female organ. But could this new globalisation of all things 'down there' explain, at least in part, why feminist Naomi Wolf's recent attempt to write 'a biography of the vagina' – including a detailed account of her own sexual responses – was judged as excessively narcissistic by so many female reviewers?

In *Sweet Freedom*, Bea Campbell and Anna Coote spelt out the challenges that second-wave feminism laid down to convention, including the idea that 'sexuality belongs to a private sphere which floats free of economic and political affairs. Another is that it is simply an expression of economic relations, which will be altered as a result of economic transition.'[18] Coote and Campbell were drawing on years of knowledge, and involvement, in the nuanced, and often fierce, debates of socialist and radical feminists respectively – the idea that '[sexuality] holds within it a fundamental challenge to patriarchy'. But re-reading their account of that second-wave feminist revolution, I find myself wondering if there is, today, a covert connection between sexuality and the laws of capitalism. Is contemporary sexual behaviour more economically driven, or shaped, than we are aware of?

Look closely at the 'unhooked' culture that Stepp bemoans and it is, by her own admission, a narrow one: a dissection of the unstable behaviours of a driven, privileged portion of US society: straight, largely white, well-educated, wealthy, American girls. Sexual braggadocio becomes another manifestation of both their born-to-rule affluence and the pressures now placed on such young women today, to be both successful economically *and* sexually. But the 'unhooked' culture also becomes a way of rehearsing a deep lack of commitment to any values but the immediate, becoming ever more practised at escape rather than loyalty. Stepp puts it this way:

> Hooking up's defining characteristic is the ability to *unhook* from a partner at any time, just as they might delete an old song on their iPod or an out of date 'away' message on their computer. Maybe they tire of their partner or find someone who is 'hotter' or, for some other reason, more to their liking. Maybe they get burned badly in a relationship or find themselves swamped with term papers and final exams. *The freedom to unhook from someone – ostensibly without repercussions – gives them maximum flexibility.*[19] [My emphasis.]

It is hard not to hear in this kind of language the echo of the new economy, with the premium it places on short-term, flexible, loyalty-free liaisons between employer and employee.

Hanna Rosin, author of *The End of Men*, has undertaken probably the most up-to-date survey of contemporary sexual mores. But she, too, takes the temperature of a limited group of young women. She, too, is looking at a narrow, privileged group – 'exceptional' woman in the making, beautiful graduates from elite universities. This, after all, draws on the core of her argument: that the exceptional-women-to-be of the next generation are leaving most men standing. New forms of sexual behaviour are about trying out the role of full-on macho style independence and seeing how it fits. In her chapter on the rituals of this new sexual behaviour, 'Hearts of Steel', she follows the fortunes of one breathtakingly beautiful girl, a graduate of Yale, who shares with Rosin not just the details of her frenetic sexual life, but her lack of dependence on men in general: 'What do I need a man for? I don't need him financially. I don't need him to do activities. I have lots of friends here. So fuck it.'[20]

Rosin takes a cool, morally neutral look at such women; she

also finds clear links between their sexual and economic behaviour. Women don't want men – or at least romantic entanglements – to get in their professional way. According to a survey undertaken in 2004 (by two students, still at college) women were already managing their romantic lives like savvy headhunters, aware that they wanted to be married by thirty. 'The women still had to deal with the old-fashioned burden of protecting their personal reputations, but in the long view, what they really wanted to protect was their future professional reputations.' Rather than struggling to get into relationships, one of the student researchers reported to Rosin, they had 'had to work hard to avoid them':[21] 'The ambitious women calculate that having a relationship would be like a four-credit class, and they don't always have time for it so instead they opt for a lighter hook up.'[22]

At one point, Rosin attends a party of highly qualified, go-getting professionals in their late twenties. She assesses the women's apparently assertive, emotion-free sexual behaviour in shrewd economic terms:

> These women consider a heart of steel a fair price to pay for their new high ranking in this social hierarchy. In eras past, the pretty women in such a corporate setting would have been imports brought in to liven up the party, secretaries maybe, or paid escorts . . . But here the women floating around in their feather earrings, thigh-high boots, and knowing smiles were social equals, at least. These twenty-eight-year-old women halfway to an elite MBA with five years of finance experience behind them and enough money to shop at Barneys, *were using their sex appeal not just to catch the man or dazzle him . . . but to challenge him in his most important domain, the work place* . . . It's even possible that women their age are using their sex appeal not just to keep up with the men, but to surpass them. If in college sex appeal is something you have to rein in to focus on your career, after college it might actually be a career-booster.[23] [My emphasis.]

Rosin posits the idea that these women might be exhibiting a new form of 'soft power' now so valued in the marketplace: what Catherine Hakim has called 'erotic capital'.

Hakim, a sociologist, has developed a theory of 'erotic capital' building on, in one sense, a commonplace observation: that a woman will often augment her worldly or professional impact by stressing, deliberately or otherwise, her feminine or sexual side, through highlighting her looks, personal elegance or liveliness. The more controversial aspect of Hakim's thesis, outlined in her recent book *Honey Money: The Power of Erotic Capital* is that women should consciously deploy their sexuality at work or in public life; she delineates no fewer than six ways in which they can do this. In her view, some, if not all, of these 'six ways' are designed to deliberately tap into men's greater need for sexual stimulation, particularly after the age of thirty. Suffice to say, Hakim's emphasis, particularly on the yawning gap between male and female sexual need, has been roundly criticised by feminists.

Is this progress? Not for the human heart, that's for sure. And given that writers like Stepp and Rosin deliberately focus on exceptional (that is, affluent) women in the making (or the un-making, judging by the high levels of unhappiness they record), we can't take these developments as typical of the experience of most young women.

Both risk severely overplaying the transformation there has been in young women's sexual behaviour over the last fifty years, in the interests of a good story. In one of the largest surveys done of 'hook ups' in the USA – quoted by Rosin – college graduates report a median of only five hook ups over four years, and an average of 7.9, while a quarter of students 'opt out' of the hook-up culture altogether. Rosin also notes that there is a strong class difference in behaviour with many young women from less well-off backgrounds remaining connected to boyfriends back home – and therefore in traditional 'dating' relationships – throughout their years of studying, even if this is seen as a failure of ambition.[24]

Of all the young women I spoke to, with ages ranging from the late teens to the early thirties, only one acknowledged she had what you might call an 'adventurous' sexual lifestyle, and even she, without prompting, said, 'I guess you could say I have been in love with all my boyfriends – yes I certainly felt something strong for them.' Another had not had a 'date' for four years; a few, in their early twenties, were free floating, but all thinking more about their future work, study plans or political involvement than finding a lover; a third group were in relatively stable, long-term relationships. Another small sub-group had had children young, a fact which catapulted them into an entirely different way of life; all of these were in stable relationships, coping with bringing up children and establishing themselves in their work lives – or just keeping afloat.

This is not a sample survey by any means but it presents a very different picture to the glamorous, dangerous world portrayed by the American writers who gain so much attention. It suggests a rather diluted, steady state, sexual revolution – or sexual evolution: an impression confirmed by recent surveys. A poll of 2,000 women undertaken for the magazine *More* found that one in four young women had slept with more than ten people, compared with one in five men who had done the same. Only 1 per cent of young women said they would want to get married before having sex, with the majority losing their virginity at the age of sixteen. More than half said they were not in love with their first partner, and only one in three believe it is important to be in love with someone before going to bed with them. Seven out of ten said they had had a one-night stand, with a fifth admitting to having had more than five casual encounters.[25] Economist Alison Wolf also stresses the relatively modest rates of sexual activity among British women. According to the latest figures (2000), only 9 per cent of non-graduate women and 16 per cent of graduate women, aged 25–34, reported five or more opposite sex partners in the last five years. Leaving aside the possibility of high, unrecorded, rates of sapphic passion, this is hardly proof of a generation of sexually uninhibited young women.[26] Could it be that the extent of sexual licence among young women has been exaggerated for the sake of sensational headlines, the stirring up of marketable moral panic?

But what of that original challenge thrown down to heterosexuality by second-wave feminism, the battle ground cleared by Koedt and Hite et al.: the right to equal pleasure in the bedroom? It's odd how risky it feels, even now, to assert female pleasure as a legitimate goal. It feels a bit technical, a little soulless but also rather crude. But then again, why not ask about the big O? Surely sexual fulfilment, in addition to more diffuse pleasures, is one of the things we should want our daughters to want? Yet it is strange how among all the cultural obsessing about 'unhooked' girls and mass oral sex in car parks, so many writers write so little about how young women actually feel about their sexual encounters and, in particular, about 'orgasm equity'.

> One Canadian study of first sexual experiences and their impact on young people's subsequent erotic lives recorded that just 6 per cent of girls as opposed to 60 per cent of young men experience orgasm during their first sexual experience. One friend remarked that the figure for the girls seemed high and for the boys seemed low!

Even the most superficial search indicates an inequality in the climax stakes. We know from one small Canadian study of first sexual experiences and their impact on young people's subsequent erotic lives that just 6 per cent of girls as opposed to 60 per cent of young men experience orgasm during their first sexual experience.[27] (Discussing this with friends, one of them observed that the figure for the girls seemed high, but for the boys seemed low!) Hanna Rosin acknowledges mutual pleasure to be an issue but notes, almost in passing, that 'men are more likely to have an orgasm during a hook up, maybe because men in college are not all that experienced yet and don't know how to please their partners, or because women don't always insist on having their sexual needs attended to.'[28] To this, she adds, rather like an anxious party hostess, that orgasm or not, equal numbers of men and women – about half in total – enjoyed their last hook up 'very much'.

Imagine my delight at coming upon the findings of the UK's 'Biggest Ever National Orgasm Survey'. In fact, this is a website devoted to the marketing of a brand of pelvic toner; apparently, there is a strong connection between a well-toned pelvic floor and a healthy variety of climaxes. Oh well. Even here we discover that nearly half of all women report 'not getting their share of orgasms'; 70 per cent never or rarely achieve vaginal orgasm during penetrative sex; only 31 per cent claim to do so often or always; 36 per cent never or rarely achieve clitoral orgasm during penetrative sex, but 80 per cent often or always achieve clitoral orgasm by self-stimulation.[29] In July 2012, the *Daily Mail* reported on an AskMen.com's Great Male Survey, which polled 50,000 people across the US, UK and Australia, and found that over 'a quarter of women admit to faking it every time they have sex'. Of women, 25 per cent were also 'not at all satisfied, because of the quality of sex', with 27 per cent admitting to 'no sex life'.[30] It's rather sobering to realise that, in pure percentage terms, sexual outcomes have not improved much since the days of Hite and co.

Rhiannon and Holly of the feminist *Vagenda* magazine, only confirm this depressing message:

> If, as was reported this week in Jezebel [the US feminist blog] women are reporting in their droves that they hardly ever achieve the big O during casual sexual encounters, then something about our culture has gone awry. This is a culture that has boldly trod where men previously feared to tread: we've discussed premature ejaculation, erectile dysfunction, and the menopausal dips in sex drive with an increasing awareness and sensitivity, all the while acknowledging that almost all of us will come across sexual roadblocks in our lifetime. We live in a world where solutions to losing your boner are plastered across tube trains, and Viagra is as well known a drug as Paracetamol. But when it comes to women being unable to reach orgasm, we are all too often sold the line that it's just part and parcel of being female, most likely our own fault for being so unlike men. The message is that cumming, if you're one of the ladies, is an addition rather than a legitimate demand.[31]

So, I remain curious, as to what, exactly, women are enjoying 'very much' in their love making or during casual sex? Is it just the sense of 'skin on skin': the thrill of intimacy itself: the amusing affectionate before-and-after banter? Fair enough, if so. But even this is not happening, if you believe the reports of women like Stepp and Rosin who conjure up an image of female detachment and cynicism, of young women playing a part while protecting themselves with 'hearts of steel'. There's nothing wrong with playing the field – surely we all want our daughters to enjoy experimentation, to learn about themselves in relationships, to find out who and what they enjoy. In Kate Figes's words, the realisation that 'you can have several different relationships with several people and that you will discover all sorts of things about the world through that relationship. That you will learn about books and art, and places and food – and yourself. Young people should be exploring.' Figes is nostalgic for the 'the fun to be had shagging about in your teens and twenties. We need sex with different people – girls and boys need it – partly in order to know how to do it. Instead it seems that girls today feel a puritanical pressure not to do it, not to be a slut.'

It is for all these reasons that I put some store by the term 'sexual evolution' rather than revolution, because I believe we still have some way to go. If the right to sexual freedom and pleasure for girls is essential, so too is their right to pursue it in contexts that feel comfortable to *them*. We, the elders, must neither unduly admonish nor leave them floundering in an ethically neutral, emotionally dangerous, social world. We must help them find the right balance of play and protection.

This is one of the arguments in the excellent *Hard to Get: Twenty-Something Women and the Paradox of Sexual Freedom*. Leslie Bell, a feminist, sociologist and psychotherapist, embraces and tries to extend the original aim of feminism. She heeds Ehrenreich et al.'s warnings that the sexual revolution must be shaped in reference to the needs and wishes of women, not men or the market, the state or religion. In contrast to the maternal conservatives, with their narratives of moral panic, Leslie Bell sees not untrammelled licence or gyrating opportunism but a generation of women caught between the lure of sexual freedom and the longing for something more real and satisfying in their relationships. Instead of an 'either/or' situation – promiscuity or prematurely committed partnership – she sees young women engaged in an ongoing struggle to honour all parts of themselves. *Hard to Get* scrutinises

> this new in-between period of early adulthood and the ways that it offers women a mixed bag: opportunities, to be sure, but also retrograde messages about their identities as sexual beings, partners, and future mothers. And while they have plenty of training in how to be successful and in control of their careers, young women have little help or training, apart from the self-help aisle in their local bookstore, on how to manage these freedoms, mixed messages, and their own desires to get what they want from sex and love.[32]

Bell believes young women are weighed down by competing cultural notions about the kind of sex and relationships they should be having in their twenties:

Be assertive, but not aggressive. Be feminine but not too passive. Be sexually adventurous, but don't alienate men with your sexual prowess. Be honest and open, but don't overwhelm someone with too much personal information. They are taught to seek out a companionate relationship of equals. But at the same time they are instructed by increasingly popular arguments from the burgeoning field of evolutionary psychology about irreconcilable differences between men and women. Meanwhile they spend their twenties hearing gloomy forecasts about their chances of marriage if they don't marry before thirty, and their chances of conceiving a baby if they don't get pregnant before thirty-five. Given the discordant nature of these prescriptions, it's no wonder that the women I interviewed and counsel struggle to square these contradictory messages with their own individual experiences.[33]

She also noted that young women, trained to be autonomous and ambitious in work, had 'trouble letting down their guard . . . difficulty being vulnerable and expressing needs'.[34] Rosin confirms this view when she observes that, 'As Meghan Daum writes in *My Misspent Youth*, her memoir of single womanhood, the "worst sin imaginable was not cruelty or bitchiness or even professional failure but vulnerability".'[35]

*Hard to Get* sorts young women into three groups: those who put their 'relational' desires aside, in order to honour their sexual selves, so blocking the development of any truly intimate relationships in which they can more fully become themselves; women who block their sexual needs, in order to make a settled relationship; and a third group, women who can fulfil both sides of themselves, and negotiate their looming thirties – when, for some, the question of having a child might arise – without 'splitting' themselves in a way that will cause damage. In Bell's view, splitting – 'a tendency to think in either/or patterns and to insist that one cannot feel two seemingly contradictory desires at once' – has become a 'widespread sociological phenomenon among young women'.[36]

Bell's case studies are as rich and complex as a good novel. At the same time, she roots them firmly in our current context: the

unsettled nature of this new in-between period of early adulthood for women, and the uncertainty and anxiety that accompany it . . . Despite all the advances of women over the past fifty years, these experiences are frequently split into masculine and feminine ones, with the masculine being overvalued socially and psychologically . . . Splitting leads some women to assume that they cannot be strong and autonomous when they are interdependent with others, vulnerable and intimate.[37]

Interestingly, Bell found that lesbian and bisexual women found it far easier to integrate their various needs and 'get what they want' from relationships than straight women.

Refreshingly, she does not believe that all the answers lie within women themselves. Instead, we need 'sexuality education' in school, and for society as whole to 'acknowledge that all desire is normal and that conflict between desires is inevitable . . . If we can develop curiosity about our desires and aspects of ourselves that don't match up with those sanctioned by our culture, we may begin to build lives in which we feel more pleasure and satisfaction.'[38] A crucial part of that learning process involves 'mentor'-style relationships, older women who are honest about discussing how they reconciled (or failed to reconcile?) their needs for relationship and autonomy; and perhaps most important of all, mothers and other carers who presented a model of the 'whole' woman in their own lives, and allowed their daughters to be 'whole' people from the start.

This is not just theoretical. Of the women she describes, the ones who were most able to integrate and satisfy their various desires had, from an early age, been allowed to express the many sides of themselves, and had not been suppressed or shamed by them. Both mothers and fathers play a part in allowing girls to feel at ease with their sexuality from an early age; fathers by not withdrawing from teenage girls, ill at ease with their growing bodies and burgeoning attractions; mothers by admiring and appreciating their daughters' sexuality rather than entering into narcissistic competition with them. Bell also stresses the importance of a work culture that gives women – and men – sufficient time to enjoy personal and family relationships without their having to sacrifice their ambition. Perhaps 'vulnerability and assertion might then be understood as human experiences, and not located exclusively in women or men.'[39] More complex representations of women in media, advertising, movies, television and books will also help create a more 'grown-up menu' of possible ways of being, for the women of the future.

Revolution has always provoked stern reaction. Ever since the so-called permissive sixties there has been a concerted effort to encourage women to return to older mores and outdated sexual manners. This movement backwards is represented by small, splinter movements like the Silver Ring Thing (SRT) which advocates complete sexual abstinence before marriage. In the UK, the SRT movement has never had much purchase. Its HQ seems, rather improbably, to be located in Horsham, Surrey. The King's Church's website, in Horsham, recently carried a report of a workshop that had tried to draw young people away from the anarchic freedoms which are tearing them apart 'physically, emotionally and spiritually . . . more than ever, Christian young people are facing a battle to remain pure in this area of their lives. SRT is an abstinence program designed specifically for teenagers that aims to educate and support teenagers about Biblical sexual purity.' The numbers enrolled were not high: 'twenty-two young people attended for a full day', suggesting some gave up the effort to contain their impure sexual desires by lunchtime.

> Ever since the so-called permissive sixties there has been a concerted effort to encourage women to return to older mores and outdated sexual manners.

We are witnessing a similar reaction against the new traditionalism, as embodied by *The Rules*, a series of popular books that encourage women to return to an imagined age of old, cultivating mystery and sexual unavailability, all with the ultimate purpose of snaring a man. No one likes a needy clinger but *The Rules* speaks directly to young women's anxiety, pinpointed by Bell, that they will never find a partner. First published in 1995, there seems no end to the ways women can be told how to snag a man. *The Rules* was followed by *The Rules 2: More Rules to Live and Love By*; *The Rules for Marriage*; *The Rules for Online Dating*; *All the Rules*; and then, in December 2012, *The New Rules: The dating Dos and Don'ts for the Digital Generation*. Some of the more absurd advice offered by these handbooks includes: Don't Talk to a Man First (and Don't Ask Him to Dance); Don't go Dutch on a Date; Don't Call Him and Rarely

Return His Calls: Let Him Take the Lead; Be Easy to Live With; Never Text, Email or Facebook a Man First: Wait At Least Four Hours To Answer A Text ('the older you are, the longer you should wait'). But reviews of the latest Digital Rules suggest that women are finally breaking free of the allure of man-catching manoeuvres. A recent feature article on the digital *Rules* undercuts the book's claim that you 'should always wait for a man to make the first move' by pointing out that 'according to a new survey, the digital generation of girls play the dating game more pro-actively with 79 per cent happy to initiate contact, with many taking the philosophy "why wait?"'[40]

Young women seem sensibly reluctant to take refuge in old relationship models but they are not, it seems, defeated or overwhelmed by their new freedoms either. Hanna Rosin argues that while

> there may be many problems for women with the casual sex environment . . . it is not a place where they drown. Young men and women have discovered a sexual freedom unbridled by the conventions of marriage, or any conventions. But that's not how the story ends. They will need time, as one young woman at Yale told me, to figure out what they want and how to ask for it. *Ultimately, the desire for a deeper human connection always wins out, for both men and women.* Even for those business-school women, their hookup years are likely to end up as a series of photographs, buried somewhere on their Facebook page, that they do or don't share with their husband – a memory that they recall fondly or sourly, but that hardly defines them.[41] [My emphasis.]

But, as I discovered when talking to women, this does not stop many young women from feeling an intense anxiety about finding a partner, exacerbated by economic anxiety. Many feel obliged to keep working 'insane hours' in case they should never meet anyone: but then they're never going to meet anyone if they keep working insane hours. 'There's this massive pressure to be partnered up.' Another spoke of this huge 'economic pressure'. And a third: 'I've been single through most of my twenties – my work doesn't help. On my last job, I was working all hours, till 9 at night, at the weekends. And then I think, "I'm going to be single for ever, I'm not going to meet anyone." A lot of women like me wake up and think,

"Oh My God, my chances have gone."' For another young woman, 'Every aspect of our lives – even our romantic lives – is very commercialised. It's all about selling to us.'

One told me:

I've been to quite a few [friends' weddings] now. Sometimes I'm looking at them, looking at people – these are my friends. And yet I am so alienated by the whole thing. It's as if I am coming from another planet. But then I was always not that bothered – it was not my goal. Women are always more congratulated for being in a couple. It shows that she – they – are well adjusted. It's what normal people do. I can see colleagues trying to work out what's wrong with me. There's a slight distrust there, at me still being single. And you know, sometimes, I wake up in the middle of the night and think 'What if I never feel like that? About someone?'

Writing on the f-word blog Ada Nkechi wrote:

I broke off an engagement at the start of 2012. It's a thing that, to be fair, few people ever expect to do once they've proposed or accepted. Comments from others created a strong sense that it took me a long time to define – that an engaged woman should be grateful. Someone offers you a ring – that's the most you can ever hope for. You're a fool to turn it down. Why would you expect anything more? There was also the bind that keeps so many in bad relationships: once you've committed, it's better to be consistent than self-aware and single.[42]

But what of the desire – or pressure – to have children? Nikki Gemmell says of herself:

In my twenties, I was concentrated on my career and never thought about kids. Then my periods became heavier. It was as if they were urging me towards something. Suddenly, I felt this tsunami of need, a need to have a child. It went against everything I had thought or known before. It was overwhelming. But we don't talk about this because it's not politically correct. I used to see women with babies as weak and pitiful.

Leslie Bell argues that parents often send contradictory messages to their daughters. On the one hand, they appear to urge their daughters to play the field but only up until a certain point; they then bring considerable pressure on them to find partners, marry and settle down, as their thirties approach. I, too, heard this several times from women in their twenties – often after we had finished the formal part of our interview, and got stuck into a drink or two.

'Oh, that's my mother on the phone,' said one, checking her smart phone:

> She'll only be ringing to tell me how anxious she is that I haven't yet met someone. Doesn't she realise that there is nothing she can say to me that I haven't thought of a hundred times myself? Doesn't she understand that I am terrified of ending up without a partner and her getting all freaked about it doesn't help me one bit?

She was distressed and irritated, yet I could imagine (and empathise with) the distress of her equally irritated mother. At that very moment, I made a mental note to myself: don't ever hassle either of my daughters about partners or when they are going to settle down or have they met anyone 'nice'. Never. Ever.

There is a new realism about the rituals of marriage itself, particu-larly post 2008. Tales of twenty-somethings blowing a lifetime's worth of savings, or a possible house deposit, on grand, showy weddings – a staple of the last two decades – have given way to lower key events. Bridal magazines currently report the latest drop in wedding day 'spends from £22,000 in 2011 to just £16,000 in 2012'. (Still, a large amount of money.) These days, the bride might still wear white and the groom a suit but there is often an attractively relaxed, playful feel to the whole occasion that befits a society where fewer people marry later, cohabitation remains on the rise, divorce figures are stable (but lower than they were in the 1980s) and there is just far less money to go round.

I also sense a more realistic awareness that marriage is a tough call, particularly as we live longer. Is this really a generation hooked on 'romanticism – the big happy ending', as one middle-aged woman said to me, 'that widespread belief that *the* person you're going to marry is out there somewhere'? It feels to me that many young women have absorbed the lessons of previous generations; they have watched their own mothers carefully, seeing what worked and what didn't work. They know what they want and don't want. Several women spoke very positively of their parents' marriages:

> I wanted just what my mum has got. She was very involved with us. It was just a way of living. But she told me she got married too young. She said to me, 'Why do you need to get married? You absolutely don't have to get married and you don't have to do all that bridal shop/white wedding stuff.'

But even the most thoughtful bride can't truly gauge what is ahead. It is not cynicism that makes an older person reflective at a young person's wedding; it is simply the weight of experience, making its presence felt in deep, honest, hopeful thoughtfulness. Divorce is probably one of the most painful experiences anyone will have to go through. Even those who stay married, and happily so, are going to experience their portion of disappointment, difficulty and loneliness. Thankfully, there is now much franker public discussion about the trials and tedium, as well as the joys and benefits, of staying within one partnership, often for up to half a century, and the challenges of raising children. Thoughtful young women who have decided to take the leap from cohabitation to marriage, perhaps as a preparation for parenthood, are inevitably optimistic, but also better prepared for what's ahead. A generation – or two – of feminist writing has thrown the window open onto the complex realities of long-term cohabitation. Magazine articles these days are as likely to stress the companionable or even pragmatic elements of modern marriage as crank up the unrealistic romance.

So, I wonder if here, too, we are witnessing a positive evolution of sorts: a more flexible notion of family than the rigid and oppressive forms of the past. In Britain in the nineteenth century, a wife was considered the chattel of her husband; if she dared to break away from him, she risked losing everything: her children, the property she had brought into the union, her reputation. Until recently, women were legally trapped in deeply unhappy marriages; there was no escape. Divorce is never easy. It is deeply painful for parents and children. But it is *possible* – and ultimately it protects women's freedom, even as single parenthood augments women's poverty. The issue here is that many fathers – not mothers – can escape their financial and other responsibilities to children, not that unhappy couples should be locked together for life. Yes, the conservative right insist on 'the iconic commitment of one man, one woman, for life'.[43] Yes, the liberal feminist is more likely to talk about 'a group of people deciding to live together as a unit and become a family. The word we have for that might be roommates or friends. But it might be two women, aged 35, who want children and can't find men. I'm supportive of different types of families.'[44] In practice, these ideas are edging nearer towards a workable middle, particularly given the recent vote to allow gay marriage. Writer Julie Bindel made me laugh when she recently said, 'Why lesbians and gay men are so desperate to enter into a system that has its roots in inequality I do not know . . . [for us] all to go to IKEA and fall out while we're there.' But in some ways, we could do a lot worse as a society than keep hovering around this tolerant-enough middle or compromise point.

For Nikki Gemmell there is

> an inherent caution and vulnerability in women, that is reflected in their sexual lives. We're still shy about many things, when we are younger. A lot of us don't have a voice until our mid thirties or forties. Life is a process of distilling. We distil our relationships into those that really matter. We shed the pretence, until we can stand and say this is who we are. We learn to let go of that carefully controlled persona that we may have built up earlier [in our twenties]. We loosen and lighten up.

She believes, 'No matter how empowered a woman's world is when she grows up, all of us go through the deep vulnerability of woman-hood – difficulties about body image, relationships, and loneliness. Every woman will go on that journey – in order to find her voice.' But, she suggests, it is likely to be committed partnership, and the trust that it engenders, that increases rather than diminishes women's sexual freedom:

> I strongly believe that a happy marriage increases the possibilities for women, in terms of sexuality in particular. A trusting relationship, of whatever kind, goes to the core of who we are. Sex is all about

surrender to the body, being honest about that surrender. It can be exhilarating. In a few relationships I've seen, you can tell there's a bedrock of honesty there.

## So what will she tell her daughter?

Make sure you can talk together comfortably. It can be easier to talk about childcare arrangements than to say, 'I don't like the way that you kiss.' Don't let anyone chip away at your self-esteem. Nothing is solid. You know, I'm excited for my daughter's future. She has so many chances. In fact, I feel they – our daughters – they *are* the future.

# 6

## Breakpoint

*In which we learn that motherhood will almost certainly come as an enormous shock to a future generation of girls educated to succeed not breed – and that society's demands of maternal perfection should be resisted in favour of a saner work world.*

In Helen Simpson's wonderful short story 'Lentils and Lilies' nubile, narcissistic teenager Jade is trying to get to grips with the works of the poet Coleridge but finds herself instead daydreaming about her future glorious career, the coming of summer and how she will never be like her fractious, working mother, 'lost forever in a forest of twitching detail with her tense talk of juggling . . . her joyless "running the family".' Heading for an interview for a summer job, at a local garden centre, Jade comes across a desperate mother trying to extract a lentil from her toddler's nose – with a pair of tweezers. Corralled into going back to the woman's house to help with this emergency, Jade is repelled by the mother's 'ragged cuticles, the graceless way her heels stuck out from the backs of her sandals like hunks of Parmesan.' In the closing lines of the story, taking her leave of the hapless mother of two – lentil still not extracted from the child's nostril – Jade suddenly asserts her own mother's superiority: 'My mother's got four . . . *And* a job', before fleeing the scene of domestic squalor.

Here, then, is a gentle probing not just of class difference or the yawning gap between youth and middle age but a dark comedy about the inevitable gap in understanding, indeed, the positive mutual disdain, that so often exists between the mother and non-mother. In just nine limpidly written pages, the parents among us are returned to our own teenage selves: arrogant and cockily determined that we will never be one of these harried, hapless mothers, living in domestic drear or running the home as a military campaign. *We* will not partner up with a man who does not do his share. *We* will not humiliate ourself with snotty, screaming toddlers in the street. *We* will not become figures of 'tendons and hawsers, a taut figure at the front door screaming at them all to do their music practice.'[1]

And yet, ultimately, the literary and human joke is surely on snooty, certain young Jade. Why? Like it or not, we, the reader, cannot help but peek into the future, and there allow ourselves a moment or two of deeply enjoyable conjecture, projecting forward to that moment when Jade, and all the young women like her, will most likely end up like one of these two women: her bossy, efficient, joyless mother or the desperate stranger wielding tweezers in the street.

Of course, young women have always dreamed that they could somehow escape the lives of their mothers. Others may long for motherhood, and for them the problem is more practical: worry about how they will afford a family or a home or even a room of their own. Many – particularly graduate women – now delay childbearing until their thirties, or later; overall, this group is choosing to have far fewer children than previous generations prompting global concern at the falling birthrate among the 'educated classes'.[2] Either way, could the new language of empowerment and expectation around girls' and young women's lives lead them to underestimate the tremendous jolt – the sense of disconnect – that motherhood brings to a life predicated on work and self-fulfilment? One journalist, specialising in parent issues, went to 'talk to a group of young women at a top university – and they all had their plans ready – about how they were going to work for so long – then marry – then take so much time off and so on.' She didn't have the heart to tell them that it just wasn't going to work out quite like that.

Writer Rebecca Asher sees the 'disconnect' at a political level too:

> Could the new language of empowerment and expectation around girls' and young women's lives lead them to under-estimate the tremendous jolt that motherhood brings?

There is this expectation of onward progression – played out in the media all the time. Girls are doing better. Young women have achieved this amazing economic push. Their earnings are closer to men. And we have this growing political consensus around shared parenting. Lots of headlines about more men becoming carers. One consequence of that is that the 'expectation gap' could get psychologically worse for women – the shock of that changing overnight.[3]

Even our politicians seem to recognise the problem these days. In a speech in late November 2012, Deputy Prime Minister Nick Clegg talked about how women are

> stopped in their tracks by our outdated ideas about women and work. We, as a society, we have got so much better at telling young women: the sky's the limit. Get a job; be independent; be the boss; run as far and as fast as your talents can take you . . . Then, suddenly, when they hit their late 20s, their early 30s, despite all their earlier momentum, despite all the endless possibility, they are suddenly stopped in their tracks. It's like a rubber band snaps these women back.[4]

But what's the big secret? After all, the complex joys and cares of motherhood are easily discoverable by anyone who cares to visit a library or click 'motherhood' on a search engine or, better still, seeks out a mother friend for an hour or two (if *she* can spare the time of course). How odd then that the deep knowledge of what mother-hood really means seems somehow to be culturally buried. Or is it learned and forgotten, over and over again? And by old and young alike.

There can be a kind of self-enclosing 'Why me?' attitude at work here, as with all big life experiences. In *A Life's Work*, Rachel Cusk's intense account of the birth and early years of her daughters, she makes the astonishing (for a writer) but rawly honest admission 'that it was my impression, when I became a mother, that nothing had been written about it all,' adding quickly, 'this may merely be a good example of that tone-deafness I describe, with which a non–parent is afflicted whenever a parent speaks.'[5] A few pages later, she concedes that 'literature has long since discovered and documented this place of which I thought myself to be the first inhabitant'.[6]

In a similar vein, one can tell a daughter that childbirth hurts but not do justice to the agonising pain. Far harder to convey the raw bodily and existential shock of giving birth: the sense of one's life suddenly being thrown in complete disarray. Rebecca Asher makes a good job of it in the opening lines of *Shattered*:

> There is a photograph of me holding my son when he is two months old. He is in rude health. His complexion is peachy, his eyes shine with liveliness and curiosity, and his impressive thatch of hair sits naturally in a boy-band twist. In contrast, I appear to be in the grip of a life-sapping disease. My skin is sallow and drawn, the grey off-set only by aubergine accents below the eyes. My cheeks are hollow. My shoulders are hunched. What has happened to me?[7]

A few pages on, she describes the days and weeks after the birth of her first child as one of entrancement and ecstasy:

> But then my husband went back to work, our baby ceased sleeping all day and the music stopped . . . Abruptly the severe challenges of new motherhood were brought home to me: the loss of autonomy and the self-abnegation were instant and absolute. The independence, affirmation and daily purpose that I'd been used to gave way to gruelling, unacknowledged servitude. *My life became unrecognisable to me.*[8] [My emphasis.]

Rachel Cusk uses a metaphor peculiarly appropriate to our modern age:

> I have the sense of stepping off the proper path of my life, of travelling forwards but at some unbreachable distance; as if I had boarded a train and could see through the window the road on which I had always been, a road with which for a while my train ran parallel before gaining speed and moving steadily away to east or west, to a vista of unfamiliar hills, leaving everything vanished behind it.[9]

I, too, was simply not prepared for the plunge into a a world of pain, blood, exhaustion. I, too, was ecstatic, enraptured, exhausted and beside myself (a good phrase, in fact, as one becomes two people, in a sense). I would compare it to being sucked in, and thrown about, by a giant wave (nature has you in its grip) or, to switch metaphors entirely, it is like enjoying a game of Monopoly and suddenly finding yourself forever sent back to Go. No matter how skilled or determined a player you are, you are simply no longer in the game.

> 'Ambivalence' is one of the most useful words in the lexicons of the new mother or indeed the mother full stop.

'Ambivalence' is one of the most useful words in the lexicons of the new mother or indeed the mother full stop. I felt completed and dismembered. Energised and enervated. But it is mostly the practical difficulties that I remember. For a few years, and particularly when I had two children under three, it was a struggle to put on a kettle and read a letter without interruption. Weekends? Holidays? These once pleasurable oases of recuperative time in a busy purposeful life became the sites of yet more drudgery and never-ending tasks.

It was not all terrible, not at all; that is not my point. But it was far, in every conceivable sense, from the world of meetings, offices, deadlines, dreams: the world of plans and purpose and pleasures that I had inhabited for nearly two decades as a young woman and as a researcher and working writer. For a long time, I could not imagine any real return to these worlds or not on what felt like acceptable terms. In some ways, I never did return, or not in the same way. Instead, I joined the largest secret society in the world where I am glad to report I have made some of my best and most enduring friendships. In this subterranean world, the jokes are first class and the sense of camaraderie quite exceptional.

Nowadays, living with teenage daughters, it interests me not just how hard it is to convey any (let alone all) of this experience but how reluctant I am to try or they to hear it. It's as if we have made a silent pact to skip over this part of an adult woman's life. As if it is not relevant, or not relevant – yet. This may well be sensible. Still, I am curious – what is this reluctance? A reluctance to encourage? Or discourage? Or is it that body-related barrier between the generations again, a slight distaste, that goes both ways, at how basic so much of human life really is: blood, shit, milk, spit, snot. Who wants to think about all this primal stuff before they have to, or, indeed, after they have pulled clear?

But there's more to it than that; it feels like news from an alien land. Here I am urging them to think about the written constitution or get to grips with Descartes, to try out swimming or saving. It's that gap again – between the life they're being set up for – out there, striving, shaping their destiny, using their brain – and this other shadowy territory of drear baggy dressing gowns, garish TV, chilled white cabbage leaves pressed into greying bras (to counteract the agony of mastitis), the head-banging misery of the early hours. It is no surprise, then, that they are not at all keen to hear about it all from me. By defini-tion, our mother's stories are stories from the past. Meanwhile, daughters are eager to forge forward into the future, make the world anew.

Read the papers, check out the headlines, read the Big Theme books, and once again you'd be forgiven for believing that a gender-neutral future is fast creeping up on us in terms of mothering and the economy. There's no doubt: new technology, the economic changes triggered by recession, feminism – all have changed the conditions of work in ways that should, in theory, be of huge benefit to women now and in the future. These provide, on the surface at least, some encouragement to the idea that we are edging towards a new kind of responsible egalitarianism.

Journalist Gaby Hinsliff has recently chronicled the ways that the 'work life balance' – already an outdated term, along with 'having it all' – is being transformed into something much more messy and modern. Now we talk about the *merge*. And no doubt, a new term or two will take over within the next year or two. The *merge* was coined by Facebook executive Emily White to describe a life, in Hinsliff's words, in which

> work and free time are no longer neatly compartmentalised but seamlessly jumbled up together. It's a world in which it's no big deal to take two hours out of the working day for something personal, but also routine to spend the same time answering emails on a Sunday: where even executives can leave at 5.30 p.m. to have tea with the children (as Facebook's CEO Sheryl Sandberg famously does) but be back on the laptop by 9 p.m.[10]

Only ten years ago, work and home life were quite distinct, with perhaps the odd late-night phone call or Sunday meeting. Nowadays, with mobiles, emails, Skype, there are multiple ways to stay in touch. There is also a new uncertainty about the boundary between friendship and work contacts: Twitter and Facebook becomes sites of exchange with people you see daily or those you have never met with whom you share interests or might want to tap for a work favour or contact. Screen time has become less of a novel activity, more of a way of life, as most people use internet and email virtually seven days a week (including time spent surfing, in desperation, for an app that can shut off interconnectivity!). Physical distance or location becomes no barrier to doing 'work'. A local mother friend of mine, who runs her own successful company, often takes work calls while shopping for her teenage children; the murmur of the bargain-hunting crowds or her own proficient working her way through the racks can be taken for an open-plan office as long as no one shouts out, 'Have you got these in size 10?' too close to her ear. Hinsliff describes being briefed by a Treasury official – a man – who was also taking care of his young children in the park; 'the conversation was punctuated by despairing shouts of: "NO, NOT IN THE FLOWERBEDS!"'[11]

Hinsliff is well placed to capture the lineaments of this emerging revolution, particularly at the higher ends of the employment market. Formerly the political editor of the *Observer*, the competing pressures of mothering and work led her to resign her job. But she quickly discovered the benefits of a different kind of working: home-based and more flexible (a word that never goes out of fashion). It also changed her husband's ideas about work, leading her to argue that more men would move away from a conventional life of working nine-to-five if they could.

According to Hanna Rosin, author of *The End of Men*, this is exactly what is happening. She identifies a new phenomenon: a group of men and women – graduates, good earners – who double their earning power and general economic dynamism when they pair off. With a similar educational and early work years profile, and similar, if not identical ambitions, these graduate couples are forging a different kind of gender future in terms of the distribution of income and roles. This kind of 'seesaw marriage' increasingly exists, at least among the top 30 per cent of graduates, but it has little to do with feminism, and everything to do with lifestyle and economic expectations:

> Couples are not chasing justice and fairness as measured by some external yardstick of gender equality. What they are after is individual self-fulfilment, and each partner can have a shot at achieving it at different points in the marriage. The arrangement got established in an era where the creative class moves more fluidly through jobs and no one expects to stay in the same job forever. It thrives in a culture that privileges self-expression over duty.[12]

Of course, the big question is – one to which we shall return in a moment – what happens after the children come along?

But it's not just top women – and men – who want to do things differently. Rebecca Asher talked to couples from across the economic spectrum for her research:

> What came across very clearly is that working-class women have the same expectations of work and home as middle-class women. They want to do just as well in their careers and they expected their partners to do their part. To say that the 'flexible working/shared parenting debate' is a middle-class one is just so patronising. They have the same cares and concerns for themselves – and their children – as middle-class families.

Recession and austerity are also re-shaping the landscape. According to the UK Office of National Statistics in January 2013, a record number of fathers now stay at home 'to bring up the children'; part of the 2.3 million people in the UK who fall into the 'economically inactive' category. That figure has shot up from 19,000 to 227,000 over twelve months and now represents the highest number of stay-at-home fathers since records first began in 1993. Again, we are looking at a lifestyle change brought about as much by the economy as sexual politics. Many men are unable to find work, others with partners on good salaries decide that it makes more economic sense for them to stay at home. (The number of women staying at home to look after children has also increased to 2.1 million, although the ONS notes that this figure has been higher in the past. Figures from the European Commission show that female breadwinners have increased their earnings by almost 10 per cent.)[13] The Fatherhood Institute argues that UK fathers' involvement in family work (in all senses) has dramatically increased 'over the last thirty years and continues to do so, with the gap between mothers' and fathers' contributions at home narrowing. British fathers' care of infants and young children rose 800% between 1975 and 1997, from 15 minutes to two hours on the average working day.'[14]

According to The Fatherhood Institute 'empirical studies of paternity leave suggest that younger generations of European men are [now] approaching paternity leave as an important component of family togetherness and personal identity' and that on a number of indicators, shared parental leave encouraged the motivation and work satisfaction, as well as the business efficiency, of both mothers and fathers. 'Sweeping fatherhood under the carpet is no longer a viable strategy.'[15] Certainly, a great fanfare surrounded the announcement, in November 2012, that the British government planned to introduce a system of flexible parental leave from 2015. Both parents will be allowed to share up to a year's leave after the birth of a child. Women will retain their right to fifty-two weeks of maternity leave and only mothers will be allowed to take leave in the first two weeks after birth. But after that, parents can divide up the rest of the time. The only rule is that no more than twelve months can be taken in total, with no more than nine months at guaranteed pay. The proposal was soon criticised by some, like Nick Pearce of the think tank IPPR, on the grounds that the opportunity to

> create a 'use it or lose it' block of leave for fathers, which all the evidence suggests is the only way of increasing the proportion of dads who take up parental leave when their children are very young, has been missed. In its absence, we can expect very little change in the UK's highly unequal division of childcare and employment responsibilities between men and women. Mothers will remain the primary child-carers, and motherhood will continue to penalise their pay and career prospects. Policy will remain shaped by highly gendered assumptions about parenting.[16]

Childcare remains a pressing concern for contemporary families. A special report from the Resolution Foundation, which undertakes research into low- and middle-income families, published in late 2012, confirms that 'the UK has some of the most expensive childcare in the OECD, accounting for up to a third of household income in some cases'. For lower paid families, 'while childcare costs represent a smaller proportion of the household income for lower income families, childcare costs nevertheless significantly erode work incentives. A second earner on the minimum wage is only £4 a week better off a week if she works full time than if she did not work at all.'

Rita Clifton was, until mid 2012, chief executive of Interbrand, one of the world's largest corporate consultancies, and is the manifestly devoted mother of two grown-up daughters. Formerly vice-chairman of Saatchi and Saatchi, she has been described as 'the doyenne of branding' by *Campaign* magazine, and 'Brand guru' by the *Financial Times*. But Clifton is also an emblem, a slice of cultural and social history, one of the early Exceptional (full-time, high-earning, corporate) mothers. Clifton, whose daughters were born in the late 1980s, acknowledges that she was 'pioneering [in that she was] the first woman of any seniority . . . to have a baby and come back to work full time.'When Clifton's elder sister had her first child, seven years earlier, it was common for women to stop working. And Clifton is honest about her own ambivalence when the time came:

> The baby was 10 weeks when I left her. It felt a huge pressure . . . I remember the last NCT meeting . . . all my mother friends, all of them were going to have several months at home with the baby and I was flooded with tears.

She is in tears as she tells me this. (So am I.) After her second daughter was born:

> The children were with a nanny . . . they were perfectly fine. I had a rush of guilt. Still breast feeding . . . had to bottle the breast milk – I was breast pumping at the office, I had milk in sachets in the freezer. It was all a bit of a cliché – bulging boobs, lack of sleep, slightly surreal. I would get phone calls and messages – the baby doesn't want to take a bottle. But you just get on with it. I didn't have a long maternity leave. Still, full-time working and babies, I felt knackered. When I look back at pictures of me in my twenties I just

look awful. My life was working/seeing the baby/sleeping. Weekends were sacrosanct . . . when I was with them, I tried really to be with them. I loved them unconditionally . . . how can I explain how difficult it was to go away? Once, I had to go to Singapore for a week and I was just bawling. On the plane, the only thing I could think of was my children. It's not that surprising. They have been on you physically all the time, taken up a lot of your mind space. You are glued to them.

Meanwhile, back at the office, all the 'guys had photos of their children – but women didn't. I never talked about the children at work. I didn't initiate any of that conversation. Nowadays there's a much more open conversation.' Did she think of giving up?

No, I nearly did three days a week . . . but once I got to the office, I could focus on the work, knowing they were at home, and secure. The last nanny we had was with us for twelve years – she was just such an asset . . . it meant I could focus on other parts of life. I haven't been a pushy mother . . . very much a nurturing mother. The girls would say, I provided 'an unconditional love, supply of cuddles. Unbridled joy.'

Clifton is the Exceptional Mother par excellence, the efficient elder sibling, or spin-off, of the Exceptional Woman, a new cultural figure that emerged from the 1980s onwards. Female celebrities began to flaunt their artistic competence, physical beauty and swelling bodies: an iconic image of this period was Demi Moore, posing naked, with a bulging pregnant stomach, on the cover of *Vanity Fair* in 1991. Madonna became pregnant in 1995, while filming *Evita* – but appeared at both the European and American premieres within weeks of giving birth. The Diva to beat all Divas was Back in Shape. The bar for modern women was getting higher.

The early Exceptional Mother had the clean lines, and often the exaggerated characteristics, of a cartoon figure. In the late 1990s, she was probably best represented by Nicola Horlick, mother of five, a round-faced, dark-eyed fund manager at Morgan Grenfell who in early 1997 was suspended after suggestions she had been in talks with a rival bank. A top banker and mother to five children? The nation fell, and fed, upon this fact, with equal parts scepticism and admiration. Should we applaud? Should we be appalled? The tabloids trailed Horlick as she pushed a buggy or fed a baby with formula milk, talking about her politics and her admiration for Labour leader Tony Blair – soon to be elected in a landslide – as she did so.

For a long time the 'career mother' was largely derided, from just about every side. Conventional society, and less confident women, judged them as bad mothers who had more or less abandoned their job of maternal care for the sake of ambition. Feminists on the liberal/left could find nothing progressive in the successful corporate figure, male or female; this was not traditional feminist territory in any sense. But as the grip of the market has tightened, and politics has shifted towards the conservative end of the spectrum, Exceptional Mothers, particularly with things to say about the economy and parenthood, have come to seem almost radical. The model itself has changed. The website Timewise Jobs has published a list of the top fifty part-time workers, The UK's Power Part Time Top 50, which, encouragingly, includes some men, and shows what is possible in this new landscape. Women like Lea Paterson, who heads the Inflation report and Bulletin Division at the Bank of England, works four days a week at times of increased work pressure, and three and a half days a week otherwise. Helen Michels, Global Innovation Director, Futures Team, at global drinks giant Diageo, which has net sales of over £10 billion across more than 180 markets around the world, works part time in order to achieve a better work life balance – 'to spend time with her son and pursue personal interests outside of Diageo'.[17]

Paradoxically, women like Clifton (and Sandberg) both reveal and conceal the work of motherhood. They offer us valuable observations of personal pain and struggle but these may not do justice to the difficulties of those women who combine motherhood with far less interesting or well remunerated work. For all our advances, are we still handing on to our collective daughters a complex, deceptive set

> For a long time 'career mothers' were largely derided, from just about every side as bad mothers who had more or less abandoned their job of maternal care for the sake of ambition . . .

of signals about what lies ahead that ill prepares them for the shock of birth, caring, and the long years of managing two kinds of lives?

Laura, a high-flying young lawyer, is trying to get her career established, and is in a relatively new relationship. She looks around her friends and peer group, some of whom have had children and she says,

> I am really disappointed in a lot of them. What I see is the approach of their wives who are my friends. Already, they are taking it all on! And the men are just carrying on working in the same way, leaving the wives holding the baby. And these [men] are the best of the crop. To describe what I feel as 'disappointed' is, in fact, a fucking understatement.

Kate is also

> worried about what's ahead. My husband is great. He definitely wants kids. But on a practical level he doesn't do much housework. I don't think he realises what's involved in having a child. He also can't do the financial stuff. I am much more practical. So that's really what I worry about – his inability to do housework. He is good at cooking – if you ask him to do it. But I've got to be identifying what needs doing – he just doesn't see it as a problem. He just doesn't even notice – that's all going to be so much more intense if we have a child. I would like him to do 50/50 shared leave. But I'm not sure it's going to work out like that. I imagine I am going to end up doing anything like 60 to 90 per cent of the work of having a child. I want him to stop and think about it before we get there. I think he'd be a really good father. So I'm not agonising. But it is all in the back of my mind.

Head teachers and high-flying executives may tell girls to 'make your partner a real partner'. But for now, this seems very much a minority pursuit. For most women, motherhood still means two things: more work, less pay. A 2009 (pre-austerity) report from the UK-based Fawcett Society, *Not Having It All: How Motherhood Reduces Women's Pay and Employment Prospects*, has analysed the 'mother gap' in stark economic terms:

> For each year she is absent from the workplace, a mother's future wages will reduce by 5%. Mothers are also much more likely than

fathers to adjust their work to fit in with their children's schedules which means they are much more likely to return to work part time: and part-time work is more likely to be low paid, and women working part time are less likely to be promoted, will have less access to training and are more likely to be made redundant.

What's more, this pay penalty is one of the highest in Europe, according to separate research published by the University of Manchester which showed that working mothers in the UK are half as likely as childless women to work in high-earning professions and eight times more likely to work part time. These figures put the UK in last place out of the six countries studied – the others being Finland, Denmark, Germany, the Netherlands and France. Poor access to childcare, and limited parental-leave options were the main reason for this disparity.[18]

> Working mothers in the UK are half as likely as childless women to work in high-earning professions and eight times more likely to work part time.

Typically, the media latched on enthusiastically to the implications of lost pay for 'top women' with the news, in December 2012, that in Britain female executives earn a staggering £423,390 less over their lifetimes than male workers who follow identical career paths. Women managers, it emerged, earn £14,689 a year less than their male counterparts, with female directors earning an average basic salary of £127,257 – compared to a male director average of £141,946 – according to an analysis by the Chartered Management Institute. Women also receive less than half of what men are awarded in cash bonuses – the average bonus for a male executive being £7,496, compared to £3,726 for a female executive.[19]

The difficulty is, we can't disentangle this pay gap from what happens at home. Yes, men and women in today's economy both work long hours, if we add up paid and unpaid work time put in by each. But there is, surely, a world of difference between hours spent at work, which may well consolidate a career, or reap overtime payments, and the circular kinds of labour involved in keeping a home and family afloat: not to mention the additional freedom afforded to a man who knows that family life is literally being 'taken care' of.

For these reasons, domestic work, in all its dimensions, remains the potentially deadly iceberg in terms of women's extra-domestic fulfilment or reward. There has been remarkably little change on this front. According to a report from the IPPR, patterns of housework have shifted only slightly over the last half century or more. More than eight out of ten women born in 1958 say they do more laundry and ironing than their partner, while seven out of ten women born in 1970 agree. 'The revolution in gender roles is unfinished,' the report said, with charming understatement.[20] According to a separate study by the think tank Demos, *The Other Glass Ceiling: The domestic politics of parenting*, fathers want to play a more active role in family life but lack the necessary skills and confidence to do so. According to special polling carried out for the report, 44 per cent of mothers said they would take the day off work if their child was unexpectedly ill and couldn't go to school, but only 3 per cent said that their husband or male partner would take the day off work in these circumstances.[21]

> The distribution of domestic work seems to have shifted remarkably little over the years, regardless of the economic contribution of women or men.

One of the puzzling features about all this is that the distribution of domestic work seems to have shifted remarkably little over the years, regardless of the economic contribution of women or men. One piece of US research drew on interviews with thirty working-class cohabiting couples. Commenting on her findings, co-author Sharon Sassler, professor of policy analysis and management at New York's Cornell University, observed that

When men aren't working, they don't see domestic labour as a means of contributing. In fact, they double down and do less of it, since it challenges their masculinity. But when men earn more, women – who are almost all working, too – feel obliged to contribute in some way to maintaining the household, generally by cooking and cleaning. The connection between masculinity and privileges is maintained for many of these men. Almost none of the women who paid the majority of the household bills were awarded the privileges that male providers have traditionally received, such as retaining control of household finances.[22]

Other UK based research confirms that in male bread-winner families or when women work part time, gender divisions are strong.

'Having children is of enormous importance, and is associated with men doing a much smaller share of household chores, mostly because the increase in total housework associated with having children is done almost entirely by women.'[23] Even when single women work full time, they do less housework overall than 'dual-career' married mothers.

A few years ago, I tackled this issue in a long piece for the *Guardian* on 'married single parents'. What I found were highly qualified women, often working part time in responsible and demanding jobs, but still taking on the full load of domestic life. One of my interviewees had a doctorate in social anthropology and worked from home, managing her own social research projects, hiring a nanny to care for the children during those hours. Her husband worked a regular twelve-to-fourteen-hour day in a new hi-tech venture. She was unequivocally positive about the role she had adopted:

> Family life is 100 per cent my responsibility. I'm 100 per cent in charge. My husband hasn't been to the supermarket in two to three years. And he doesn't intend to go. He says if I don't want to do the shop, then we can pay someone else to do it. His working life is so intense, he has so much stress, I don't resent him at all. [He] is the best dad I know, and that is so much more important than whether or not he rinses his noodle bowl. He gets up at 5.30 a.m. so as to get his work done before his hour with the kids in the morning. In the evening, he rushes home to be able to put them to bed by 7.30 p.m.

A second interviewee had met her husband when, in their twenties, they worked in the corporate world; both rose steadily through the ranks. When her husband was offered work abroad, she gave up her job in order to stay at home. She described her life as 'fairly stressful. Emotionally, you're married. But you do all the family stuff, you cope entirely alone. The daily school run. Entertaining his parents. Sorting out the holidays. Buying the birthday scooter and putting it all together.' She smiles ruefully, 'I don't get adult company in the way I should. He doesn't get the daily pleasures, hugs, that would make him feel valued. If you don't have very strong communication, then [it can feel] as if his only role is to provide the finance.'[24] Not surprisingly a lot of these women talked about it being a 'deal' – a deal that wouldn't last for long. This was a particular period of their lives as a couple – where one person (the woman) would pay attention to family – and the other person (the man) would pay attention to money, worldliness and status. That seemed to dovetail with economic realities, to make a kind of regressive sense.

Strangely, however, the 'deal' did not seem to alter, or not that much, even when the woman was the chief breadwinner. Some women seemed to oddly relish this crazily heroic and exhausting double role. Why? One said, 'By doing everything in the family, I've always felt I was in the driving seat. Being in control is very important to me.' Another interviewee worked full time, as did her husband: but it was she who was entirely responsible for domestic life. She wrestled with her fury – 'about twice a year, I get so angry, I can't sleep. I'm churned up. It seems so unfair.' However, she had come to accept, she could affect no real change in her husband's behaviour.[25]

In *The End of Men*, Hanna Rosin follows a typical 'see-saw' couple called Steven and Sarah. Sarah goes out to work and Steven looks after the children. Rosin hung out with the family for a couple of days, listening to a tale of a modern woman who 'aced' law school and networked her way into great jobs and a man who feels that 'I don't have to rush . . . I can do more of what I want. I don't care if I make money. I don't have to because my wife is the one feeding the family.' So far, so modern.

But what happens when Sarah gets home from work? The passage is worth quoting in full because it says so much about the deep-laid imperatives of motherhood. Rosin – rightly – writes it as a sort of low-level detective story, as in 'hunt the real family dynamic':

> Just before six, Sarah walked in from work, sat down to take off her sneakers, and then got right back up again. It's hard to describe what happened next . . . Within minutes Xavier was up in his high chair, his butt now lathered in cream, eating blueberries. Strawberries appeared on the table to be cut for a pie, along with flour and butter . . . Chopped meat came next . . . and a cold beer got to my hand. She set the tables, bathed the baby, laid out the burgers, put together the pie. Did I mention she was seven and a half months pregnant? It seemed as if the rest of us had until that point only been lazily

squatting in this house, and now the space reverted to its rightful owner who was whipping it back into shape.[26]

Rosin's observations speak to a deep truth about the difficulty of separating out 'house' or 'domestic' work from other kinds of work within a family or even of attempts to measure who does what. Cleaning, cooking, washing up: these are practical tasks that can be apportioned more fairly, and certainly are, compared to our mothers' and grandmothers' day. Analysis by the IPPR has suggested that the greatest move towards domestic equality is happening in homes with mothers in higher-paid occupations; there has been less change in the distribution of unpaid work among women in skilled (manual and non-manual) occupations.[27] But, in general, it is clear that it is still women who perform – or who arrange for these tasks to be performed, if they outsource them to other low-waged women. Many professional families now hire paid help in the home; nannies are a crucial component of the new economy. It has been estimated that over six million people employ domestic help of some kind, over a million more than a decade previously.[28]

But it is not so easy to outsource all the nebulous, multiple personal tasks of family life, such as remembering family birthdays or helping with children's homework. This involves a kind of emotional care and attention: automatically registering the moods, needs, concerns of everyone within the family, and trying, as far as possible, to balance them. Yes, more men are now taking on more of these responsibilities, and many writers – mothers and feminists – have written about women's 'gatekeeping' in respect of their children's lives, their inability to give up their domestic role: a sort of exhausted power play.

But I wonder if mothers face another difficulty in relation to men as more equal partners? When a woman keeps doing traditional work and manages a family she is a figure of significant personal and cultural power. Exhausted, run ragged, short on sleep: but a mythic creature (if only to herself). When a man gives up his worldly or work power, and takes on the jobs of the domestic sphere, he is viewed by many as a hybrid or oddly unclassifiable person. I am not talking about a man who takes a baby out in a pram or a child to the park for a Sunday kick-around. I am talking about a father who does the washing, does the shopping, organises the play dates, picks up the children every day from school. Others do not know what to make of him, how to pigeon hole him, how to deal with him. He is often excluded from the company of women that can make motherhood such an enjoyable, if complex, nether world. Few men have access to this, or similar, companionship. Mary Catherine Bateson puts it like this: 'When a man accepts the vulnerabilities associated with a woman's position, he is doubly vulnerable. For a woman it is familiar territory.'[29]

'It's not the physical work that exhausts me, it's all the emotional labour. Are they settling in at school? Are they happy with themselves? I talk to my husband about the minutiae and he glazes over as if I am this tediously obsessed woman. He's dealing with the Big Stuff, out in the world.'

Whether it is women – or some men – who do this family work, it remains difficult to convey the quantity or quality of the burdens involved to younger generations and so prepare them for parenthood. You can read Allison's Pearson's bestseller *I Don't Know How She Does It* a dozen times but never come to grasp the totality of the care and concern for our children, the way it invades every waking moment. Writing Lists just doesn't begin to explain it. As one prominent feminist said to me, 'It's not the physical work that exhausts me it's all the emotional labour. Are they settling in at school? Are they happy with themselves? I talk to my husband about the minutiae and he glazes over as if I am this tediously obsessed woman. He's dealing with the Big Stuff, out in the world.'

Ultimately, it is the compound effect that is the killer, the years and years of boxing and coxing, leading, possibly, to a spirit-sapping diminution of energy and ambition. Christina Wood is the head of department in a large challenging school – and she described her daily life to me as follows:

It is very hard to combine being a teacher and a mother. If I work really hard at school and put in the inevitably long hours it takes to plan, create resources, teach, mark etc., I feel guilty for being away from my young son and not being there for all his precious moments growing up. If I dedicate more of my time to my son, and gain a bit more of a work-life balance, I feel guilty about the pupils who deserve a teacher who is fully devoted to them and the huge amount of time and energy that is required to work at such a challenging school. *I therefore do not have a work-life balance.* I rush from teaching to try to spend some quality time with my son, then rush to work long into the night, giving up sleeping, to allow me to get the work done. [But] however hard I work there is always new work that needs to be done, the workload is immense and not sleeping cannot be sustained long term. I am made to feel guilty if I need time off to care for my son if he is sick. This leaves me feeling under pressure and unsupported. Bringing up your children and teaching other people's children are the most important things in the world and combining the two will always be tricky but needs to be carefully handled if both are to be combined effectively. [My emphasis.]

I recently came across an anonymous blog by a female scientist which seemed to sum up what many women feel, not at the outset of parenthood, but a decade or two into the reality of juggling ambition, children and partnership: the tiredness, the resentment, the retreat into conservatism, and the self-criticism and endless questioning about paths taken and not taken. Here is an edited version:

I have beautiful and smart children, who are unfortunately prone to ear infections and food allergies that made the early years of each of their childhoods very challenging. I love them dearly, but there is a lot of work involved. A lot of worrying, and a large mental load involving scheduling various doctor's appointments, taking time off work for each of them, making lunches, getting them all ready for school, picking them up from school, making dinner, doing dishes, giving baths . . . Why doesn't my husband do more? He does things around the house, cleaning and laundry. But I cannot battle over chores any more. Also, he is happy. He has time to play World of Warcraft to his heart's content, he can sleep in on weekends. Who am I and how important is my career really that I would have the right to ask him to sacrifice much more of his comfort and happiness? For all I know, I could be working even more and I would still not be happy. The difference would be that I would never see my kids or him, and that he would likely be miserable too. Now, at least one of us is happy, that's something I suppose.

In *Half a Life*, Gaby Hinsliff observes that, within most same-sex relationships, the familiar power struggles over what was once called housework simply do not arise, suggesting that the battle for 'domestic democracy' is still to be fought by our daughters – the heterosexual ones, at any rate. Will they face the kind of internal conflict as this anonymous blogger or of the mother I interviewed who suffered insomnia through her fury at the inequality in workload? Or will they decide, as this woman had, to 'channel her anger', to learn how to count her blessings. 'Lovely children, meaningful work and a real connection with my husband. I'm very lucky.' Really?

So where are we heading? Are the mothers of the future going to find it easier to balance all these different demands? Within the UK, discussions about flexible working and shared parenting have become a settled part of our vocabulary but not, yet, our practice. Rebecca Asher, author of *Shattered*, believes that the Coalition promise of 'shared parenting' is massively overstating what is actually on offer:

> Of course, some sort of political consensus around shared parenting is a good thing – but no one will actually sign up to the means to deliver it for significant numbers of families. The government legislation in this area is weak. Lots of businesses would say, 'It's not up to us to integrate women into work.' At the same time some feminists baulk at the idea of shared parental leave, believing that it undermines mothers' rights.

Currently, the British government is committed to a 'strictly voluntary' approach to the issue of more flexible working. In its written evidence to the recent Women in the Workplace Select Committee, the government stated unequivocally:

> The voluntary, business-led approach is the best way to encourage employers to drive culture change and tackle the complex issue of equal pay, except where a business is found to have discriminated on equal pay. Businesses themselves are best placed to identify the key barriers to gender equality in their workplace and take steps to tackle

them. The best businesses are already doing this – and by sharing their success, they will inspire others to follow.[30]

But Karen Mattison, a mother of three sons, and founder of Women Like Us and Timewise Jobs sees a real problem with this voluntary approach:

> You get a lot of companies who are using flexibility to keep people. But when that person leaves their job, the job will be advertised at five days a week. It's like there is a default to a full-time job. Political correctness determines that they should say they are offering flexible work. But the fear in companies is: 'We don't want *everyone* to ask.' I went to one big law firm (in an attempt to get them to advertise their jobs on a more flexible basis) and they said, 'Look at the way our firm works. We have clients who will give us a problem at 10 p.m. and they want to be able to go home, go to sleep and for us to have worked out a solution by 5 a.m. or 7 a.m. the next morning by the time they've got up. If our people are working flexibly, we are certainly not going to be telling them that.'

This profound reluctance was confirmed by a recent study by the communications company O2 which highlighted 'a clear disconnect in what businesses say and do, and employee perceptions of the policies and support that are in place to help them'.

Looking at the current landscape, there seems, too, a danger of going backwards. It is illegal to discriminate against pregnant women or to make a woman redundant while she is on maternity leave. But there are, it seems, ways to make new mothers – already exhausted, lacking in confidence – unwelcome in their old jobs. UK research company OnePoll questioned 1,000 women in February 2013 about their experience of returning to work; the results were quite shocking. Almost a third of new mothers (30 per cent) felt they didn't fit in any more and two in five felt they lacked support, with almost 20 per cent feeling that no one understood

> Almost a third of new mothers (30 per cent) felt they did not fit in any more and two in five felt they lacked support, with almost 20 per cent feeling that no one understood what it was like juggling work with new motherhood. (Survey by OnePoll, February 2013)

what it was like juggling work with new motherhood. Nearly one in ten said the stress affected their relationship with their partner. Only 3 per cent had sought legal advice over maternity discrimination; 10 per cent had sought help from their HR department. And seven of the women surveyed had lost their job while on maternity leave.

According to Samantha Mangwana, an employment lawyer at the leading UK law firm Slater & Gordon, which commissioned the research, these findings were 'sad and shocking'. 'Women are suffering in silence,' she said:

> A common case is that a woman goes back to her role and all her clients have been given to other people. And they are not returned. So everything she has built up over the years is gone. Or they are simply being made redundant ahead of worse-performing men. The big issue is that women are somehow seen as being less committed to their employers because they are now mothers. Many companies are settling out of court because they don't want to be seen to be treating pregnant women or new mothers like this. But the awful thing is that I see the same major companies again and again and again, writing out these cheques – accompanied, of course, with a confidentiality clause.[31]

In a disheartening twist some employers, including some senior women, are now clamping down on more parent-friendly work practices, initiating a backlash against a revolution that has barely begun.

And in a disheartening twist some employers, including some senior women, are now clamping down on more parent-friendly work practices, initiating a backlash against a revolution that has barely begun. In early 2013, Marissa Mayer, the chief executive of Yahoo, declared that all 11,500 Yahoo employees are to come to work in the office, on the grounds that working from home meant that 'speed and quality are often sacrificed'. (Mayer herself has had a nursery built adjacent to her office so that she can see her own child during the day.) Alexandra Shulman, the outspoken editor of British *Vogue*, has also weighed into this debate in separate interviews. In one noted contribution, she argued:

The reality is, if you take time out and have children, it does damage your trajectory in some way. I know it shouldn't, I know there should be a way round it, but I think it's really hard. We have a lot of people [at *Vogue*] who have been fantastic all through their pregnancy, then gone off, had the baby, not known how long they were going to be away, decided to take the full year and either come back pregnant or come back and been pregnant again very quickly. So effectively, you're sort of out, really, for two or three years and that does make a difference. You can't pretend it doesn't.

Shulman has also echoed Mayer's views on more flexible work arrangements:

Working from home is exactly that. Working in the office is something different . . . Invariably my reaction is the same. Sorry, but no. I believe in the collective creativity of an office. Some of the best stories in any publication I have worked on have come out of a glancing remark somebody has made about their night before, or a piece of gossip, or a joke. The daily download of chatter within the office feeds into what we produce in an incalculable way. Having half the team sitting at home, fiddling around on a search engine from the kitchen or pasting up mood boards from the sofa does not replicate that.[32]

Shulman's arguments seem reasonable. But they also underline a fundamental shift in the relationship between employer and employee that has been taking place over the past three decades, and which could restrict the chances of younger women combining children and work. As the writer Lucy Mangan recently observed, 'in the general absence of old-fashioned things like trades' unions (so effectively dismantled in the seventies and eighties by those who had much to gain by their neutering), employers wield enormous power over their workforce and – human nature being what it is, especially when allied to the prospect of making money – require very little encouragement to abuse it. Employment rights – and their close cousin, anti-discrimination legislation – have been hard-won over the years. They have never not been under threat, and the threat is increasing as the economy grinds to a halt.'[33] It makes me wonder if Sheryl Sandberg, and her passionate belief that more women at the top will enable more women to *get* to the top, has got it all wrong after all.

Rita Clifton also 'wants more women to be running more organisations'. But at the same time, she believes there's still a

> challenge for women in the corporate arena. I don't want to go back to Pretending. We need an honest debate about what's happening in the workplace rather than more legal regulation . . . a human conversation about how and what you want and want for your life. Do women 'Leave Before They Leave?' I'm not sure that really happens until they start to have children. But motherhood is a preoccupying thing . . . takes up some mind space. That's not to say you can't do a great job of doing your job. But 'work-life balance' – I have a problem with that term. It's as if work is the thing you have to get through.

She supports flexible working:

> Although I think you probably have to do four days and if you're doing four days then you are working full-time because you are always going to do long days. The difficulty with women who are on maternity leave or at home, on part-time contracts, is that they have to be open minded about taking calls, showing that they are connected. It's a give and take. It's challenging for women to be away for such a long time . . . maybe up to nine months or a year. The risk is that they get disconnected from the business.

In Clifton's view, the market will sort it out, because it needs to keep talented women:

> We need more women in the future to be running organisations – to be role models – and women of a certain age. Women might bow out of the workforce from say thirty to forty-five, to have their families, but then be ready to come back for a few decades in their early to middle middle age.

Academic and life-long learning specialist Tom Schuller takes a similar view of the way forward for the next generation:

> I think you have to take the life course perspective . . . Parental leave focuses on a specific part of the life course, when we need to look

at it in a longer-term context. The equality thing only makes sense over the life span. With the retirement age getting later, a working life will last much longer. So there are new issues and new opportunities for women in their forties and fifties. Lots of older people are now taking part in training. There used to be real drop-off among older people. But now we all realise that we have work in front of us. Later life careers are far more open. But whether organisations are open to that . . .

He leaves the end of the sentence hanging in the air.

Karen Mattison also agrees:

Once you've got out of these executive roles – it's very hard to get back in, fifteen years on. But things have changed in recent years. Women *expect* to get back to work now. So that faces a [professional woman] with three routes. One: carry on full time, the so-called Alpha Woman/Beta Man approach, with your husband at home: effectively you have swapped roles. Two: don't work at all. Or three: go down the middle way, working part time, job sharing, a route which still doesn't really exist when it comes to the better paid jobs. I think that this is where we are starting to see some change and for me that's what The Power List was all about. The common belief that you can't do a senior role less than full time is actually wrong. The problem is that many who have succeeded in this and are working in senior part-time roles are doing it 'under the radar' and the role models in UK plc can be hard to find.

So important does Mattison think it is to increase the supply of highly skilled part-time jobs, she has made it her professional task to concentrate on the recruitment end of the market. Having set up the impressive Part Time Power List, she now wants to 'grow the supply' of well paid (over £40,000 a year), flexible or part-time jobs for the thousands of people – men as well as women – who want them. Currently, the imbalance between supply and demand is striking. Her timewisejobs website is currently advertising 180 jobs at any one time. She has 40,000 professional candidates on her site every month searching for this kind of work.

The other big idea of the future, Mattison believes, is the job-split, which differs subtly from 'the older idea of a "job share", where two people did one job'. The problem with that is that when one person leaves, the other person has to go full time or they have to find a new partner who can divide it along lines that suit them:

> Companies don't tend to be keen on job sharing; they don't carry many people in that role. But job splits take a job with two distinct components, say like marketing and PR. The job is worth £50,000 a year – and you divide it up and and put the job out to two different people. It's a big part of the future.

Mattison continues,

> One of the lessons for me over the past couple of years is that we can't just sit and wait for the dream part-time job to appear in the company we want to work for. We have to change the conversation with these businesses and this is what my focus is entirely on now. Instead of asking if they have part-time roles, I now talk to them about whether they are open to flexibility for the right candidate. Often the answer is yes but the business is just not communicating it to prospective employees. This is a huge opportunity for them to attract the kind of high calibre talent they need. For many experienced professionals, having a flexible working arrangement is the deal breaker that would convince them to move to another company. Too often it is not advertised as an option by businesses and they simply don't apply.

And what of the bigger political picture? Will our daughters – the mothers of the future – be dependent on modern-minded recruitment agencies or third-sector entrepreneurs like Mattison rather than the state and society to improve their chances of combining work and children? As long as the demands of the market take precedence over human well-being or women's needs, it could well be. According to Rebecca Asher,

> One of the reasons I find where we are in the UK so frustrating is that we have so much good evidence in policy terms about what works. We could cherry pick the best policies from around the world. We know that well-remunerated, ring-fenced maternity and paternity leave encourages men to take leave. And that's so important because it is in those early weeks and months that habits and dynamics are established between mothers, fathers and children. We know that 'the right

to request' isn't enough. In lots of European countries people have a right to part-time working. We have a wealth of research which shows the benefit to business of working flexibly, in terms of what parents put back into the workforce in commitment, productivity and longevity. And well-subsidised, high-quality childcare of course. But that agenda is so ideologically driven at the moment. It is ruled by de-regulation. 'Stack it high, sell it cheap.' That's not a good idea because it won't work on its own terms and parents and carers don't support it.

Given what we know about the value of keeping women in employment, retaining their skills and how good it is for the economy, Asher thinks we have made astonishingly little progress. 'I do feel we go round and round the houses. I think my mum would have had a similar conversation thirty years ago. It gets more and more frustrating.'

Anne-Marie Slaughter came to a form of political radicalism through motherhood:

I strongly believe that women can 'have it all' (and that men can too). I believe that we can 'have it all at the same time.' But not today, *not with the way America's economy and society are currently structured.* My experiences over the past three years have forced me to confront a number of uncomfortable facts that need to be widely acknowledged – and quickly changed.[34] [My emphasis.]

Changing work practices means 'fighting the mundane battles – every day, every year – in individual workplaces, in legislatures, and in the media'. Some of these changes, she argues, are rather 'prosaic' yet, given the current stasis, they sound revolutionary: 'My longtime and invaluable assistant, who has a doctorate and juggles many balls as the mother of teenage twins, emailed me while I was working on this article: "You know what would help the vast majority of women with work/family balance? MAKE SCHOOL SCHEDULES MATCH WORK SCHEDULES." The present system, she noted, "is based on a society that no longer exists – one in which farming was a major occupation and stay-at-home moms were the norm. Yet the system hasn't changed."'[35]

'You know what would help the vast majority of women with work/family balance? MAKE SCHOOL SCHEDULES MATCH WORK SCHEDULES!'

A recent special report by the British think tank IPPR published in April 2013 argued that to revive twenty-first-century feminism, a childcare revolution and greater access to quality flexible work is needed. 'The last wave of feminism certainly delivered for some professional women, but others have been left behind. The next wave in the United Kingdom should be less about how women can succeed in a man's game and more about how to change the rules of the game. Feminism needs fathers. Men should work more flexibly, take greater responsibility for caring for their children and do more housework. The state should offer universal pre-school childcare, which will pay for itself over time by increasing the UK's female employment rate and boosting tax paid by working mothers. The route to gender equality requires society to change and men to voluntarily do more of their fair share.'[36]

Others have argued for an overall reduction in the working week, in an attempt to balance out the excessive hours of some, and widespread unemployment on the other:

> Imagine a new 'standard' working week of 21 hours. How would it feel to wake up on a chilly weekday morning? More time in bed, more time with the kids, more time to read, see your mum, hang out with friends, repair the guttering, make music, fix lunch, walk in the park,

writes Anna Coote of the New Economics Foundation.

> While some are overworking, over-earning and over-consuming, others can barely afford life's necessities. A much shorter working week would help us all to live more sustainable, satisfying lives by sharing out paid and unpaid time more evenly across the population. Ideas about what is normal can sometimes change quite suddenly – as with not smoking in bars and restaurants. The weight of public opinion can swing from antipathy to routine acceptance, usually when there's a combination of new evidence, changing conditions, a sense of crisis and a strong campaign.[37]

A more humane working environment would benefit both mothers and fathers. But if this is to happen, it needs women *and* men – now and in the future – to fight for change. As Rebecca Asher concludes, with a deep sigh:

Mothers have to take some of the blame because we have bought into the idea that it's an individual problem to be individually solved. Parents – mothers and fathers – need to recognise their collective power as citizens, voters and consumers. It would be great if there were a more effective, active parents' lobby – a proper grass-roots campaign. Not a niche or professional thing, but an authentic, broad-based parental voice lobbying for change. We need to persuade policy makers that raising a child is a communal responsibility: parents together with meaningful support from government and wider society. That's the challenge for the future.

# PART III

Rebellions and Resources

# 7

# How Should a Woman Be?

*In which we consider how our daughters might think about issues
such as ambition and anger in order to enjoy life on their own
terms — oh, and how they should recognise and counter the dark
art of male condescension and squash anyone who fails to recognise their true, glorious value.*

Backbone. Resilience. Optimism. Endurance. Building 'character' is
all the mode these days. Schools, teachers and parents are exhorted
to shape the personalities, not to mention stiffen the backbone, of
their charges at every turn. Several books have recently been published
extolling the importance of personality, even if the emphasis on
character is inextricably tied, as everything is these days, to the state
of the economy. According to Hilary Wilce, author of the forthcoming
*Backbone: What Children Need, Aren't Getting and How to Give it Back
to Them,*

> In a competitive and fast-moving world, tomorrow's adults will have
> to draw deeply on their personal resources to learn new things and
> navigate life's constant changes. I already see this daily in my work as
> a personal-development coach. Academic attainments still matter, but
> degrees and postgraduate qualifications are now two a penny, and it's
> what's inside the individual that ultimately shapes careers and lives.[1]

Yet it can feel peculiarly difficult to think about the character
issue, in either general or gendered terms: and parents are well placed
to understand why. First of all, who could agree on what a good or
strong character *is*? (Dictionary definitions range from possessing
'moral and ethical strength' to 'the quality of being individual in an
interesting or unusual way' to 'strength and originality in a person's

nature'.) Clearly, temperament, education, good or bad luck all play their distinct part in creating human personality which is why you can find such different characters, and fates, within the same family.

On the other hand, it is impossible to say what makes a good or strong person without resorting to a largely uncontentious set of off-the-shelf traits: Backbone. Resilience. Optimism. Endurance. Etc. My own list would include: sound judgement, a sense of humour, a necessary toleration of ambiguity and ambivalence (but not to a self-destructive degree); awareness and mastery of one's emotions; some sense of the underlying direction of one's life combined with both an ability to display interim life-affirming spontaneity and the ability to stop or change course; kindness; a certain toughness . . . Easy, you see? Seriously: here, as in so many areas of human endeavour, context is all. There are clearly moments to deploy humour and moments to risk exposing vulnerability; it is pointless to display generosity towards the fundamentally mean spirited or unreciprocal; when does tolerance of ambiguity and ambivalence shade into self-deception? Sometimes, the only answer to a relationship or situation is not continued loyalty or yet more effort, but the courage to leave . . . and so on. *Not* so easy, you see.

It is for these reasons that literature, the deep elaboration of character within authentically complex contexts – the difference in my view between Great Books and Great Box Sets – will always provide a more useful guide to the ambiguity of human existence, including the difficulties of being and growing up female, than any amount of Cognitive Behaviour Therapy or self-help books. 'Just be yourself', 'Respect yourself and others will respect you' have far less long-term impact than a considered attempt to understand how Dorothea Brooke in George Eliot's *Middlemarch* or Isabel Archer in Henry James's *Portrait of a Lady*, both highly intelligent, sympathetic women, could end up living with men who drained their very life-force, in marriages from which neither, because of a mix of social and psychological reasons, seemed able to engineer an effective escape.

Sometimes, when my daughters and I are sitting round the kitchen table, talking over a knotty friendship issue or discussing people – one of life's great pleasures – I will tell them: anyone who really wants to understand friendship or sexual passion or integrity at work, will have

to set aside *Friends* or *Gossip Girl* and read Jane Austen and George
Eliot, most of Edith Wharton and pretty much all of Willa Cather.
(You should even give *Eat, Pray, Love* a go, for what it has to say about
savouring life's pleasures and slowing down.) I love the work of some
of the more established male authors of the twentieth century: F. Scott
Fitzgerald, Nabokov, James Baldwin, Philip Roth. Reading the works
of these men will surely help our daughters understand how some
men think about some women, beneath the veneer of whatever
etiquette each generation employs. At the very least, you will come
away with a grasp of the brilliant, empathic humanity at work even
in the most misogynistic strains of high literary culture.

Growing up female, however, brings up particular problems and
themes of a more daily sort: and young women – all women – are
going to need additional tools in order to tackle these. Every generation holds these conversations in their own distinct terms – and I
have no doubt our daughters and even their daughters' daughters
will do just that – but looking back over the last hundred years,
similar themes appear to emerge over and over again for each generation of women. What is the best means to self-
fulfilment? What about the Problem of Anger?
And – more fun, this – how to deal with the
age-old issue of male condescension? And in
keeping with the circular nature of women's
lives, it is striking how often issues connected
with ambition, anger and male condescension
overlap in a woman's life.

> It is striking how
> often issues
> connected with
> ambition, anger and
> male condescension
> overlap in a
> woman's life.

When the young Doris Lessing arrived in smoggy grim post-war
London in 1950, carrying a young son, and the manuscript of her
first novel *The Grass is Singing*, she was not thinking about how to
Lean In or where to meet the right people, of how to network with
an eye to becoming a future Nobel Prize winner. She was simply
hungry to write and to love, and to be part of politics. Intellectual
energy, obsessive creativity, the longing for love, curiosity: these were
the distinct elements of her 'ambition'. Writing about her political
youth, in the 1960s and 1970s, activist and academic Lynne Segal
quotes her friend Sheila Rowbotham: 'I never had a notion of a

career . . . I just thought you lived for politics and earned enough money to survive.'

In today's 'market facing' world, of course, self-fulfilment seems to have become entirely redefined as, or narrowed down to, a form of worldly ambition, managerial authority or the dreaded 'aspiration'. And how much less lovely it sounds too; the descriptors themselves so much shorter, sharper, more brisk; thrusting rather than reflective. This shift in, and shortening of, language reflects a sea change in thinking between the generations too. As I have said, issues of career, success or winning more money seemed remote, irrelevant and distasteful to many women of the 1960s and 1970s for whom the political origins of feminism, and its links to the left and the labour movement, took precedence. As I came to young adulthood in that world, I inevitably imbibed many of its values; it was one of the reasons that the 1980s and all its shoulder-padded thrustedness threw me into a bit of a (decade-long) bad mood. Here were women wanting things – sex, money, fame, power – and wanting them just for themselves, not for the health of society or in the name of the collective good. In one way, it was easy to dismiss it all: not my sort of people. But even then I knew this question of ambition was not so simple; why *shouldn't* women want approbation, power, money?

In part, we did not think of the more conventional question of 'careers' because, on the whole, either our mothers, if middle class, did not work, or if they did, they had a more contingent place in the workforce, doing part-time, low paid work that brought scarce outer world reward or respect. We, their collective daughters, had little exposure to, or experience of, either female worldly ambition or authority, so we did not know how to think of it. Ambition was something that belonged to young, pushy men, of any social class. Look at the culture of the 1950s or the 1960s; the new determination belonged to young working- or lower-class men, like Joe Lampton in *Room at the Top* or the real-life David Bailey. Women were their muses, not their peers – let alone their superiors.

How things have changed. Most young women today have mothers who work and all young women are the daughters of women who want more than they may have achieved. So a younger generation has, in myriad ways, been exposed, without realising it, to all the joys and contradictions, frustrations and rewards of 'women in the workforce', often in positions of some power. As Lennie Goodings argues in *Fifty Shades of Feminism*:

> The fact is we are everywhere and in every walk of life: there are thousands of us in law, medicine, business, education, the police, media, even in government. But it's as if that fact has not penetrated into everyday consciousness: women in power are not regarded as ordinary. They are thought of as remarkable and not portraying the usual state of things. Is that why women shy away from claiming their position?[2]

As we have seen, this is the argument of Sheryl Sandberg, and her exhortation to ambition is setting the tone of the early twenty-first century; but it is perhaps more accurate to see her, in her person and her proposals, as reflective of a fundamental shift in women's earning and public power that has, in some way, ground to a halt. Sandberg identifies the problem as female self-doubt and deference to (outdated) male attitudes. Young women of today, therefore, have to press on, to become 'pushy broads', to ask for what they want. And deserve.

According to a senior woman in publishing,

> My feeling is that it is much more okay now for women to be ambitious. It's not such a male thing anymore. Women see it as their right to want to achieve success in spite of the barriers that I'm sure exist in many professions. I really only know the publishing world in any depth and women have always been successful in that world, but at the cost of being paid less, receiving less respect from their male colleagues and having to be twice as good and work twice as hard to get as far. So that old cliché still stands. We've all watched the smart young men ricochet into prestigious positions leaping over more experienced and equally qualified women who stand back and wait to be recognised.

As the daughter of an American, I have a sneaking fondness for 'pushy broads'. I have certainly long felt impatient at the way that girls are always taught to be nice, to be receptive, to think of others; to put others first. *The Tyranny of Lovely* as one recent book title puts it. I would not want my daughters to sit by while men who may not have their talent or skills shoot past them in terms of earnings and authority.

I don't want them being 'good' and low paid. Being paid what one is worth, and what the man next door to you is being paid, is actually nothing to do with ambition but with economic justice. We do not like a man less because he earns what he believes he is worth; nor do we, I suspect, think about how he got to that place in human terms. Nor do I want my daughters to lack the courage to acquire – and demonstrate – real skills and knowledge. I want them to have a go at leading, or managing, other people if that's what they want to do.

In a brilliant essay in her collection *The End of the Novel of Love*, Vivian Gornick describes what the absence of ambition actually can mean. She dissects the late-nineteenth-century domestic, economic and psychological world of Clover Adams, wife of the historian and professional intriguer Henry Adams. Clover was the original 'salon-iste', part of the privileged and clever Boston Brahmin world. She brought together intellectuals and public servants in her husband's world and beyond; they discussed national and world events – and each other – with caustic brilliance. Yet the difference between her and her husband – and her husband's world – was a simple but profound one. Every day, the men 'went out to do battle with the world; doing battle with the world allowed them to do battle with themselves; doing battle with themselves they brought their miseries under enough control to achieve sufficient detachment; achieving detachment they did the work that gives human existence its meaning.'[3] Unlike her husband, Clover Adams lived in a private world of unrealised potential. With no channel for her intellect, her ambition or her organising impulses, her 'miseries' became suicidal. No doubt there were several contributory reasons, but her sense of uselessness was surely one. On a late Sunday afternoon in early December 1885 she committed suicide by swallowing cyanide.

In a poignant footnote to *The Feminine Mystique*, Betty Friedan makes note of an unpublished joint doctoral study of 'Fifty College Educated Women' in the post-war years. She writes:

> These fifty educated women had been full-time housewives and mothers throughout the years their children were in school. With the last child's departure, the women suffering severe distress because they [had] no deep interest beyond the home included a few whose actual ability and achievement were high; these women had been leaders

in community work . . . The authors' own orientation . . . makes them deplore the fact that education gave these women 'unrealistic' goals (a surprising number, now in their fifties and sixties, still wished they had been doctors).[4]

So why do I *still* cavil at that 'ambition' word then? As always etymology is a place to start. The *Oxford English Dictionary*'s first definition is good and plain: 'a strong desire to do or achieve something' (although it is interesting that it reinforces gender difference in the examples it gives: 'her ambition was to become a model'; 'he achieved his ambition of making a fortune'). The *OED* also notes that the word derives from Middle English – and ultimately from Latin, *ambire*: 'to go around' (canvassing for votes) or, in modern parlance, to put oneself 'out there'. But the American English dictionary *Merriam-Webster* leads on the worldly theme: 'an ardent desire for rank, fame or power' (here, the example given is 'her ambition is to start her own business') or 'a desire for activity or exertion'. A third definition links it to 'craving favours, vainglory, and popularity'.

The unspoken, slightly shameful, fear that lurks around ambition is that it cuts a historic and meaningful cord between women and relationships in a variety of senses: that the quest for meaning or the imperative to care will wither in the race for self-promotion. This is slightly different from, but connected to, the more conventional concern, that a woman might not be able to manage it 'all'. Tom Schuller writes in his capacity as a parent of two daughters,

> Does 'giving every encouragement' mean guiding or pressing them to aim literally as high as possible? This might be the only acceptable answer. But is it an unacceptably pessimistic line to suggest caution about very high ambitions because of the pressure that this puts on women, combined with the doubtful probabilities of actually getting to the top?[5]

Mary Catherine Bateson cuts to the heart of this double bind:

> No one who is passionately engaged in his or her work limits it for long to forty hours a week. Positions carrying the greatest challenge or responsibility are predicated on this assumption. It is often in the second shift or late at night at the office that the really creative work is done.

People of talent and ambition do enough work for two and are unlikely to invest vast amounts of time in other activities. Anybody can live two lives – few can live three at once . . . The fact that many women work a second shift while their husbands work only one is deeply unfair.[6]

It may be that older women, we anxious mothers, are of limited use with our worries about 'self-interest' pushing out our daughters' ability to create happy relationships, have children, sustain friendships or just enjoy a bit of time to themselves. Here, we have to draw on the growing example of women who work hard, enjoy life, or exercise authority without losing the human touch. Surely, one of the key qualifiers, if not caveats, is that finding contentment has to be a meaningful value in itself.

From my many conversations with younger women over the past years, I am left in no doubt that they – from fire officer to struggling single parent, top CEO to young media whizz kid – are unlikely to forget or forgo that. But on hearing how difficult it remains to win self-fulfilment or the job you deserve in today's world and on receiving anguished confessions about how 'giving up' seems the only way to go, if only for a while, we must not on any account say 'I told you so'. This is just another way of saying, the answer to the difficulties thrown up by ambition for today's young women lies not in their character but their worldly circumstances, the answer lies in politics. Of course, any woman who is genuinely serious about what she does will have to face, as equivalent men have always done, issues of authority, responsibility and failure. A partner in a law firm or a top barrister bears an often heavy responsibility for intimate aspects of others' lives; she will face intense professional pressure – and might feel a sense of personal blame – should she 'fail' a client in a high-profile divorce case or a complex criminal trial. A surgeon can save lives but may not be able to do so. A headteacher could face an inspection that leads to the school being put in special measures and losing its valued place in the community for years to come. A writer risks endless rejection or humiliatingly bad reviews. In a recent blog about Marissa Mayer, the head of Yahoo,

> In a recent blog about Marissa Mayer, the head of Yahoo, one woman observed, with some awe, 'She had the courage to do what she had to do – she didn't care if she was liked or not.'

one woman observed, with some awe, 'She had the courage to do what she had to do – she didn't care if she was liked or not.' Such a quality would scarcely be remarked upon in a man.

But even an abundance of 'inner authority' is not going to save any individual from difficult decisions; the woman who leads, or manages, may well have to refuse demands, cut pay or even sack employees. Nor is there refuge from ordinary, ignominious failure, such as: seeing others promoted or favoured over you, losing a job, falling out with a powerful superior. Historically, women have avoided dealing with this kind of difficulty by not admitting to 'wanting' anything in the first place. To spend one's life on that blurred border between real drive and achievement, in a kind of dreamy I-could-have-been-anything-if-I-had really-tried state, can be, as Simone de Beauvoir so ruthlessly observed, a form of bad faith. To acknowledge ambition, and to go for it (however it turns out) is, at the very least, an advance on narcissistic defensiveness.

Of course, some kinds of ambition – of a political, artistic or creative sort – are going to take different forms; they will not conform to the classic *Lean In* model. As Stefan Collini observes 'what if the potential people have is to become esoteric, unsaleable poets?'[7] In *Composing a Life*, Mary Catherine Bateson constructs a slow and deeply subtle argument about the disrupted but deeply creative reality of so many women's lives. Women have to handle the competing demands of love and friendship and children, as well as manage the distortions of male and institutional condescension, and their own, sometimes painful, lack of self-esteem. She writes of herself, and four friends, all from intellectual and privileged backgrounds, all of whom have pursued intellectual or creative ambitions. These are not simple stories. Each of these lives has involved enthusiasms pursued, abrupt stops and starts as a result of emotional concerns or responsibilities, including the having of children, but also the loving of husbands or partners: often startling personal understandings – or rifts – have enriched their professional selves. No female life is linear – or not in a male way; that is part of its richness. All the women Bateson writes about have achieved a great deal, but they are both deeply fulfilled, by the balance of so many competing demands, *and* frustrated: frustrated at the diversions, disruptions, missed chances, unfair treatment, pulls of family life, that have made it so much harder for them to pursue work and creative passions.

A writer friend of mine, who has never earned much money, talks about herself as follows:

> I have never been a conventionally ambitious person – climbing up the corporate ladder, making loads of money, having a posh house, all of that makes no sense to me at all. Seems vacant and somehow sad. However, being ambitious to realise one's own potential seems vital to me, as a human being. So, I want to be the best writer I can possibly be, not because I might win the Booker, or make a million sales (sigh) but because of the deep satisfaction it gives me, to know I have given of my best, and that the result is the absolute best I could have done at that time. Ambition, for me, is to be – and to become – fully oneself, with all the learning, studying, crafting, working, failing and trying again, that that entails.

One young woman I interviewed told me: 'I thought I had fatal limitations when I was growing up. I thought I wasn't ambitious because the idea of success was so tied to a job and career. But actually I *was* ambitious, because I didn't want that. I wanted to live differently.' The story she tells about herself is not about job and career moves, but a refreshing story of defining herself by taste and culture and relationships. She is, and always was, proud of the kind of 'music, books, films' she liked, 'high-end culture'. When she started on her Masters, she moved in with a group of girls and it was a very happy household. 'I guess I'd put it like this. I'm interested in meaning not materialism.'

There is one more thing to add here, something about the inevitability of a female life being of a more 'patchwork' nature. Even if the kind of political changes that I would like to see, in terms of the organisation of work and the economy, were brought in tomorrow, and work and personal life were in greater alignment, women might still need, or want, to think of work in a different way; the reminder of the limits – in all senses – of conventional, driven, male-shaped ambition.

Mothers can possess an irritating certainty that they know their children better than they know themselves and that should play a key, if possibly covert, part in deciding what their children should do in, or with, their lives. On the contrary, I believe we owe our daughters curiosity: the chance to be, or become, strangers, even to us, as we inquire of, and show ourselves willing to hear, wishes and dreams we may never have imagined or of which we may not even approve. It seems to me, then, that the kind of questions we should be – always – asking our daughters are, 'What really animates and interests you?' 'What do you enjoy doing?' 'Can you find a way to pursue what you love or are intrigued by?' And perhaps, later on in their lives, we might ask helpful questions such as: 'What compromises are you prepared to make – and how can I help you to figure out which compromises are worth making and which seem like a form of self-sacrifice?' When Shelby Knox, the young American feminist who made her name fighting for proper sex education in her Texas high school, came to New York to see what she could make of her life, she was lucky enough to meet Gloria Steinem. While Shelby was humming and hawing about what to do with her time, the question that Gloria Steinem asked her was 'What do you really, really want to do?'

> I believe we owe our daughters curiosity: the chance to be strangers, even to us, as we show ourselves willing to hear wishes and dreams we may never have imagined or of which we may not even approve.

One of the impressive things about former minister Estelle Morris, whom I interviewed (see previous chapter) is that she has put her experience of ambition, leadership, success *and* set-backs, at the service of young women just starting out on their work lives. 'Here I am a feminist, my ideas formed in the 1960s and 1970s, so what role can I play?' She finds it exciting to see younger women 'redefine the feminist narrative in their own ways. So I ask myself, "How might you help?"' And one way she can help is by mentoring young women:

> Sometimes I'm good at just talking and listening. I'll ask questions – and I'm also good at connecting up information from different sessions. So I will ask, 'How did it go?' I always say to women, 'What's your ambition? How far do you think you can go?' I also say to them, 'I think you could. You *could* do this or that.' Also, when they have a problem I can help them to see it in a wider perspective. I can ask: 'What's the next step?'

We would do well to warn them that life is very likely to change course – in so many interrelated ways, and often abruptly – over the years. We should also warn them that disappointment, mistakes, despair are part of the weave of a working as well as a personal life, and that bright, superficial mantra along the lines of 'love yourself' or 'look on the bright side' are best abandoned as tools for living early on.

One of the very minor regrets of my own life is that I listened too politely and too long to people who did not know, or did not care to know, me sufficiently, even as they dared or deigned to offer quick, cheery and utterly useless (to me) advice on some particular work or personal issue. I feel an affinity here with Bateson, who takes a long time to come to her own judgement of personal and professional situations. We need to help our daughters reach their own understandings, in their own way, according to their 'lights', not ours: the ability to think out all sides of a situation, good and bad, and then come to a decision – should I go on? should I quit? should I change my behaviour in one particular way? – is a vital element of a strong character. Far better that than to think one must toil on in all circumstances, in the most traditional female ways, with a bright fixed smile on our faces (but probably radiating a kind of suppressed fury) so that others should not be disturbed, for even a moment, by our legitimate difficulties.

Women and anger, it's insane. Female anger is unruly, base, frightening. The Mad Woman In the Attic. Taming of the Shrew. Fatal Attraction. In these stories, it's clear it would be better for everyone if these women were tamed. Female anger is seen as madness. To be pitied. I do get angry a lot – for feminist reasons. I often think – 'well, that's the old husband gone.' I've decided it's a sacrifice I'm willing to make. You have to make a bargain with yourself. Living by your feminist principles, means social isolation.

These are not the words of a feminist martyr. They were spoken to me in a tiny bar behind King's Cross, London, on a chill spring evening by a smart, political young woman. In fact, they surprised me so much, they sent me home to conduct a short experiment; to investigate (some of) the ways that feminism has interrogated anger, as a specific subject in women's lives. I started by taking down twenty feminist books published over the last seventy years, covering a range of themes – sex, politics, anthropology; of differing political stripe – liberal, socialist and radical feminism; and representing different kinds of authors: white, black, middle-class, working-class, lesbian and straight. The earliest book in my collection was *Male and Female* by Margaret Mead, but the pile included *The Feminist Mystique*, Valerie Wallace's book on *Black Macho and the Myths of the Superwoman*, Australian Susan Maushart's *The Mask of Motherhood*, and coming right up to date with Hanna Rosin's *The End of Men*. Flicking through index after index I was puzzled and intrigued by what was in there and what was not. While there was a scattering of regular entries for autonomy, ambition, anomie, androgyny there were remarkably few direct references to anger, or its close relation: aggression. Instead, I found myself skipping, with great interest, straight from the American Revolution through to Susan B. Anthony, from Hans Christian Andersen straight to Judith Arcana: or following a trail from Androgyny to Anthropology, Maya Angelou to the Angry Brigade.

Of these twenty books – a random sample, I concede – there were only three in which I found a specific entry under 'anger' or 'aggression'. The first was in Andrea Dworkin's mighty *Sexual Intercourse*, a discussion of how much men hate women when they are having sex with them, seen through the lens of Tolstoy's relations with his wife. The second was a lengthy passage on the role of rage in psychosis in Juliet Mitchell's intricate and authoritative *Psychoanalysis and Feminism*. Finally, there was Mead's *Male and Female*; but, as with Dworkin, the passage in question referred to men's, not women's, anger.

I claim no scientific objectivity for my experiment. Yet it interests me. After all, righteous anger is often the chief handmaiden of women's liberation, in all its forms: anger at a clutch of prejudices expressed against, and limitations imposed on, women. The suffragettes and suffragists were united in their fury at the assumption that they were not full citizens, and were disallowed the vote. Second-wave feminism emerged from young women's anger at the way they felt they were treated by an emerging radical class of rebellious young left-leaning men, and the oppression of motherhood and the diminishing of women by the wider culture.

Anger is also clearly an animating emotion in terms of creating and calibrating the feminist *message*. The tone of debate in the 1960s and 1970s was much more rancorous and confrontational than it seems to be today. Healthy irritation is there in much feminist writing. In *A Room of One's Own*, Virginia Woolf is coolly and brilliantly cross about the men who write condescending books about women and curious about the anger that these men themselves display towards the female sex. I have my mother's original Penguin paperback of Betty Friedan's *The Feminine Mystique* on my desk, its battered cover carrying a quote from a *Life* review which describes it as 'an angry, thoroughly documented book that in one way or another is going to provoke the daylights out of almost everyone who reads it'. When I picked up Nina Power's recently published *One Dimensional Woman* I felt and responded to her animated annoyance at the narrow, commercialised conformities of our age, including a 'me! me! me!' sort of feminism.

> Anger often comes into its own when a woman is older, coming towards or passing the final 'breakpoint' of middle age: menopause. It's as if she suddenly meets her pre-pubertal self again, gazing clear-eyed out at the world as it really is, less preoccupied now with how that world sees her . . .

But anger often comes into its own when a woman is older, moving towards or passing the final 'breakpoint' of middle age: menopause. It's as if she suddenly meets her pre-pubertal self again, gazing clear-eyed out at the world as it really is, less preoccupied now with how that world sees her. The years of intricate connection and compromise, around sex, love and family, are not exactly behind her but they no longer feel quite so pressing. The balance of the pleasure and pain incurred by sexual and romantic involvement are clearer, the decision about children made, and irrevocable, and unless she is a very elderly *prima gravida*, most of the juggling and exhaustion of bringing up a child out the way. Confidence is buoyed by experience but an inner stubbornness has grown too, a refusal always to keep the peace, keep the job, keep the goodwill of the more powerful. Sometimes the anger is all the more potent when expressed by those who have most loyally played their part or played the game, only to find themselves thrown off course by what they know to be rank injustice.

★

I could see that stubborn liberated glow the moment I met Miriam O'Reilly, the British television presenter who fought the BBC over age discrimination, when she was dropped from her presenting job on the grounds that she was too old – at the age of fifty-one. I met O'Reilly to talk about her case about a year after she had won it; the most noticeable thing about her apart from her air of determined merriment, and occasional glimpses of vulnerability, was her shock of creamy white hair. At some point in her long campaign for justice, O'Reilly decided to stop dying her hair its trademark black (dyeing one's hair being de rigueur for older women on television). Her natural colour suited her skin, and highlighted an aura of personal liberation.

The story began for O'Reilly when she was told that her contract at *Countryfile* was being terminated:

> My executive editor simply told me when he called me into his office that the network wanted to 'refresh the line-up'. He made no reference to my age at that point. He didn't mention anyone else. I only found out a week later that three other middle-aged women presenters had also lost their jobs. He (my executive editor) later said (which he denied at the Tribunal), 'One day I'll be told I'm too old to do my job and will be shuffled off to retirement.'

Later, when it became clear that age was the issue, O'Reilly was told:

> The television audience don't like older women. The conventional idea is that TV is a visual medium and people need to be visually attractive. Older women aren't attractive. I do think it's absurd, and I knew it wasn't true. But really it's all about prime-time ratings, an out-of-date view that older women won't put bums on seats.
>
> I was fifty-one. I am at the top of my game. I have won many news awards. The kids were off my hands. It was too early for me to be shuffled off into retirement. I made my feelings clear. I spoke out in private. Soon the consequences became clear. I had been warned to 'keep my head down', but I could not.

She was offered only one programme out of eight on *Costing the Earth*, a BBC Radio 4 series she had been presenting alongside *Countryfile*:

I expected to get four, as I shared the series with Tom Heap, but I was only offered one – 'The Environmental Cost of Ageing'. At the Tribunal the producer of the programme told the judges that although 'it looks bad now' at the time he thought it was 'funny' to offer me that one programme only on that theme. I knew they were making fun of me and declined to do that programme. I was told it was that programme or 'nothing'. It was a clear attempt to rub my nose in it. The judges were very critical of this. As a result the BBC was also found to have victimised me because I spoke out internally about age discrimination.

She could also see the implications for younger women:

> One of the things that has been bugging me is the way that everyone plays down the problems of older women and how even young women fall into this trap. It's as if younger women project their fear of the consequences of their own ageing onto other women, rather than tackle the structures that diminish us all.

The fear is particularly strong in the media. According to a Women in Journalism survey, *The Lady Vanishes at 45*, 71 per cent of women are worried about being forced out of their careers as they reach their forties and fifties. 'Old age' is now considered to begin at forty-five – 60 per cent of the over forty-fives have experienced direct age discrimination. The survey has found that 49 per cent of women see *no* older, senior role models in their offices, and another 13 per cent only know one. Seventy per cent see older men outnumbering older women at every level.

O'Reilly could have brought the action without speaking about it, but she wanted to throw it open for public debate:

> What's the point of doing it, if I don't go public? The most worrying part was the financial implications. There were escalating financial costs and for a variety of reasons I was not working as much as before. The solicitor and barrister reduced their fees, but even so. The worst thing was I could not help my daughter with her studies. I could not help her financially. She really respected me for having the courage to take a stand.

The tribunal decision came in January 2011. O'Reilly had won her claim of age-related discrimination.

At the time I questioned whether I had really 'won' because of the personal toll of bringing the case. With time I came to realise it was a massive victory for the individual. I have laid down a marker to broadcasters and other employers that you can't treat women unfairly for something they have no control over: getting older. The BBC said my case was a 'turning point' and pledged to put more older women on TV. The former Director General, Mark Thompson, publicly said my tribunal win was an 'important wake-up call' for the whole industry. We are seeing the beginnings of that change with Mary Beard and the white-haired Margaret Mountford presenting a BBC1 prime-time programme on Pompeii a couple of weeks ago. Victoria Wood recently explored our love affair with tea, in two programmes, again on prime-time BBC1. It was rare for any older woman (apart from Anne Robinson) to be sole presenter on a prime-time BBC 1 programme before my case. It shows you can stand up for your rights and win. My mother died before the results of my case came in. The most important thing for me is to know I 'did something' about the discrimination. My mum would have been very proud of me for that.

O'Reilly is now deputy chair of Labour's Commission on Older Women, set up by Harriet Harman, Deputy Leader, to consider the experience of older women in work, as carers and in public life. Research compiled by the Commission has shown that women over fifty comprise just 5 per cent of on-screen presenters. O'Reilly's fight continues.

Anger does not always have such a clear outlet, object or outcome. It can feel cloudy, tricky, threatening, particularly for women, judging from the vast array of handbooks for sale out there. *The Dance of Anger: A Woman's Guide to Changing the Pattern of Intimate Relationships / Women, Anger and Depression / Every Woman's Guide to Managing Your Anger / The Anger Workbook for Women / The Anger Habit in Relationships: A Communication Handbook for Relationships, Marriages and Partnerships.* Perhaps these writers know something feminists

> Anger holds a particular taboo for women as part of the age-old obedience and niceness package; women need to find a way to throw it off or re-channel it more productively.

don't. Or perhaps feminist thinkers think the point is too obvious to labour. Anger holds a particular taboo for women as part of the age-old obedience and niceness package; women need to find a way to throw it off or re-channel it more productively.

On a personal level, however, anger is a little bit more tricky than that. In some cultures – or families – anger finds free reign. A woman I spoke to in Leeds said, 'In my family we were – and are – always shouting. Everyone gets their views off their chest – there's no bar on it at all.' Other forms of fury don't need encouraging. One middle-aged woman whom I interviewed said, 'I grew up with a fiercely angry mother and, as a shy little girl, felt the full force of that fire, whether the anger was justified or not. As a result, I am fearful of anger. It is a very potent, and potentially very destructive emotion.'

I still find it shocking to lose my temper; afterwards I reproach myself for days (particularly if I get angry with anyone who is not part of my immediate family); equally I do not much like being shouted at or spoken to sternly by anyone. One learns quickly in life how each person has a different trigger or point of provocation: what will infuriate or ignite one person will leave another amused or unmoved; it is as well to know that about oneself before bellowing at someone who said something that sounded like something your sister said to you twenty years ago.

The need for us all to tread very carefully in terms of our anger is intricately illustrated in an essay by black novelist Taiye Selasi, in which she charts the plaited effects of an apparently casual conversation with a fellow guest at her best friend's wedding: 'the world's whitest wedding'. Her interlocutor is the 'third and presumably final husband' of the bride's grandmother (an important detail):

'And where are *you* from?' he asked in that accent I've only heard on Beacon Hill, in films about the Kennedys, and drinking with my agent. Boston Brahmin, baritone. A bit of extra weight on 'you', as if the question mark belonged to me (the questionable thing), not 'from'. I gave the answer I always give, the answer I'd give if you asked me now, refined by years of daily practice, available in multiple languages. 'I'm not sure where I'm from! I was born in London. My father's from Ghana but lives in Saudi Arabia. My mother's Nigerian but lives in Ghana. I grew up in Boston.' Here I'll pause for reaction

– soft chuckles of confusion, some statement along the lines of
'You're a citizen of the world!' – then open the floor to any follow-
up questions about any of the countries I've mentioned.

But there was something in the follow-up questions – Selasi is
the daughter of her Ghanaian father's third wife – prompting Percy,
the Brahmin with the baritone voice, to say, 'Your father had three
wives at once?' which shook her to her roots. She could not pick
up her glass without shaking hands, she retreated in sobs and despair
to the bathroom – and later to see a kind of 'healer-cum-therapist-
cum-psychic-cum-life coach' after returning from the wedding in
Jamaica, in 'emotional disrepair, unable to sleep or eat or stop crying,
all because of one comment'.

> 'I wasn't ashamed! I was angry!' I raged. 'He's a third bloody husband
> himself, for chrissake. If I were white, he'd never have thought my
> dad had three wives at once.' Ileane, beside me, pressed on my chest.
> 'Why does this make you so angry?' she cooed. 'Because he's racist,'
> I cried. This may well not have been true. The truth came next. 'And
> he's right.'

What followed was a long unpicking of the story of her parents'
relationship – she did not meet her father until she was twelve – and
her need to return to, and reassess, her own connection to Ghana, the
land of her father. 'Intellectually, I perceived myself as a product and
champion of modern West Africa. Emotionally, I perceived myself as a
West African polygamist's daughter. What I needed was some other
way to know myself as African, apart from as heir to my parents' hurts.'[8]
Anger can be a thrilling risk, for to express it cleanly and in the
moment cuts directly across the grain, and habits, of womanly care
and preservation of connection. On the contrary it is a brutal form
of cutting off, a heady chance to unmask oneself, to suddenly state:
this is who I am, or who I am not. It is a glorious opportunity to
say: stop; the simple plain-speaking *no*, after years, possibly, of the coy
and pleasing, *oh yes, okay then.* When Vivian Gornick witnessed a
terrible quarrel between friends, there was 'the sickening dry excite-
ment I felt that evening, the awful sense I had that the world as I
knew it was cutting itself to pieces even as we spoke'.[9] Anger can
often feel like dealing the final blow to a situation or relationship;

there is no going back. That is its threat and its exhilaration. (It is, too, why an anger suppressed is truly deadly.)

I do not have sons, but I suspect that many mothers handle the expression of anger in their boys a little differently: feeling pride or fatalism, but no sense of the natural order upturned, a future imperilled by the refusal to keep quiet. An angry man may not be much fun; but he does not have a great deal to fear from the charge of over-assertiveness or face the same risk of psychic or actual separation. Indeed a woman — mother, sister, partner, wife — may well cheer him, soothe him, or help repair ruptured relations.

Who will do this for our daughters? How many young women or those who care for them feel, as that young woman in the bar feels, that her anger means social and romantic isolation, imprisonment in the attic of social unacceptability?

As a parent, I have not, and would not, encourage suppression of irritation or rage. Observing young children, one perceives the pulse and purity of the emotion. Getting cross is such a normal and sane response to pain, worry or a sense of diminishment. It not only has its uses, without doubt; it's a necessary weapon in the psychological arsenal. Dismissing one's children anger — particularly girls' — could, too easily, lead them to transmute the emotion into unhealthy anxiety or later into depression. Being too nice, and inauthentically so, poses the greater risk.

Even so I would counsel a kind of caution, but for human, not female specific, reasons. Within relationships, where these is a sense of commitment, safety, reciprocity, the expression of anger seems to me essential. It is not only a claim of justice, but it moves relationships along, as eleven-year-old Tessie told Carol Gilligan:

'When you are having an argument . . . and you just keep it inside and don't tell anyone, you never hear the person's point of view. And if you are telling someone about it, you are telling it from both sides and so you hear what my mother said, or what my brother said. And they can say, well, you might be mad, but your mom was right, and you say, yeah, I know. So when you say it out loud, you have to listen . . . fighting is what makes relationships go on [in] the face of trouble, and the more fights you get in and the more it goes on . . . the stronger it gets because the more you can talk with that person.'[10]

Without this dialogue, the risk is that relationships ossify or fester from unhelpful silences. Anger helps ease the flow of affection – and understanding – between those who care about each other.

But in other relationships, the mother in me would urge forms of compromise, to encourage anger, within discernible limits. Taiye Selasi's emotional and cultural detective work around her own fury, at a single social remark, is exemplary in this regard. Equally wise is this rather different piece of advice, presumably for less charged situations, from one woman I talked to:

> I have learned that a cool and controlled expression of anger goes a very long way. Ice, rather than fire. Setting of boundaries in a reasonably calm way. I have also learned that, however hard it may seem, a feeling of anger at something that someone has said, needs to be expressed somehow, and in the moment. Festering over wounds is no good, but a real and immediate response – finding a way to express the anger in terms that will not annihilate the recipient, but will show a measure of how you are feeling – seems healthy to me. It always helps to not say 'you make me feel . . .' but, rather, 'I feel . . .' In other words don't apportion blame but be honest about one's own feelings.

My mother used to advise me to 'use anger as fuel', to employ the emotion to productive purpose. The technique is well illustrated by this story from a working mother:

> When my children were young, I spent a lot of time with other parents. It always irked me that virtually none of the fathers ever inquired or showed much interest in my work, yet I always seemed to get drawn into the details or their latest project or work proposal or whatever. For a while, I felt absolutely murderous. I loathed their assumption of *my* attention coupled with a lack of reciprocity which also seemed to mirror the difficulties I was having at work. It took me time to realise that I did not have to enter into or sustain conversations with these rather egotistical men; it was bad time management on my part. Instead, I could utilise my time and energy to better use. For myself.

In *Composing a Life* Mary Catherine Bateson gives a long description of a painful, if productive, period of her life when she was a university administrator at Amherst College. It is, on one level, a story of the imperfections of humans who come together for the purposes of running and reforming an institution. At another level, it is a morality tale about patriarchy, about how men both include and exclude women, including the way that they exclude the women that they include. It reminds me somewhat of Sandberg's *Lean In* although it is very different in tone. We need more accounts of power like this, accounts that describe the experience of a woman in the subtlest of terms, separating out the many elements that are necessarily involved in the workings of any large and powerful institution: the way the 'grandfathering' patriarchy and discrimination deal with strong women, the individual strengths and weaknesses of the individual woman drawn into the institution, and the alchemy between all of these factors. Bateson describes these in reflective, rueful prose. But once she had been asked to leave the college, on what reads like the most unjust grounds imaginable, she notes that:

> Anger was an achievement, a step away from the chasm of despair. Women in this society tend to be disproportionately damaged by such experiences, because we are too ready to accuse ourselves of failure and too reluctant to surrender trust once it is granted, whether to a spouse or an institution. Often, American men learn to project their disappointments outwards . . . women tend to internalize their losses.[11]

I like the idea of anger as 'achievement'. I recognise in it the clean, sharp finality of the sensation that I myself feel when I have long toiled to understand or 'make right' a difficult human situation. I can see my own part in what has happened but I can see, too, that others have their own motives, their need to cling on to certain meanings, that make, finally, no ordinary compromise or happy-enough resolution possible. (Some people are just like that: they need manageable amounts of difficulty; it is a habit of mind or feeling.) *Enough!* says a voice in my head. Irritated but not bitter. I am relieved, finally, to stop trying. Case closed.

As for the more public uses or expression of anger, I note that in the recently published *Fifty Shades of Feminism* several of the contributors make reference to anger (although there is no index to mark the fact). Writer Tahmima Anam sounds remarkably like that young woman in the bar in King's Cross:

> You cannot be angry. You will want to be angry. If you are angry, you will be called An Angry Young Woman, or worse, An Angry Old Woman, or even worse, An Angry Feminist. You will be called a bitch. You will take comfort in the company of your woman friends, but sometimes you will feel painfully, irreparably alone.

The good news, also reflected in *Fifty Shades of Feminism* and many other places, is that young and old women are using their anger to social and political use once more. I discuss this in the next chapter.

Backbone. Resilience. Optimism. Endurance. Penelope Fitzgerald, the Booker Prize winner, clearly possessed a few of these qualities – and more – judging from Julian Barnes's recently published essay on the writer in which he wrote, with a devastating coolness, about the 'diminishment' that this great but modest author received during her professional life – largely at the hands of men. 'Even so,' Barnes writes,

> when public recognition came, it followed no obvious trajectory, and was attended by a certain level of male diminishment. In 1977 her non-fiction publisher, Richard Garnett, informed her dunderheadedly that she was 'only an amateur writer', to which she responded mildly, 'I asked myself, how many books do you have to write and how many semi-colons do you have to discard before you lose amateur status?' The following year, after having been shortlisted for the Booker Prize with *The Bookshop*, she asked her fiction publisher, Colin Haycraft, if it would be a good idea to write another novel. He jocundly replied that if she went on writing fiction he didn't want it blamed on him, and in any case he already had too many short novels with sad endings on his hands . . . The BBC's resident book-heads also treated her condescendingly: radio's Frank Delaney told her she 'deserved to win because my book was free of objectionable matter and suitable for family reading'; while television's Robert Robinson gave her patronisingly little airtime on *The Book Programme* and scarcely concealed his view that she shouldn't have won. And after she died, even her memorial meeting was disfigured by the turkey-cocking of a young male novelist.[12]

Barnes's essay has particular impact because it takes on the question of male diminishment as an issue of simple respect, or its absence, between human beings. We can only speculate as to how much of the condescension of discouragement directed at Fitzgerald was the result of conscious gender prejudice. Regardless, she herself was clearly not (overly) put off by the behaviour of such (retrospectively) hapless others. Let's hope – or indeed, presume – she was one of those women who find motivation strengthened by others' apparent lack of interest. Casual diminishment does wonders for one's inner determination, I have always found.

> Casual diminishment does wonders for one's inner determination, I have always found.

'Oh lordy, will it ever end?' a friend wrote to me when I asked her for any specific examples of patronage. '[It] is everywhere and it must be challenged . . . but I do know that male condescension makes me ANGRIER [!] than almost anything else I have to deal with.' Ask most women for their experience of being 'put down' and they will come out with an array of diverse examples – and the odd witty way of responding.

Often, the condescension will take the form of humour and one finds oneself on the receiving end of a not very funny or – slightly trickier, this – some actually quite funny jokes that have at their heart the diminution of women or the female sex. Blonde jokes are the worst, says my blonde daughter, and I shall have to trust her account as one is less on the receiving end of this sort of humour as one ages. I have some sympathy with those who argue that tackling humour with anger or politics is not the way to go; like using a full pail of water to put out a match and likely to show up the challenger in the wrong light. Far better is to strike a witty light of your own, if you can, and quickly enough. In *Fifty Shades of Feminism* Kathy Lette argues that, in order to deal with this kind of male humour, women have to 'think like a bloke':

> [T]he average man keeps fit by doing step aerobics off his own ego. So be confident and assertive. If a man tells sexist jokes to embarrass or unnerve you, fight back. Ask him if he knows why 'dumb blonde' jokes are always one liners? So that men will understand them . . .

If you're in banking, try asking if he knows the difference between government bonds and blokes. Government bonds mature.

How to deal with the more direct put-downs, those 'Calm Down, Dear' remarks or the physical gestures that go with the 'What a Silly Thing You Are' package – such as the pat on the head, or the laughing tap of the arm? If in doubt, do nothing; a withering glance, a pregnant pause before sweeping on with a more substantive remark. (Doing absolutely nothing is often an excellent fall-back position.) The braver among us will coolly take on the demeaning put-down:

> I think the best challenge is not to rise hotly to the bait, but to laugh at it and then proceed to pour cold water on the situation. To treat it with the contempt it deserves. A new male singer has joined our singing group. He is not very good, but that doesn't stop him telling the other (female) members of our section how to do it! I challenged him once, but he continued to do it. When I challenged him a second time, he said, 'Oh you're very bossy aren't you?' when in fact he had been the one bossing others about for weeks. I just laughed and said, 'Yes I am.' Since then – I simply avoid him. *I have kind of castrated him in my mind and have noticed that, whilst he still tells others what to do, he doesn't ever challenge me.* Who won this? Not sure.

Some women develop careful clever strategies, such as Valerie Stevens, who wrote to tell me how, back in the 1980s, she was appointed to

> [the] chair [of] the Board of the Greater Manchester Bus Company. The Director of Engineering was a young man in his early thirties and he understood the new non-sexist world. We devised a plan to test the level of disbelief that a woman could know anything about buses. We often used to visit exhibitions and as we visited the stands we waited to see which salesman (it was always a man) would talk to him or me. We graded them by their technique. We visited one stand selling disability adaptations and the salesman talked at length to the Director even when I asked questions. He finally finished his sales pitch and said would we consider buying and Neil turned to me and then to him and said, 'I don't know, you had better ask her – she is the boss.' It worked every time.

A relatively recent problem, particularly for women writers, is outright misogynistic attack, increasingly on the internet, where the anonymity of the accuser/abuser allows them to reveal their woman hatred with full force. Most female writers have plenty of experience of this, ranging from the ordinarily abusive to the outright threatening. I have several of my own examples here, such as a blog (apparently responding to something I had written) which was entitled 'Melissa Benn: pig ignorant and stupid with it.' (As if the 'stupid' functioned as a kind of weighty qualifier, rather than a mere diluted repetition, of the original insult.) A few years ago, my picture was put up online with a number of other female contributors to the *Guardian*. Internet users were encouraged to vote for the least attractive of the 'dogs' on show. And here's one sadly all-too-typical, if unusually restrained, example of the kind of comment my journalism has attracted over the years; this, posted beneath an article in the *Guardian* on free schools, in autumn 2011: 'This is Melissa, daught of the Rt Hon Anthony Wedgwood-Benn . . . doesn't deserve to be listened to or taken seriously . . .' [*sic*]

Online verbal attacks on women and, increasingly, the menace of actual violence, have grown in recent years. UK journalist Suzanne Moore observed, 'Obviously any woman who writes about feminism will be well versed in online hatred . . . Technology has made it much easier to abuse people such as me. You can do it in your mum's bedroom . . . I cannot repeat some of what I have received, except to say that it involves graphic descriptions of dismemberment, blood and excrement.'[13]

Shifting public attitudes to such abuse were reflected in the arrest of a man in late July 2013 following attacks on feminist banknote campaigner Caroline Criado-Perez. Perez was subject to a barrage of rape and murder threats after she attended the Bank of England's unveiling of the new £10 note with Jane Austen's image on it.

Moore rightly puts all this vitriol in a wider context:

There is an enormous amount of woman hating out in the world (listen in to the way people talk on a bus or in a classroom) but couple this with a populist disdain for a media elite. Cross-hatch this with a growing sense of powerlessness of many men in our economy – the sight of a woman being paid to speak out is like a red rag to a bull. Certainly, I have been struck by the intense class hatred online;

I do not know if it is 'worse' than the woman hatred; but I do know that it intensifies the woman hatred.

The police acted in the case of Caroline Criado-Perez, a welcome new approach to the intensification of misogyny on social media and a better answer, certainly, than expecting – or suggesting – that women desist from participating in online public debate.

But there is one final category of frustrating condescension that is, in some ways, the hardest to deal with. I can describe it in only the most general of terms, as a sense of deep and growing unreality – a spreading sensation of invisibility – when speaking to a particular person: usually, but not always, a man. It is as if one's words are incapable of making a human connection even though the spoken-to may well nod or reply. Yet one gleans the powerful, but again entirely instinctual, impression of ghostliness, of utter insubstantiality. There is no way of confirming, testing or countering what is, after all, just a sensation but the eerie hollowness of such exchanges, the absolute absence of an answering human echo, is a useful clue as to what is really going on. How frequently have I longed, in such situations, just to turn on my heel and walk away! Maybe one day I will.

In an essay in *Approaching Eye Level*, Vivian Gornick describes a dinner she hosted, at which a dynamic feminist intellectual takes on

> an old communist, a man who takes for granted that what he has to say will be always be of central interest. His life has been formed by a conviction that everyone in the room is a student of his – they're either young, more inexperienced, less intelligent, or else a woman or a child . . . Men like Kayman had been dominating the table since time began: it was only natural he would have expected the people at this dinner party to defer to him as well. But now there was another personality in the room as strong as his own . . . it was her turn. Everyone could see that, no? And it turned out: no.[14]

But who in life knows, really, whose turn it is, or how to wring justice out of a conversation in which those present cannot gracefully find ways to engage with each other? The point is; at this dinner, these people refused to play by the rules, and the scene quickly got ugly. Another male guest accused the female intellectual of 'interrupting', of not letting the great man get a sentence out. Another guest cries out, 'Can't we have a civilised exchange at the dinner table anymore?' To which the female intellectual says, 'If civilised means one person at the table gets categorically ignored and is to remain silent about it then, no. I guess we can't have a civilised exchange anymore.' As for Gornick, she believes she is glimpsing 'as though for the first time, the death of sentimental affection between women and men. The familiar arrangement between us was at an end. Our backing off, our silence, our turning the other cheek . . . was over.'[15] By 'our' she means women's.

Gornick is writing about an era – of feminist challenge – pure anger – the re-ordering of relationships – that came. And went. Like so much of original feminism the question of the terms of the debate between men and women, in private and public life, have been papered over, buried deep, the traces kicked clear. This particular, intriguing, infuriating aspect of original angry – for it *was* angry – feminism has not been disinterred; women still seem to allow themselves to be rendered invisible, or at least more silent in private and public conversation, these days. Sit in a meeting – and ask for questions from the floor; they will overwhelmingly come from men. (And it is interesting how many experienced female speakers say it is harder to ask a question from the floor than to speak from a platform, because at least from the platform one's intervention has been officially sanctioned; one is deemed to have something to say.)

> Sit in a meeting – and ask for questions from the floor; they will overwhelmingly come from men.

Thinking about this problem sent me back to a seminal text of second-wave feminism: Dale Spender's *Man Made Language*. This shortish paperback is a wonderful piece of the rapidly receding cultural feminist past. When first published in 1980, the book illuminated for many the politics shaping that most natural of exchanges: male and female speech. Here Spender challenged the stereotype, that

> women talk a lot . . . it is not surprising that investigation of sex differences in language should have begun by looking for the excessive talkativeness of women. However, here, perhaps more than in any other research area, findings were in complete contradiction with the stereotype of women's language. There has not been one study which provides

evidence that women talk more than men, and there have been numerous studies which indicate that men talk more than women.[16]

And again, 'In mixed-sex conversations, it is primarily males who interrupt females.'[17]

She then went on to make an interesting observation:

The concept of women as the talkative sex involves a comparison: they must talk too much against some sort of standard or yardstick and we have erroneously assumed that the measurement of women is in comparison to men. But this appears not to be the case. The talkativeness of women has been gauged in comparison not with men but with *silence*. Women have not been judged on the grounds of whether they talk more than men, but of whether they talk more than silent women.[18]

Personally, I am not so interested in the 'science' or even the surveys that track the back and forth of male/female conversations, particularly not when it takes us into *Men are from Mars and Women are from Venus* type territory. For the moment, I simply note Spender's claim that for some men (and who knows, maybe some women?) a talkative woman is one who talks *at all*. It is certainly a plausible enough interpretation of some situations I have encountered. It can sometimes feel as if any woman who makes her claim to equal space or time with the men is literally 'speaking out of turn'.

Add to this the fact that a woman in mixed company (and Spender finds the surveys and science to back up this argument too) often subconsciously plays a facilitating or supplementary role, in relation to male talk. (A woman may also do this with other women but the facilitation/support is more likely to be reciprocated.) So, again, when she chooses to speak her mind, and at some length, she is breaking a number of rules simultaneously, including the assumed ties of 'sentimental affection' between the sexes, in the social world, and thus risks, like Gornick's female intellectual friend, being judged a kind of monster. Or a bore.

For every minute she speaks she is travelling further from that lodestar of absolute silence; she is disrupting the stereotype of the lovely, (largely) silent muse or cheerleader, who enables the public expression of a man's ideas or feelings on any range of situations.

253

How odd then that the sharp perceptions of feminists such as Spender, should, over three decades later, have all but disappeared, their traces kicked over, yet leaving numerous sparky, thoughtful, opinionated young or not-so-young women feeling odd, angry, lonely or occasionally in despair when in mixed company. Has the world changed that much?

Julian Barnes does not record Penelope Fitzgerald's replies to the men who tried to put her down. But, of course, her answer was to win the Booker Prize and become a Proven Worldly Success; in her case, the joke was on those who slighted her: the editor, the publisher, the 'turkey-cocking' man who spoke at her funeral. Given that this avenue of retribution or its equivalent, in whatever world, is not open to most women, this must remain a minority strategy, a unique riposte.

But it occurs to me now that a book is a good metaphor in terms of an answer to a presumption of any kind of superiority, male or not. It is an unarguable answer: a proof – if not the actual pudding. It makes me think of the fifteen-year-old schoolgirl who told me, 'The boys like to patronise me in maths, and ask me if I need any help; I love the look on their faces when we get back the exam results and I've done better than them.' Like revenge, achievement is a dish best served chilled. But as I have noted in earlier parts of this book, it's only a partial victory. Why shouldn't a girl write the books, ace the maths *and* speak her mind, at length, to a table or a hall full of respectful men as well?

> Like revenge, achievement is a dish best served chilled.

# 8

## Stand Up and Stand Out

*In which we celebrate the achievements of modern feminism and
lay down a few gauntlets for the future . . .*

Like it or not, feminism has a PR problem that needs sorting . . .
young women are telling us that 'feminism' is a dirty word, for a
variety of reasons, perhaps most significantly because it's 'angry' it's
not 'sexy' or 'feminine'. Young women also expressed the feeling that
feminism wasn't really 'for' them – that it was too complex and
alienating and that they didn't have the correct terminology . . . we
need to go further than this and try and think about ways in which
we can get young women thinking about gender inequality.[1]

Ah yes, that old image problem. I do not doubt the veracity of this
judgement by Rhiannon Lucy Cosslett and Holly Baxter, the witty
and irreverent founders of *Vagenda*, on young women's attitudes to
sexual politics. Feminism – women's best collective chance to preserve
and extend their rights and interests – has always had a bad press; the
fight for change has always been represented as
hard and unfeminine, until, that is, the battle is
won on a particular issue, and all fall in line. Still,
the carping at the underlying philosophy and the
complex human practice – summed up by the
F word – drones on. In the wise words of philosopher John Stuart Mill, one article may 'be to
the public mind no more than a drop of water
upon stone' but it is the *repetition* that does the
harm, and that grinds everyone down into irritated disengagement. 'Has feminism gone too far?'
'Is feminism to blame for the breakdown of the

> Feminism – women's
> best collective chance
> to preserve and
> extend their rights
> and interests – has
> always had a bad
> press; until, that is,
> the battle is won on
> a particular issue, and
> all fall in line.

family?' 'Is feminism irrelevant to modern women?' (And it is really not hard to uncover a hundred such titles as these.) In fact, it is extraordinary that anyone, let along young women, can break through this wall of both vicious and subtly nuanced propaganda.

At another level, though, the *Vagenda* writers' question strikes me as odd, coming at a time when there seems have been real resurgence – if not a mighty explosion – of both feminist activism and argument. Helen Lewis of the *New Statesman* said recently, 'It feels as though there's a greater energy to the feminist movement now than I've experienced before in my adult life; there's a critical mass of women who just won't shut up about the things they care about.'[2] According to Natasha Walter, writer and founder of Women for Refugee Women: 'These are exciting times – there's a strong sense of pride in activism that I really don't remember being there before.' In August 2010, the *Observer* magazine published a major feature on Meet the New Feminists, 'Women from Around the world on causes that inspire them'. Interviewed around the same time, Kat Banyard of Feminista noted the rapid growth of UK feminist grassroots groups. The newer organisations – among them, Object ('challenging the sexual objectification of women'), Women for Refugee Women, End Violence Against Women (self-explanatory), Everyday Sexism (a terrific Twitter campaign), Turn Your Back on Page Three, No More Page Three and Expert Women – have joined long-standing organisations like the Fawcett Society and Women in Journalism, to create a strong media and political presence in recent years.

When a group of women stood outside the *Sun*'s offices, displaying a giant collage that compared the way men and women are represented in the tabloids, one journalist summed up the difference between the two with the single word: 'clothes'.

What's most striking about this new period is how issues of representation of women or the lack of representation of women or the grossly *distorted* representation of women have taken top billing, with violence against women coming a close, and connected, second. Much of the energy for these campaigns has come from a new generation, radicalised by their own anger at the slights and spite of old and new media. When a group of women stood outside the *Sun*'s offices, displaying a giant collage that compared the way men and women are represented in the tabloids, one journalist summed up the difference between the two with the single word: 'clothes'. (As in: men are allowed to wear them; women must be stripped bare.) There's also a new wit and creativity to recent actions. SlutWalks deliberately played on the scornful double standards shown towards scantily clothed younger women and/or promiscuous women: I had some interesting arguments with older, sterner friends about these demonstrations, and their underlying premise. On the Muff March young women donned outrageous costumes and outsized merkins to make their point about the new standards of artificiality in relation to the female body and the rise of designer vagina surgery: the women marched down Harley Street, home to the cosmetic surgeons and doctors who have serviced distressed women down the decades.

For those of us who remember the British Labour MP Clare Short's doughty attempts to get rid of the *Sun*'s Page 3 – and the victimisation she suffered from the paper as a direct result – it has been strange to see this particular political project revived and with such great success. But politics works like that sometimes: you might spend years pushing forward on an issue with little apparent success and then suddenly, a seeming shift or new turn of events, and the wall comes down. The actress Lucy-Anne Holmes only started her campaign against Page 3 by chance, last summer, when she picked up a copy of the *Sun*. 'It was the summer of the Olympics and the country was gripped with sporting fever.' As Holmes opened the paper, she was 'glad to see there was no topless woman on Page 3, just stories of victorious athletes, such as Victoria Pendleton, Jessica Ennis'. She leafed through the sports coverage contentedly, until she reached page 13. There she found 'a massive picture of a girl in her pants', she says. The typical image had just been moved back. 'It made me really sad. It was the biggest female image in that issue, and I think pretty much every issue [of the *Sun*] for forty-two years.'[3]

Holmes started up a Twitter account, a Facebook page and a petition to try and get Page 3 stopped. One of her tweets – 'Seriously, we are all so over Page 3 – it is so last century' – got a response from Rupert Murdoch, or the people who write his tweets for him, agreeing that, 'you may be right, don't know but considering. Perhaps halfway house with glamorous fashionistas.' Holme's petition had, by spring 2013, secured 85,000 signatures.[4] Looking back, one can already see the discrete elements that came together so fortuitously: the temporary weakness of the Murdoch empire, the glory of the Olympic female athletes and the rising anger, in general, among young women, at the way they were being represented in the press.

Something was shifting. As Kira Cochrane observed in 2012:

Over the past few years, and particularly the past few months, anger about the media portrayal of women, in terms of visibility, sexualisation and humiliation, has grown at feverish pace. Along with the campaigns to end Page 3 are projects to highlight the paucity of female experts in broadcasting and the dearth of older women on TV, to make it easier for journalists to find female speakers, to show how media sexism affects women on a personal level, and clarify just how it feeds into a culture in which women's confidence is undermined, ambitions narrowed, and experiences of rape and violence disbelieved. There's a growing sense this could be a watershed moment, when coverage genuinely changes for the better.[5]

Liz Kelly, a campaigner for decades against violence against women, made the same observation in her contribution to *Fifty Shades of Feminism*: 'The last few months have been remarkable for the sustained national and international debates on sexual violence.'[6] Nina Power told me, 'Rape culture has been exposed and condemned in unprecedented ways in recent months, which is extremely good news, though it doesn't go far enough yet, as we know the police still don't take rape seriously enough and convictions are very low.'

When talking about the representation of women, in the media, in the public sphere, one never strays very far from this matter of women's bodies: and particularly, attractive women's bodies. While I was writing the book I became aware of a Ukrainian group called Femen who conduct their protests bare breasted and have put on a 'Topless Jihad Day' in Berlin, Kiev and Paris. 'We're free. We're naked. It's our right. It's our body. It's our rules and nobody can use religion, [or] some other holy things, to abuse women, to oppress them,' declared Alexandra Shevchenko, one of Femen's leaders. I'll admit, I have wrestled with uncertainty about the methods of feminism, not to mention suspicions that they are a sophisticated outrider for a new Armando Iannucci comedy, but there is no doubt that they have garnered more publicity in their short life than the committed campaigning of most women's groups. Mainstream opinion has always had a keener interest in feminist arguments coming from attractive exponents. The writer Rebecca West, a dark-eyed beauty, was one of the most influential spokeswomen of turn-of-the-century feminism. The suffragettes Emmeline and Christabel Pankhurst were well connected, charismatic women who gripped the nation's imagination with their uncompromising boldness. The young, strikingly lovely Germaine Greer talked about fucking and pornography, and always got more attention than the low-key British feminists who debated the history of the co-operative movement or trade union organisation. Naomi Wolf started out writing about beauty, and has recently turned to close consideration of her own sex parts. She gets far fewer favourable reviews these days – ultimately no woman who argues for too long for or about feminism gets an unstintingly good press – but she, like Greer, has always commanded attention.

From late 2012 onwards, it seemed as if public attitudes to sexual assault and violence were shifting quite dramatically. Here, again, we must note the long-term impact of women's campaigning on this issue, the challenge posed by feminism of the seventies to the 'sleaze' of that period: sleaze that has turned out to have a violent underbelly. It feels as if every day brings a new, shocking story of male violence against women or young girls, and the arrest of many established celebrities and public figures. Even so, I find myself wondering how much of the media's fascination with these stories is caught up with the idea of fallen men – even fallen heroes – rather than injured women. Liz Kelly identified a sea change in public attitudes to sexual assault following the revelations about British television presenter Jimmy Savile, a national treasure turned national bogeyman. Frequent scandals about child abuse in the Catholic Church have now established without any doubt that this powerful institution has for many years wilfully ignored a serious problem within the priesthood. In contrast, women's suffering is considered more routine, less newsworthy. We are compelled by the transgressors, not the pain experienced by the victims. The much reported comment by a *Newsnight* producer on evidence presented in a continuing scandal in a North Wales care home that it was from 'just the women' illustrates the casual but habitual oversight of women's evidence. And there was even a hint of the 'fallen man' theme following the horrific Delhi rape case, when in late 2012 a young woman was gang-raped and thrown naked from a bus, and subsequently died from her injuries. This particular case provoked world-wide distress and anger, even as it sparked discussion about how much easier we find it to condemn rape in other countries.[7] But while the butchery in this case was not disputed, here, too, due consideration was paid to the part played by a growing sense of disenfranchisement felt by young men in India's many cities, languishing without proper jobs or futures.

The shocking disregard of female testimony, particularly when the women concerned are in any way fragile or vulnerable, was demonstrated by the appalling catalogue of child grooming and abuse perpetrated by a gang of men, who lived in and around the Oxford area, for nearly a decade. During the 2013 trial of the gang, it emerged that despite the police being alerted several times to clear evidence that young girls, some in their early teens, most of them in care, were being plied with drugs and drink, serially beaten and raped and sold to men around the country, the authorities turned a 'blind eye' to the girls' claims on the grounds that they were 'tearaways'. In May 2013, the emergence of a catalogue of mistakes and 'missed opportunities' in the case of Maria Stubbings, strangled to death with a dog-lead by her ex-boyfriend (who had a known history of violence against women, including a murder conviction, and had already been jailed for assaulting Stubbings), led her family, and other families similarly affected by official failings in relation to domestic violence, to call on the Home Secretary Theresa May for a Stephen Lawrence-style public inquiry into police action, or inaction, in such cases. Shamefully, the same scenario – a series of appeals from a terrified woman that are met by a lack of an effective official response or significant errors, leading to the woman's death – has been repeated down the years. Two women a week die in England and Wales as a result of domestic violence: that this figure has stayed steady for fifteen years says as much about official complacency as it does about the violent nature of some men.

And whose bodies, whose injuries, are more newsworthy? What to do about Page 3 will always generate a discussion or column. Compare this to coverage, or its lack, of female genital mutilation (FGM). According to Rahila Gupta, up to 140 million women and children are living with FGM worldwide, with 21,000 at risk in the UK alone. Some writers have recently tried to link and compare the growth in the number of women opting for labiaplasty (also known as female genital cosmetic surgery) in the west with FGM. Rahila Gupta rightly rejects this theory. Yes, one might be able to identify a kind of parallel set of patriarchal 'standards' imposed on the female body but it is vital to draw a distinction between women 'choosing' labiaplasty and the fact that FGM is largely imposed on girls at some point between birth and fifteen years old: 'they are powerless victims.'[8] Once again, we have to ask: why does the press devote more attention to the Page 3 issue than to that of real violence perpetrated on real women? And the answer is easy to see: an attractive woman talking about how the breasts on Page 3 make her feel bad about her own breasts, is a perfect example of the kind of recycling of outrage that is a staple of our culture.

But contemporary feminism is not just confined to a clutch of campaigns. It is there in the reporting, columns and feature articles of a number of journalists: Hadley Freeman, Beatrix Campbell, Caitlin Moran, Helen Lewis, Laurie Penny, Charlotte Raven, Julie Burchill, Suzanne Moore, Kira Cochrane, Tanya Gold, Hannah Pool, Julie Bindel, Ellie Mae O'Hagan, Zoe Williams, Joan Smith, Deborah Orr, Libby Brooks, Viv Groskop, Natasha Walter – and many more. All are singular voices imbued with a feminist perspectives, rather than representatives of a 'women's movement'. It is there in the resurgence of student feminist activism. Helena Horton, a student at York University, described to me the 'three feminist groups' currently on campus:

> One for campus issues, WomCom, which has done stuff like 'Show and Tell' which was an anti-sexual stigma art and literature exhibition, anti-sexual harassment campaigning and getting the campus involved in One Billion Rising. One for women in politics, Tell, which is

trying to improve the representation of women in campus political societies by campaigning, offering support, holding talks and events, and holding public-speaking training and confidence boosting for women, and generally being a supportive network, it's called GAP, gender accessible politics. [And then] one for international feminist discussion and campaigning: York FemSoc. They all have at least thirty active members.

Horton added:

> I think we're pretty tame, anger-wise, compared to other unis but I am doing an angry anti-Page 3 campaign at the moment on campus to remove the *Sun* from our Union shop and this is going to referendum next term so I'm currently ramping up support for that. WomCom haven't gotten involved though as they think it's too controversial.

And what of the rise of a certain kind of global feminist elder – women like Gloria Steinem, the indefatigable US figure of the second wave who has continued campaigning through the decades and whom I last saw talking on *Channel 4 News* about the patriarchal nature of monotheism, part of a discussion around the London events for the campaign One Billion Rising. (One could sense newsreader Jon Snow's bemusement at the unlikely turn of the conversation, but also his willingness to let the discussion wander a little out of control through his respect for Steinem.) Feminists International would also include Angelina Jolie, a United Nations special envoy for refugee issues, standing in a black shift and white pearls, in April 2013, praising a 'long overdue' decision by the G8 foreign ministers to commit $35 million to tackle rape and sexual violence; or Hillary Clinton, who as US secretary of state, was, in *Guardian* journalist Madeleine Bunting's words, 'the most powerful politician to advance an explicitly feminist agenda' highlighting the use of sexual violence in war or the unacceptably high level of abortions of female foetuses in China. Sheryl Sandberg, of course, urging women to 'lean in'. Eve Ensler, of course, mobilising one billion to rise. And a newcomer to the charts, Australian former Prime Minister Julia Gillard, whose speech berating opponent Tony Abbott – 'I will not be lectured about sexism and misogyny by this man' – was watched around the world within minutes of it being posted.

Everywhere, feminism is appearing in previously unexpected places, pervading our culture, creating a sense of commonality: a more diluted, less politically partial, but nonetheless powerful kind of 'sisterhood'. In early 2013 I chaired a discussion at the Institute of Education on socialist feminism over the past three decades: one of the speakers, twenty-seven-year-old Rosie Rogers, stood up and proclaimed, 'I'm Rosie and I'm a bundle of things. I am a feminist, a writer, a sister, a daughter, an activist, a chunk of UK Uncut, a Twitter feed, a Facebook profile, a bit of Labour, a lot of the Green party, a bit of Lib Dem and sometimes even a bit of a Tory. Every day I am a bit of all these things and more. I don't want to be put into a box of being this or that. I am transient, confused and often lost on what I believe or think but I know who I am and what I stand for.' Many in the audience clearly did not know what to make of this contribution.

Even the Girl Guides, with half a million members (and a long waiting list) has, under new leadership, taken on a new feminist timbre. Chief Executive Julie Bentley told one newspaper, 'I want to help young women to understand that all too often they will be presented with stereotypes of what a successful woman is, and it will be largely defined around their physical appearance.' She talked about how

> two-thirds of girls believe women are still judged more on their looks than their ability and one in three would consider plastic surgery to improve her experience. The celebrity culture makes them [girls] feel under pressure to look a certain way – look at the results of our study with so many even prepared to contemplate plastic surgery. Confidence, self-esteem, and inner belief are going to determine what they do with their lives, not looking nice. Guides in 2012 are more likely to be navigating a muddy ravine, going overseas to help on an Aid programme or going to one of our pop concerts.

Or, as they announced in the spring of 2013, explicitly endorsing the anti-Page 3 campaign.

There is too new strain of militancy among educators about young women's lives and choices. Helen Wright, formerly head of the Girls'

School Association, takes a resilient, respect-yourself approach to young women's lives and writes no-nonsense pieces with titles such as 'It's better to be the Plain Jane than the prettiest girl in class' and 'Encouraging girls to like themselves is at the heart of what we do'. Helen Fraser, the chief executive of the Girls' Day School Trust, made a public splash when she suggested that girls need to be as 'ambitious' in their relationships as they are in their careers. Female pupils need to find a man who will not only 'help around the home' (discuss) but would act as 'cheerleader' for their career. Fraser suggested that modern girls can have it all – career, marriage and motherhood – but they need the right kind of man to accomplish it. Without him, they risk hitting the 'nappy wall', a particularly inelegant metaphor to add to an already clumsy crop.

It was one of those moments when I realised how much mainstream politics had changed. On the morning of 14 February 2013 I clicked a link on Twitter. Stella Creasy, MP for Walthamstow, east London, had posted a short film highlighting the 'flashmob we will be holding . . . for One Billion Rising' ('One Billion: the number of women who will be raped or beaten in their lifetime'). Not a word spoken, just a thumping soundtrack, but handwritten black words posted on white card: the video itself, a pastiche of Bob Dylan's 1965 promotional film for his *Don't Look Back* Tour, one of many such imitations, but still done well. Creasy is quite the joker, and the video came alive, not just through the music and the words, but through the comic faces she pulled to accompany her message, 'We call on all governments to make ending violence women and girls a priority. Sound Good?' (cue comically quizzical expression) 'We Would Love it If you joined us at 11 AM' (cue a pantomime tap on her watch and a face as if to say: yes we can). It's hard to say what moved me so much about the video. The cause? The context? (The video was filmed in the high-ceilinged, chilly grandeur of Westminster Hall, the cavernous space in the Houses of Parliament where great world leaders are honoured.) Maybe it is *that* cause in *that* context: the energy of a mass feminist campaign being endorsed from within the gloomy, grandfatherly House of Commons. Or lively Creasy herself, young enough to be my daughter.

But then I am old enough to remember what 'real' politicians are supposed to look like. Once upon a time, in Britain, as elsewhere in the world, a woman in politics was a courageous, isolated figure. Snowy-haired Jennie Lee who with Nye Bevan, Minister of Health in the post-war Attlee government, formed possibly the most fiery, radical, socialist partnership ever. Flame-haired Barbara Castle, a tough operator, and a charismatic speaker, scourge of the trades' unions on whom she tried to impose pay controls in the 1970s. These pioneer female politicians were often distinguished by low key, facilitating spouses: quiet men in the background, and no children. In those days, not 'having a family' was considered the price of the political ticket. Very slowly that started to change. MP Helene Hayman famously breastfed her baby son at Westminster in the mid 1970s. Harriet Harman, Deputy Leader of the Labour Party, fought the 1983 election in a dark blue maternity smock, the first of three pregnancies.

Another sea change in British politics came in 1997, with the arrival of just over a hundred Labour MPs to Westminster. (And no, I'm not going to use that famous but disparaging term.) Among them, Oona King, a talkative, ambitious, personable north Londoner who had won a parliamentary nomination just weeks before the 1997 election, serving as an MP until 2005. In 2008 King published her diaries of the period, *House Music*. Reviewing the book, I observed then:

> Love her or loathe her, Oona King once seemed to signal a genuinely new type of politician. This was less to do with the cluster of New Briton labels that attach to her – black, Jewish, female, young and funky (I doubt there is another MP who clubs till dawn) – than her exceptionally informal public personality, that mix of mockney ebullience and in your face frankness. Watching her on *Question Time* is a bit like listening to a friend ruminate across the kitchen table. Gravitas just doesn't come into it.

Rowenna Davis, twenty-eight, a councillor in Southwark, a broadcaster, would like to go into Parliament. She points to a new generation of women MPs and candidates who are not prepared to compromise their femininity/womanhood in order to comply to a masculine definition of leadership. She talks of one particular prospective candidate as being like 'Tigger': 'Very bouncy, able to talk of things really openly.' Davis also believes that today's political women are informed by feminism, but keen to step out onto the national stage:

> There is a sense of compassion, an ability to value relationships, family, friends, nurturing, caring, but mixing that with aspiration, thriving and leadership. We are saying we value both of these aspects as much. One is not better than the other. I don't want to live my life in that purely competitive and individualistic way but I do want to go into politics.

Does it matter if we get more women into Parliament in the UK, particularly as we have become so cynical about politics in general?[9] Of course it matters. Women MPs may not have the apparent independence of action or glamour of some other feminist spokeswomen. Their job often involves them in much of the nitty-gritty of people's lives but that also means that they stay connected to a wide range of experiences through their constituency work. Before 1997 only forty female MPs had ever held ministerial office.[10] Yet well over forty of those women clustered around Tony Blair in May 1997 at that famous photo call at Church House ended up serving as a minister in some capacity. By the start of Blair's third term, the figure had doubled to eighty, with women holding about one-third of all government posts through the Blair years. According to Claire Annesley, a professor of politics at Manchester University, 2008 marked 'the peak of women in senior political positions, when Brown appointed Jacqui Smith as the first female home secretary and promoted several women in the government'.[11]

Mainstream politics is such a theatrical affair, with its endless behind-the-scenes drama, stoked by a press pack that follow the leading players from triumph to disaster and back again, that it is easy to forget the more low key, vital executive and legislative work that goes on in Parliament. The intake of 1997 may have been mocked for their bright, structured jackets but they also made a difference, as Polly Toynbee noted soon after New Labour's first term:

> Only look at the budget to find their handiwork. Maternity pay, child care, part-time workers' rights, lone parents' new deal and a score of

other recent measures did far more for women than for men. Ask women MPs and most will say: 'We did that.' Do you imagine, they ask, that Gordon Brown had babies on his mind when he came to power? Poverty, yes, in the abstract, but without understanding that means women. Where are the manifesto commitments to most of the things that he has spent his money on? It was ex-single mother paymaster general Dawn Primarolo – in a key but silent, back-room post – who required the Treasury to calculate the gender effect of all its actions. Women were not a central pitch back in 1997, but an afterthought and a disastrous afternoon's photo shoot with the prime minister. Remember how Tony Blair forgot to appoint a women's minister at all, calling Harriet Harman back in a hurry to add it to her brief?[12]

When Tessa Jowell was elected to Parliament in 1992,

There were more MPs named John or Jonathan than there were women in Parliament. This was Westminster post-Margaret Thatcher. Her impact on our politics and the way the country was represented was nonexistent . . . Our early legislation introduced longer maternity leave and strengthened maternity rights. Domestic violence, rape crisis centres and safety on public transport became routine debates rather than languishing on the fringes. A concerted effort to ensure decisions in the public sector did not discriminate against women led to Labour's gender equality duty, which the coalition looks set to undo. Not only did the content of our politics change, but to some extent so did the style. A crèche replaced one of the bars in Parliament and hours were changed to make it easier for members to balance work and childcare.[13]

We can trace the impact of women in British politics directly to various of today's initiatives: Creasy's campaign to bring better sex education to schools; Lisa Nandy's campaign against benefits cuts; Diane Abbott's concern about the rise of 'McParenting' and Fightclub culture. Some Tory women MPs now identify themselves as feminists. Amber Rudd joined with Stella Creasy to campaign for improved sex education. Louise Mensch, until her recent retirement to New York, spoke forcefully on the issue of female representation in the media.

Yet all the evidence points to women losing ground in public life. A major report, *Sex and Power*, published in early 2013 found:

[T]he advancement of women in the senior ranks of politics . . . has gone into reverse, with Britain rapidly falling down the international league tables for female democratic representation . . . in western governments, only Ireland and Italy had fewer female representatives in 2010 . . . at the current rate of progress, a child born today will be drawing her pension before she has any chance of being equally represented in the Parliament of her country.[14]

> In Britain, women make up only 22.5 per cent of MPs, 12.3 per cent of council leaders (in England), and 17.4 per cent of the Cabinet.

The report outlined how women make up only 22.5 per cent of MPs, 12.3 per cent of council leaders (in England), and 17.4 per cent of the cabinet. Only a third of public appointments are female; women account for 15.6 per cent of high court judges and 5 per cent of editors of national daily newspapers. And while generally better represented on devolved regional bodies, even here figures have fallen: from 50 per cent of women candidates elected in 2004 to 40 per cent last year. In Scotland, the figure has dropped from 39.5 per cent to 34.09 per cent. Trades' unions are now made up of half women, half men – yet women only lead three out of ten trades' unions, although the new General Secretary of the TUC is a woman, the first in its history.[15]

Frances O'Grady sees Westminster as the

last bastion of patriarchy. Women MPs put up with incredibly demeaning behaviour. Some MPs behave like teenage boys, fuelled by testosterone. There is a lot of hatred of women in there. I disagree with Nadine Dorries, but I thought she gave a very interesting response to the attack that was made on her by them. [Dorries's exact words were as follows: 'Unfortunately, I think that not only are Cameron and Osborne two posh boys who don't know the price of milk, but they are two arrogant posh boys who show no remorse, no contrition, and no passion to want to understand the lives of others – and that is their real crime'.] For all the change there has been, the business of politics remains inhospitable for women and in many respects we seem to be going backwards.

Is this why so many women in this country, and around the world felt a shiver down their spine when, in the autumn of 2012, Australian Prime Minister Julia Gillard lambasted opposition leader Tony Abbott in Parliament, after he accused her of condoning the denigration of women? In a powerful and emotional speech, Gillard forcefully denounced the misogyny and sexism many believe to be deeply embedded in the Australian body politic: a form of misogyny, as Gillard made clear, that she has experienced throughout her public life. (Like many around the world, I watched the speech online, with mounting delight, and immediately showed it to my daughters; I had never before seen a woman in a position of such power speak out in such resoundingly clear terms about the indignities and patronage routinely suffered by women in public, and private, life.)

But how much, I wonder, does a bruisingly adversarial political system reinforce the continuing high levels of gender inequality in British political life? Look across at some of the Nordic countries, where a mix of greater encouragement to women to join in all aspects of public life and a more consensus-seeking approach to government, has promoted a more welcoming model of political participation. What, exactly, is stopping us from doing the same?

According to Rowenna Davis, women are still 'being judged by their appearance'. She continues:

> That's very hard for women to handle. Yes you have to look perfect and neat. But it's also very hard to be considered beautiful and intelligent. If you are a beautiful woman – you must be an airhead. I think Louise Mensch suffered from that in one way. And at the other end of the spectrum, someone like Ann Widdecombe had the piss taken out of her constantly, because she was not a conventional sort of woman or politician.

Roxanne Halsey, a volunteer at EAVES – the campaign against violence against women – has said that her work has demonstrated to her clearly how sexism in the media affects women. The mocking coverage of female politicians, for instance, knocked her confidence, and left her feeling that: 'This is what happens to women who are prepared to be in the public eye – you get insulted by both men and women.'

Davis also believes that in political – and media – culture in general, women remain more tentative:

> You really have to encourage a woman to speak. She has to be *asked*. She has to be told that she can. Within the area that I work in – broadcasting – if you ask a woman to appear on a programme she will say, 'Are you sure you want me? Are you sure you don't want x?' or 'I'd like to know more' – or perhaps, 'I need more notice'. That is my day-to-day experience. Whereas I've known men who have appeared on certain programmes simply ring up the producer uninvited and say, 'Look, just to let you know that I am available on Friday, if you need me.'

Hannah Calman, thirty-two, works in a political research. She is also involved in local politics and is thinking of standing to be a councillor. What she appreciates about politics is that it puts her in touch with people:

> My partner and I are your classic professional couple. So we wouldn't normally go into local housing estates. But it's great to do that, to talk to people about the state of the flats, where they live . . . I feel much more connected to the area in which I live.

She describes her local (Labour) party as vibrant, and women taking an equal role. But she can also see that there are not enough 'women councillors': 'In my view that's because of children – home responsibilities. You get very active young women, but not so many older women and very few ethnic minority women willing to stand.' She says her local party 'agonises about its lack of women all the time'.

Would she think of going into national politics? 'I'm much more interested in being a councillor. I could see myself as a leader of a council one day in the future. But as an MP? No.' Why not?

> I'm not overly confident. You have to do presentations, media stuff, broadcasts . . . being an MP looks horrific. I hear horror stories about selection meetings, and meddling from the top down. You've also got to be well networked – put so much effort into it – be really committed. I think it takes a level of confidence I don't have. I don't want to spend the next five years doing that.

She says that she sees, in her area, 'a group of middle-class white women – articulate and confident – who will all be fine, and I am sure we will see them applying for, and getting, a seat eventually.'

Calman identifies the complex mesh of interconnecting issues that still stop women entering politics at the higher level: lack of confidence, lack of perceived connections, concern about the commitment of time it involves and worry about combining it with a satisfying home life. Although there have been reforms to the hours – no more late-night sittings, or extended periods in the bar for the drinkers – politics remains an all-consuming activity. Oona King's diaries make clear that the parliamentary life is a hugely demanding one, with surgeries filled with desperate people looking for practical help, long hours in the chamber, the demands of the media, party meetings, single issue campaigns, a possible stint on the increasingly powerful select committees, and all of this before taking on any sort of junior or ministerial job. You couldn't help but feel for Oona King when her otherwise saintly husband announced he was leaving, fed up with never seeing her. (He stayed in the end, and the couple adopted three children after King lost her seat.) David Cameron and Michael Gove might have talked about 'sharing the school run' during the 2010 election campaign and Ed Miliband might appear in magazine photo-spreads showing him enjoying relaxed time with his wife and two young sons. But the fact is, it is impossible to be party leader or Prime Minister and have much real time for, or with, your family. One of the most irritating aspects of current political coverage is the disproportionate, and often distracting, attention paid to leaders' wives compared to the negligible, and negative, attention paid to women standing for elected office.[16]

But with more women in paid or professional work is it now, paradoxically, less likely that they will get involved in politics than it was a generation ago? Margaret Hodge, sixty-eight, a mother of four, and now the powerful head of the Public Accounts Committee, told Jenni Murray of *Woman's Hour* how her political career began when, after just six weeks feeding her first child, restless and unfulfilled, she wanted to do something with her time.[17] Nowadays, a woman in Hodge's position would probably be back at work within a month of the birth, juggling childcare and work commitments, and would not even have the time to think about voluntary or political activity for a few decades.

For campaigner Fiona Millar, there are a number of more general reasons why we may see 'women coming into leadership roles later in their lives; because of the inequalities early on . . . A lot of women just won't be interested in getting involved until their children have left home, left school.' A lobby correspondent in the 1980s, Millar then worked in the Leader of the Opposition's office from 1995 to 1997, and was a special adviser at Number Ten from 1997 to 2003. She explains:

> Politics in general, but being an MP in particular, is not a job compatible with family life. I know the hours have changed but there are still a lot of ten o'clock sittings. Regional government, which seems to have more ordinary office hours, is ahead of us here, and I think that is why they have more women involved. But the Westminster system means, that if you live in the constituency – which a lot of parties now ask their candidates to do – then you are probably going to have to be in London for part of the week, in order to be at the House – and you will not see your children for half the week and just go back there at the weekends. I am not criticising anyone who does it. I think more women should do it. I just think we should recognise that it is a very difficult choice. Given that most women take the weight of domestic life and childbearing, they do the lion's share, even now, it's so much weightier a decision for them. But our democracy suffers if more women aren't involved at the highest level.

But, Millar believes,

> Because we are all going to live so much longer, women will start coming into these positions in the last twenty years of their working lives. That also makes it important that women keep their hand in during the middle years, because it is very very difficult to get back into any role or job if you have given it up. I don't think a lot of women realise that when they do give up work to have children – how hard that is. But institutions need to understand, that older women have a lot more to offer. I have got more to offer politics at fifty-five than I did when was thirty-five.

★

One of the most absorbing discussions I had for this book was with Estelle Morris, the former UK Secretary of State for Education in the New Labour government of 2002–2005, who resigned in 2003, because she felt she was not 'good enough'. Morris became caught up in a political row about the grading of A levels and, over a series of days in which she felt increasingly compromised and unfavourably commented upon, in the press and elsewhere, she decided the personal pressure was too much, she decided to step down and be honest about why she was doing so.

Her decision caused a storm of comment – much of it unfavourable. When I mention on Twitter that I am about to meet her, somebody comments to the effect that she 'let women down'. In private conversations, people talk about the way that she 'put back the cause of her sex' for decades, as a result of her resignation. I – and many other women – did not take this view, although I was disappointed to see Morris relinquish power (when I don't believe any man in her position would have done so) and believed it was a loss to the government, not least because her determination to seek consensus made her an excellent minister. She was, in the jargon, a bridge builder, a 'people person'.

Meeting Estelle Morris, who now sits in the House of Lords, in her office, I am struck by how very different she looks in the flesh to the way she does on television. She seems less tentative, more robust; she has an indefinable air of authority but she also comes across as the kind of person it would be fun to know, to have as a friend. Making this observation, she says she believes that 'politics has become part of the celebrity culture and the focus is on the person rather than your role in politics. For women, it all becomes about their lifestyle, their clothes, and that this is very much a generational shift in politics.'

She proves to be very open during our conversation about the months leading up to her decision to resign and her thoughts about it in hindsight. We met in the autumn of 2012, soon after the tenth anniversary of her resignation, 'It's funny I was thinking about it on October 23rd . . . Do I regret it? I'd do the job differently now but given where I was at the time, I don't regret resigning.'

'There's a bit of arrogance in me,' she says at one point:

I was confident about managing education policy and working with the public and the profession but less confident with the broader media. I also detested Number Ten politics. Until I became Secretary of State, my predecessor David Blunkett (she was his number two for a period) managed those relationships – all the political correspondents and Whitehall – and I managed education relationships – bridge-building with the professionals.

She also noticed that if Blunkett 'felt that things had got tangled between special advisers within the department or Number Ten he would speak directly to the PM. For some reason I did not do that.'

Morris was also an MP in a marginal seat and that creates its own difficulties, she says, adding without side, 'and remember most women aren't sitting on strong majorities'. She says she also wishes that she had thought herself into the job more:

Michael Heseltine famously wrote his ambitions on the back of an envelope when he was young. It's easy to be critical of that but now I think that helped him think himself into the job. I was fighting an election [in 2001] and I was simply thinking, 'I have got to win the seat.' I was obviously aware of the press speculation that I would be offered the post and I did think about it but not enough to be really prepared when I was actually offered the job.

She would never have turned it down:

When Tony Blair offered me the post, I was hugely excited, but the job starts straight away and I didn't, for example, have advisers in place. I had a close knit group around me who shared my aims and ways of working and I should have made them official advisers. That would have given me a firmer platform on which to start and strengthen my ability to work across Whitehall. In the end it did wear me down – not enjoying that press and political game. Afterwards, talking to supportive MPs they said, 'We didn't know you were feeling under pressure. You should have asked us.' But I never thought to ask.

Rather poignantly, she adds, 'And I shouldn't have stopped swimming. In order to deal with things, I needed to do the very things that helped me keep a sense of perspective.'

'As a result,' she says, 'when things began to go wrong, I felt that

I was no longer in control and needed to sort it out. Otherwise I was going to be the sort of politician you despise.'

She describes the difficulty of being hounded by the press, of having her photo taken when she was on a walk. 'I was thinking, "Why am I doing this?" The lack of space was awful.' Although she believed, and still believes, resigning was her only option, it did take some time to adjust:

> I did feel isolated and the diary was empty for a while. Some people thought I'd let women down and I can see why they would think that. What I'd hoped I had done was to make a case for a different sort of politics, one which many women would relate to. Women in politics shouldn't have to do politics in the way men have for generations. That struck a chord with the public and led to a debate. But it's not changed things in the long term and the argument still needs to be won.

The *Sex and Power* report makes recommendations focused on improving the 'pipeline to power' including improving civic education in schools; creating proactive champions of minority groups to encourage participation; establishing equal representation on media panels; setting quotas in candidate selection; and launching a government campaign to improve female representation at the 2015 general election, as well as improving the monitoring of who becomes a candidate and why.

All important – but all, bar quotas, capable of generating more sound and fury than action. Improving civic education in schools is laudable – but given the scale of cuts in the education budget, this is unlikely to be implemented by harassed heads and teachers, trying to keep severe school inspectors' judgements at bay. As for 'A government campaign to improve female representation at the 2015 general election', it is hard to see how such a campaign could be effectively or convincingly led by a party – or a government – that has signally failed to promote or encourage significant numbers of women and is led by a Prime Minister who, in an unmasked moment, tells a troublesome female backbencher to 'Calm Down, Dear'. Only quotas – the enforcement of change – look likely to lead to more numbers of women.[18]

Boardroom quotas are the new (political) black. Everyone is talking about them these days, for good or ill. An experienced female political lobbyist said to me, with some impatience, 'I can't stand the way that most female MPs are obsessed with getting more women in the boardroom. There must be something else to talk about.' Apparently not. But it is also in keeping with our times; top down, trickle down, feminism. Take Christine Legard's comment about how the financial crisis might not have happened if you had had 'Lehman sisters' instead of Lehman brothers. David Cameron seemed to concur with these sentiments when he spoke at a Northern Future Forum Summit in Stockholm, Sweden, in 2012, claiming that there was '"overwhelming" evidence that companies are better run if men and women work alongside each other':

> [T]he real nub of the issue is how do we accelerate, how do we fast-forward to having at least 30 per cent of boards made up by women . . . That's where you get down to quotas, *which I don't think you should ever rule out*. A fear of legislation seemed to work wonders. [My emphasis.]

Voluntary efforts in the last year have resulted in a new record high for female representation on the boards of the UK's 100 largest listed companies. The proportion has gone up from 12.5 per cent last year to 15.6 per cent this year and early in 2013 Vince Cable, the Business Secretary, even promised personally to contact the eight FTSE 100 firms that still have men-only boardrooms on the grounds that politicians must 'challenge the paternalistic culture and silent assumptions about women's priorities that are ultimately keeping the glass ceiling in place'.

Boardroom feminism may not get anyone onto the barricades, but I have some sympathy with the idea; the pressure for parity in business is a reflection, after all, of a generation who have risen to power and influence, and don't see why they should be left standing outside the rooms where power is wielded. Norway is one of the few countries in the world to have imposed 40 per cent quotas on its boardrooms. (Which promptly led to 40 per cent of businesses avoiding the new law by converting to private limited companies; two-thirds later admitted that the quota rules were behind their decision to switch.) In December 2012, I went to a packed meeting at the House of Commons to discuss the origin and impact of this policy. Supporters of quotas are convinced that gender justice is not just ideologically important but helps promote better business decisions, and has a positive impact on the nation as a whole. Those opposed think that it hampers the free reign of business and has led to too few women becoming too powerful. One opponent, Mai-Lill Ibsen, a Norwegian banker, says, 'I'm against quotas. They are discriminatory in a way. I feel we [women] are so strong we don't need that.' Some opponents have made much of the so called 'golden skirts' problem, where due to a lack of experienced women, some women gather absurd numbers of directorships. But Ibsen herself rejects this argument – pointing out that no one talks about the 'gold suits issue'.

Academic feminist Agnes Bolsø has led a research project into the Norwegian initiative. She argues:

> We found that the new make-up did influence the decision-making process. Greater female representation seems to make meetings a little more pleasant, the preparation material is tidier and more comprehensive, and the processes more formal. Our respondents call it professionalization . . . It is very hard to analyse the impact on profitability, and research on the economic effect of more women on boards is inconclusive. What is beyond doubt, however, is that the policy has paved the way for women to influence corporate decision-making. They have formed networks and are actively administering their share of the power to make decisions. The experience women gain from corporate boards is qualifying them for executive jobs. Norwegian women's representation on the boards of listed companies was 3% in 1993, 7% in 2003 and is now 42%. Lawmakers who are committed to gender equality should take note of this.[19]

Several people at the House of Commons meeting observed that narrow male-dominated cultures may have been part of the problem that led to the global financial crisis. Even the Swedish prime minister recently said: 'A male atmosphere creates more risk and a greater risk of corruption.'

What about parity in political decision making? The *Sex and Power* report urged:

> Political parties should take immediate action to increase the number of women candidates at all levels of election with a view to fielding as many candidates from as wide a variety of backgrounds and communities as possible . . . this should include active consideration of positive action measures in selection processes.

But Labour's women-only shortlists policy has been controversial. Currently, the party plans for roughly half – fifty-two – of its selections in 108 targeted seats to be women only. As for the Conservatives, as Yvonne Roberts observed, 'David Cameron's A-list of candidates for the last election has been abandoned and not much is heard of Laura Trott, his lone adviser on women, while his promise of women making up a third of his Cabinet is now seen as a pipe dream.'[20]

Something about contemporary feminism nags at me. I like *Vagenda*'s light-heartedness but fear perhaps that some of the new politics is too accommodating of those who find feminism 'angry' or 'difficult'. Has politics really become so like advertising that everything should be made digestible and as if brand new; an entire complex history wiped out like old stock? I agree with Ellie Mae O'Hagan:

> If being sexy and funny are the two cornerstones of a new feminist movement, we may as well all pack up and go home now. At its core, feminism should be angry. It should be angry because women are still being taken for a ride. Like the women in *The Feminine Mystique*, we are being sold a lie of equality in a society where the odds are politically, socially and economically stacked against us.[21]

But there's something more. However impressive and inventive the grassroots campaigns of recent years, it feels, perhaps inevitably, markedly different to former incarnations of women's liberation. I do not mean that feminists today do not work together: far from it, a number of activists have told me that there is a sense of groups working well; I saw that in practice at the UK Feminista lobbying of Parliament, where there was a warm, collegiate atmosphere. In part, it's about the difficulty of getting a sustained message out there; more people should know about this extraordinary welter of activity. When I ask Natasha Walter why there is not greater awareness of feminist activism, she says,

> Well it may be because although there is a lot going on, we're not seeing the changes we want to see. Yes, we're aware of sexual violence – but we need to do more about the way that sexual violence is reported, and the way that survivors are treated by police and the criminal justice system. And the lack of support services.

But I think it goes deeper. Every historical period throws up its own specific social, economic, political context. Feminism today is bound to pursue different themes and a different tone to the struggles of earlier times. In the late nineteenth century and the early twentieth century it became focused on an overriding and crucial objective, the right to vote. In the late 1960s and early 1970s it was inevitably bound to the progressive left and counter culture – adding its own interrogation of relationships, sexuality and domestic politics. We are now living in a period when, to return to O'Hagan's phrase, 'the odds are politically, socially and economically stacked against women'; so surely modern feminism has to reflect that and campaign directly to improve the conditions of most women's lives – even if that means taking on some women who have risen to powerful positions? (For that clash, too, is bound to come.) Part of what undoes so many female lives – and will fell our daughters, if we are not careful – is a slowly growing set of compound disadvantages, mounting difficulties and hurdles, both tangible and elusive that may come at them from every angle. And part of that is about the growth of international financial power, and the shrinking of the state.

That is why one of the strongest, and profound, challenges to real power in recent years has not come from feminism but from the new social movements, such as Occupy or UK Uncut or recent student campaigns against privatisation such as those held on the campus at Sussex University. The police appear quite a lot in the account of Melanie Strickland, a twenty-nine-year-old charity lawyer, who went down to the Occupy camp at St Paul's because she had a 'sense that something was wrong – with society. I slept there a dozen times. Definitely a life-changing thing. Validated what I'd been feeling for a long time, this vaguely empty feeling, the sense that there's a lot wrong with the world. I wanted to say to people, "Come to St Paul's – people are just telling the truth".'

Strickland told me how she came to feminism through these campaigns:

> Through my involvement with UK Uncut, and meeting other women, taking part in teach-ins and so on, I learned how the cuts dispro-portionately affected women. I learned about how women are the victims of domestic violence and low wages and discrimination. Women feel the brunt of the cuts partly because caring work is grossly undervalued. We occupied a Starbucks opposite Angel tube in London because Starbucks don't pay tax which funds essential services like rape crisis centres and networks to support women affected by domestic violence. One of the girls stood up and said, 'Right, we are going to turn this Starbucks into a women's refuge.' We shut it down and had a teach-in on the cuts, with just twelve of us. We were asked to leave but we didn't. The police were quite sympathetic, and we stayed for an hour. They recognised that we had strong moral arguments.

Strickland is outraged that some companies can just 'choose' not to pay tax. She also explained how she felt our lives had become so commercialised:

> It's all about selling to us. And yet life is quite a struggle. I personally won't ever be able to afford a place in London. I look at a lot of my friends and it's like they feel they need to acquire things. When I was growing up you didn't have all these things. People are so worried about how they are perceived.

Getting involved in politics has also made her more aware of being a woman and what that means. 'In the beginning the camps at St Paul's were really mixed in every way. Race. Gender.' But as things settled down, Strickland said,

> We had to watch it, you know, that white men over thirty didn't take over. I wouldn't have called myself a feminist – not a term I'd really have used. I have only very recently realised that a lot of injust-ice is directed at women. I learned that through Occupy. Nowadays when I go to political meetings, I regularly notice I am the only

woman there. I am in a minority. There's a real lack of diversity –
everywhere – in boardrooms, government, in institutions. Women
don't tend to reach those places where they are going to make decisions. Why? Part of it is nature. Men are naturally more confident.
They will stand up and talk even if what they are saying is crap.
Women don't do that often, and they aren't comfortable with conflict.
They want to bring people together.

Talking to Strickland one can feel her making all the connections.
Her analysis of society seems more all-encompassing and messy, less
discrete and efficient than one-issue campaigns. But she has also
found herself at the sharp, if not quite, dangerous edge of modern
politics. As Laurie Penny recently observed,

> Right now, as millions of people stare down the barrel of job losses,
> benefits sanctions, destitution and desperation and the rich are given
> tax cuts, I hear a lot of people asking why there isn't more resistance
> going on. Well, here's why. There was resistance, and it was brutally and
> systematically put down. The students, the street-organising anti-cuts
> campaigners, the Occupy movement. When people speak about the
> Occupy camps and anti-austerity protests of 2010–12, it is with a tone
> of regret, as if somehow those grassroots movements just fizzled out
> because those involved didn't know what they were doing. On the
> contrary: they were cleared out, arrested and beaten back by police,
> just like the students at Sussex.[22]

Some aspects of women's empowerment have been more easily
co-opted by capitalism than others. Increasing sexual freedom for
women encourages new markets. Capitalism has no problem with
*Fifty Shades of Grey*; that's Fifty Shades of Profit. The struggle, as I
have tried to argue, is to keep sexual freedom and expression meaningful, and equal, for women. For Nina Power,

> There has obviously been a kind of mainstreaming of elements of
> feminist ideas and rhetoric – 'empowerment', some limited forms
> of sexuality, and so on, and, more dangerously, feminism has also
> been used as a justification for imperialist wars (the 'West' will
> 'liberate' women from their oppressors through war). Partly the
> mainstreaming has a strategic component – it opens up the horizon
> for feminism – but I think the term becomes problematic when

many things are called 'feminist' that are actually ultimately destructive for women.

It may also be that to many women, young and older, some kinds of feminism might even appear as if they underwrite inequality. The *Observer* noted with prescience:

> The lack of women in the bishopric, the boardroom, on television
> . . . rightfully needs addressing. However, arguably, what requires even
> more urgent action is the profoundly inequitable manner in which
> the cumulative clout of growing unemployment, changes to benefits,
> the rising cost of childcare and significant cuts to services such as
> support for the elderly is hammering women in particular. Progress
> in the boardroom may yet prove to be the consolation prize for the
> loss of many of the gains women have won in the past 40 years.

I do not think we should put the blame for the growing inequality between women at feminism's door; after all, many of the arguments for more women in the boardroom are explicitly made in order to improve the situation of lesser paid women, although whether they will or not is another matter. But reading the *Observer* editorial, one can immediately grasp how little *those* problems – growing unemployment, changes to benefits, the rising cost of childcare and significant cuts to services – are likely to resonate with young women now, even though it is exactly those same problems that will, almost certainly, come to limit or define many of their lives later on. And as inequality has grown, it is even harder than it once was (and it always was) to talk about 'women' in any abstract way. An asylum seeker stripped of benefits has less than nothing in common with a woman struggling with the subtle sexism of middle-to-high management, although both may suffer the effect of male disregard (or violence) in their lives. What does a cleaner or call-centre worker fighting for the living wage have in common with a woman keen to become a non-executive director, apart from the fact that the non-executive director might then press for better conditions for the company's women workers?

Economic crisis breeds fear, and women feel the fear. Female obedience is reinforced by austerity, recession and repression. Low pay, insecure contracts, worry about losing even a poorly paid part-time job keep women obedient. And that fear has now spread to younger people, and younger women. A recent British Social Attitudes Survey presented an interesting picture of a rising generation who are more progressive on race and sexuality and have a far greater sense of global connection ('A 23- or 24-year-old Londoner is more likely to be concerned about Mumbai than Newcastle') but are less supportive of the NHS or the welfare state. This 'sense of cosmopolitan outreach' means young people today have more a sense of shared interests (largely expressed through the internet) than the ties of geography. Their sense of individualism is far stronger.[23]

> Economic crisis breeds fear, and women feel the fear. Female obedience is reinforced by austerity, recession and repression. Low pay, insecure contracts, worry about losing even a poorly paid part-time job keep women obedient.

But could it be that this generation is so individualistic because there is so little of the common inheritance – once known as public services or a sense of solidarity – to draw on? According to James Ball and Tom Clark, 'A rising generation that finds college expensive, work hard to come by and buying a home an impossible dream is responding to its plight, not by imagining any collective fightback, but by plotting individual escape.'[24] So many of the women I interviewed accepted that they were never going to be able to afford a flat, let alone a house. Faced with these basic life issues one could see how feminism would take a back seat. It is sometimes easier to be bold and rebellious in times of general optimism and economic buoyancy. In hard times, people go inwards.

Ultimately, what threatens women's future is growing inequality, the shape of the economy and the health of the state. That does not diminish the importance of campaigns against distorted representation or male violence: far from it. But it does mean, in the words of Nancy Fraser, the American academic and theorist, that feminists of the future are going to have to struggle not just for the politics of recognition – that is, campaigns taking on unfair representation and unequal treatment – but for redistribution – campaigns that take on issues of economic fairness, state subsidy of 'caring' for the young and elderly and the health of our public services. In Britain, according to Natasha Walter,

'Just as there is action needed now on sexual violence, so there is action needed on inequality and poverty – generations are now condemned to a poverty that we thought we had tackled with the last government.'

The novelist and essayist Zadie Smith has recently written about her personal experience, as a citizen, of the state:

> I can only really account for it by reaching back again, briefly, into the past. It's a short story about debt – because I owe the state, quite a lot. Some people owe everything they have to the bank accounts of their parents. I owe the state. Put simply, the state educated me, fixed my leg when it was broken, and gave me a grant that enabled me to go to university. It fixed my teeth (a bit) and found housing for my veteran father in his dotage. When my youngest brother was run over by a truck it saved his life and in particular his crushed right hand, a procedure that took half a year, and which would, on the open market – so a doctor told me at the time – have cost a million pounds. Those were the big things, but there were also plenty of little ones: my subsidised sports centre and my doctor's office, my school music lessons paid for with pennies, my university fees. My NHS glasses aged 9. My NHS baby aged 33. And my local library. To steal another writer's title: England made me. It has never been hard for me to pay my taxes because I understand it to be the repaying of a large, in fact, an almost incalculable, debt.[25]

Just before she draws up this convincing list of what makes up her 'incalculable debt', Smith claims, of herself, that 'I retain a particular naivety . . . which must seem comical to many people, particularly younger people.' Re-reading her list, I think it is not Smith who is naive – after all, she *knows* that the British state made her – but rather it is those whom that state might help un-make in the future who are the true innocents, all those citizens-to-come who do not even now know what they might have had or might have been because those possibilities now belong to history. That makes me sad.

A little later, Smith quotes the social democratic historian Tony Judt:

> 'We have freed ourselves of the mid-twentieth-century assumption – never universal but certainly widespread – that the state is likely to be the best solution to any given problem. We now need to liberate

ourselves from the opposite notion: that the state is – by definition and always – the worst possible option.'

We need now to 'think the state' in different ways, for a new century, and the new conditions of women's lives.

Frances O'Grady believes the tough challenge in the UK is

to defend the decent welfare system in the face of constant onslaught from right-wing newspapers, government ministers, and their advisors and spinners . . . to create a new economic model to replace the one that fell with Lehman Brothers. There is surprisingly broad consensus that we need real change.

Nina Power too believes that new movements will arise:

I think that the possibilities for solidarity are there – especially in the wake of the cuts where we know that women have been hit hardest in a number of ways (in terms of benefits, job losses in the public sector etc.). I think there is a sense of enough is enough: women have often been at the forefront of protests and uprisings, and I imagine we'll see more of that in the years to come.

Power's phrase 'enough is enough' is echoed by Helen Mott, an active member of the Bristol Fawcett Society coming up against

the fact that women are taking the brunt of the cuts and protesting against the appalling price that women are paying for not really being considered at the (political) table. When Bristol Fawcett recently lobbied the candidates for Mayor of the city – and there were four-teen men and one woman standing! – only two of the candidates made the connection between childcare and a thriving economy.

For Tess Lanning, part of the 'solution for the future should involve raising the quality and the status of the jobs that women do'. She talks of the need for a 'new funding settlement that supports a high-quality social care system, in which you have a living wage and well-trained staff. But we also need to challenge the idea that this is necessarily "women's work." High quality, affordable childcare for children from the age of one would prevent women from being shut out of work for long periods of time.'

I asked Helen Mott what she thought local government needed to do, in terms of resources and reforms.

Well, violence against women – the need to protect and enhance the services for women and girls affected by gender-based violence, to keep the specialist nature of support and to protect the expertise that resides in these organisations and that feeds into vital prevention work. That's very important. Secondly, the need to support caring responsibilities. We need a recognition that childcare should be affordable, and also an understanding of the burdens of elderly care – that women are largely shouldering these burdens, and their lives are curtailed by cuts in services. Finally, we have to address poverty and the low pay of women. We now have strong campaigns in Bristol supporting the need to pay the living wage.

Mott herself decided to stand as an independent candidate in the May 2013 elections because she felt that the women's voice needed to be heard:

There's a kind of ideological agenda about national politics. The idea is that men are people, and women are seen as a kind of collateral. But you can only do so much waiting for the men in power to step up. I thought, 'Perhaps it is we women who need to do that.'

One of the most heartening things about the Bristol scene in 2013, says Mott, is the involvement of women of all generations:

Recently we had a retrospective exhibition 'SisterShow Revisited', exploring feminist activism in the 1970s. The Bristol Festival of Ideas brought together grassroots feminist activists from then and now. Many of the women from SisterShow were active and influential in the second-wave movement. They reminded us that Bristol, for instance, had a refuge and women's centre in 1973. Some of these women are now in their seventies and eighties and are still very much engaged. At the same time, our feminist networks in the city are connected to young women in schools and at the university where they have a lively feminist society. So, the engagement spans several generations.

★

Paradoxically, the digital revolution may make a younger generation feel both more powerful and more lonely. I watch my daughters. They can get in touch with anyone without having to leave the house. 'Conversation' can be carried on palm to palm, sitting cross-legged on one's bed. I don't want to exaggerate this development: teenagers and young people do go out, a *lot*. But does that illusion of control, a sense of one's life as something within one's hand, make the messiness and unpredictability of human contact seem not just difficult, but a bit passé? In a similar vein, social media can create an illusion of democratic access and community. Traditional politics means you have to pester people to get their actual signatures on a petition – now we just have to fill in a couple of lines on an email and ping it back. Once, if I wanted to challenge someone powerful, I might have to do that old-fashioned thing: petition to lobby them at the House of Commons, or write a letter, or go somewhere in a delegation.

The value of human contact is not easily characterised or measured, but there is surely an alchemy of political means and effect; the sheer power of being together, the conversations generated in the course and conduct of a campaign, is part of the enduring power of all politics, including feminist politics. It is humanly cheering. Uplifting. (At such times, I really do feel as if 'we are all in it together'.) But in this new discrete, efficient age of hyperlinks and 140 characters, could some of that get lost? Twitter, BlackBerry and Facebook are all powerful tools. But they can so easily be isolating ones. Lucy-Anne Holmes tweeted – and got a response from – Rupert Murdoch. I would like to know: did Holmes send her tweet when she was sitting in a room full of other anti-Page 3 campaigners? Was it the product of excited consensus? Or was she alone when she tapped it out and then received the tycoon's response?

But there's a bigger point. Politics, of whatever kind, is an art, and a habit, that needs to be cultivated. Enlightening and potentially affirming, it reminds us of our common humanity and, as many of my interviewees bore out, provides a space for personal relationships that challenge so many of the empty values of our time. As I hope I have shown, girls are often subtly discouraged, for complex reasons, from finding or using a public voice. Susie Orbach believes one of the achievements of second-wave feminism, and a gift bequeathed to younger women in terms of example, is the ability to speak, and in more authentic terms, in public.

Even so, I believe there remains among, and within, many women, particularly older women, some unarticulated sense that to 'speak up' or to 'speak out' crosses an invisible but inviolable boundary. Is it just fear or is there a deeper belief perhaps that it is immodest to think one's opinion worth any more than someone else's: rude to disagree (a matter on which we still give our children mixed messages) and reckless, or at least insensitive, to put forward proposals that might disrupt the status quo or impinge on someone else's choices and conflicts.

I think it too easy to name this as innate conservatism, or worse, cowardice. For women, the preservers of much domestic life after all, often have an awed respect for the conditions in which others live their lives as well as the efforts, compromises and sacrifices so often required in order to preserve this same private, family and community life: and they possess a similarly well-grounded respect for the possibly profound implications of any kind of political change. Of course, this very awareness of the fragile web of human relations is what makes women's contribution to political debate so vital, if only more could find a way to speak up, truthfully – including in defence of their – our – own interests.

> We need to move away from the traditional rhetorical, quasi-Oxford-Union/parliamentary form of public discussion and explore other ways of holding conversations.

Either way, our daughters may need help and support in order to learn to speak up and speak out for themselves; collectively, we need to move away from the traditional, rhetorical, quasi-Oxford-Union/parliamentary form of public discussion and explore other ways of holding conversations that encourage greater participation from all sides. Some of the most important political movements, and moments, exist, almost by definition, outside mainstream, parliamentary politics; in so many ways, national politics is defined by what it *cannot* truthfully debate or do, as much as by what it can. In fact, those of us lurking in the suburbs of mainstream politics can often speak more honestly of the reality, and cause, of social problems: even as we exercise limited influence and power in terms of change. As Gary Younge recently wrote in relation to the 2012 US presidential election, 'Given the hours of coverage and the billions of dollars devoted to the election, it's stunning how few of the nation's most glaring problems are being discussed.'[26] Either way: we must not leave politics or public discussion to our fathers, husbands, brothers or sons while unwittingly silencing our daughters in the name of good manners or urge compliance for the sake of maintenance of relationship.[27]

# Epilogue
## What Should We Tell Our Daughters?

When I was a child, my mother used to wave me off to school in the mornings, positioned at the window of a room on the first floor in which she sometimes worked. Just before I reached the red postbox in our street I would turn to scan the face of the house. There she was, a shadowy talisman, a smiling harbinger of good luck. Inherited habits die hard (or in my case, not at all) and when my daughters were younger, I, too, would take up position at our first-floor living room window pantomiming encouragement from on high. I've forgotten at what stage I stopped rushing up the stairs to do my waving thing; at the moment, I suppose, where it seemed distinctly more embarrassing than appropriately supportive. But even though my girls are now in their late teens, occasionally I will hear the reverberating bang of the front door – why can they *never* learn to close it quietly? – run upstairs, sneak up to the right-hand side of the bay window and watch as, individually or together, they race off down the streets, towards a meeting with their friends, their futures.

A mother's continuing, occasionally covert, concern for her daughters is nothing new. We can see it at work in one of the most poignant genres in literary and social history, letters from mothers to daughters written down the centuries which frequently mix a heartbreakingly brave cheerfulness with tenderness and an occasional naked desperation. Mary Wollstonecraft's *Letters Written During a Short Residence in Sweden, Norway and Denmark*, her account of the travels she undertook around the Nordic countries in the late eighteenth century, with three-year-old Fanny, her illegitimate daughter, part of an attempt both to earn money and win back her lover's affection, reverberates with explicit and recognisable anxiety at her daughter's possible fate:

You know that as a female I am particularly attached to her – I feel more than a mother's fondness and anxiety, when I reflect on the dependent and oppressed state of her sex. *I dread lest she should be forced to sacrifice her heart to her principles, or principles to her heart . . .* I dread to unfold her mind, lest it should render her unfit for the world she is to inhabit – Hapless woman! what a fate is thine! [My emphasis.]

There is a gayer note, if an underlying desperation, in the famous letter that the poet Anne Sexton, who committed suicide, wrote to her daughter Linda, designed to be read when Linda reached the age – forty – at which Sexton herself was writing:

Life is not easy. It is awfully lonely. *I* know that. Now you too know it – wherever you are, Linda, talking to me. But I've had a good life – I wrote unhappy – but I lived to the hilt. You too, Linda – Live to the HILT! To the top. I love you, 40-year old Linda, and I love what you do, what you find, what you are! – Be your own woman. Belong to those you love.

It is difficult to untangle the deep personal unhappiness of Sexton's and Wollstonecraft's stories from the cultural presumptions of their age: and therefore not to recognise a distinct difference of personal and cultural tone in the way we talk of, and to, our own daughters today. For all the pressures and prohibitions, that tone feels both more robust and optimistic. After all, there are ways, now, to escape unhappy love affairs and marriages and dreary domesticity; an illegitimate baby is not a social shame; it is legitimate (if not de rigueur) to enjoy sex, earn a living, follow our dreams. We would not now dream – would we? – of wishing, as did Daisy, the beautiful protagonist of Fitzgerald's *The Great Gatsby*, drunk and goofy on the dulling anaesthetic, that her new-born daughter would grow up to be 'a beautiful little fool'? Ageing for women no longer means a long decline into fussiness and the indulgence of grandchildren, poor hearing and passivity: far from it, a woman in her forties, fifties or sixties today is recognisably different from many of the middle-aged women of my childhood. Completely new models of womanhood are available to us all, at all stages of our lives. I don't just relish all this. I breathe a huge sigh of relief.

But it is not that simple. If I allow myself, for a moment, to look down from above, as if from a political magic carpet, I would say we are, in the modern western world, living through a prolonged social and cultural in-between, a kind of twilight period in terms of women's lives. Yes, there is no longer the presumption that a woman should, without question, seek the economic protection of a man or the married state, although she may well do so. Family life has been utterly transformed over the last fifty years. The liberalisation of divorce laws, acceptance of diverse sexualities, abortion law reform, the widespread availability of contraception, limited forms of child support, feminism itself: all these changes have transformed the land-scape in which women learn, love, work and reproduce.

But new complexities will surely arise, with profound implications for our collective daughters. Over the next few decades it seems as if the already significant gulf between female 'winners' and 'losers' will only grow, not just in economic terms but in a range of other ways. Increasing numbers of highly paid professional women will have fewer children (or none at all); they will buy in more of their 'domestic comforts', employ other low waged women to cook and clean, care for their children and their elderly relatives. Their free time, if they are parents, will be largely taken up with 'intensive mothering'; they will spend more on consumer goods and they will probably eat and even sleep less than their lower paid sisters. In many ways these women's lives now more closely resemble those of their privileged male peers. Eager to merge their incomes, hearts and genes with equally favoured males, we may be witnessing the emergence of what Alison Wolf has called a new breed of 'super families'.

> Over the next few decades it seems as if the already significant gulf between female 'winners' and 'losers' will only grow.

Wolf broadly applauds this development although she acknowledges the losses to community, civic and even family life that has accompanied women's increasing entry into full-time employment. While I would welcome the expansion of women's professional capacities, and their just reward, it is hard to see how much this development has anything to do with feminism – bar the growing restlessness of senior women, angered at the continuing stress of combining work and corporate life. Such strains will undoubtedly continue to exist; it may be that future generations of would-be female high flyers will opt out, disillusioned at the continuing battle to reconcile children and career. On the other hand, perhaps the soft spoken rebellions currently led by women like Sheryl Sandberg in the States and Helena Morrissey here, will lead to lasting institutional change.

But what of the growing army of middling- to low-waged, or unemployed, women? What will happen to our 'esoteric, unsaleable poet' or the classroom teacher or care home worker? How will they manage their lives – and who will help them to do so? As the writer Toni Morrison has said,

> Two parents can't raise a child any more than one. You need a whole community – everybody – to raise a child. The notion that the head is the one who brings in the most money is a patriarchal notion, that a woman – and I have raised two children, alone – is somehow lesser . . . Or that I am incomplete without the male. That is not true. And the little nuclear family is a paradigm that just doesn't work for white people or for black people. Why we are hanging onto it, I don't know. It isolates people into little units – people need a larger unit.[1]

For the new elite, that larger unit will be created by their ability to purchase the labour of a new 'servant class' to cook, care and clean for them. But for the less well off, as I have argued, protection once provided by the state is now rapidly shrinking. We may never, in the UK, have developed the collective protections and steadiness of some of the Scandinavian countries but universal child benefit, children's centres and more generally, free education and health, have all helped several generations of women bring up a family, alone if need be. But now, in the twenty-first century, the foundations of our imperfect welfare state are under attack and it is clear the ways in which some women will suffer for it. We might well see the introduction of small, but incremental, charges in health and education and no significant expansion of relatively low cost social housing while the growth of means-tested benefits will surely bring a new shame at state dependency and sharpen the divisions between haves and have-nots.

The next generation could face a bleak social landscape with two profound consequences for them. Unlike their richer sisters, who can underwrite the risks of sexual and social freedom, relative or absolute poverty could return poorer women to a form of neo-traditionalism: thrown on the mercy of men once more as a result of financial hardship. There may well be a renewed assault on abortion rights, widely available contraception and sexual health programmes, a revived sexual puritanism and a return to the notion of the 'dignity' of marriage as the only vehicle for childrearing. Secondly, a shrinking state and women's higher rate of unemployment could risk placing greater burdens of care (of the young, the sick, the elderly) on poorer women, keeping them confined to women's work, at home. For the veteran activist Selma James, 'It's almost unbearable to wake up to a world in which the welfare state that has defended us from the worst excesses of the market is being destroyed. The only way to hold on to the last vestiges of entitlement, and even reverse defeats, is to fight like hell.'[2]

Whoever they are, we owe today's young women a vigilant refusal to return to outworn gender stereotypes, as well as an active commitment to their flourishing and true independence. In late spring 2013, as I was finishing this book, I heard from Yvonne Sharples, the spirited and talented head of Parklands school in Liverpool. She wrote:

> I am just drafting my farewell speech to [pupils] as they prepare to leave school. I plan to quote from Martin Luther King who quotes from Marianne Williams' *A Course in Miracles*: 'Our deepest fear is not that we are inadequate. Our deepest fear is that we are powerful beyond measure. It is our light, not our darkness, that most frightens us. We ask ourselves, who am I to be brilliant, gorgeous, talented and fabulous? Actually, who are you not to be? As we are liberated from our own fear, our presence automatically liberates others.' I believe this is 'what we should tell our daughters'.

Feminism, which led to so many of the changes that we all benefit from today, still has an important job to do – to fight like hell, particularly for the less powerful. It simply cannot be written off as a dated utopianism or a movement whose job is now complete. But our commitment to the next generation will need to go beyond empty talk of fostering 'aspiration', too often a thin coating of mere wishful thinking on a mass of unwelcome realities, particularly for young women coming from poorer backgrounds. 'Scaffolding', a term used in education, is a process by which a teacher shows, and models, the learning required, until the pupil has gained the required competence. Put another way, an individual hugely benefits when someone else makes it their explicit job to show them how to do what needs to be done, supporting them, even as, in Samuel Beckett's famous words, they 'fail, fail again, fail better'. *That* is the way to learn. But it takes high levels of persistence, a consistent and steady form of encouragement, and an adult ear – or three – tuned to the specific needs of this specific person. To any parent of a daughter reading this, I would only say: think carefully (and without undue self-criticism) about whether and how much we really offer this kind of support to our girls and how we can do it more, even – especially – when our daughter/s appear at their most 'difficult' or 'demanding'.

Some believe that we should encourage more and more women to seek worldly success: status, glamour, material wealth, the chance to be part of the 'right' social networks. I would place a greater – or countervailing – weight on the importance of genuine emotional and intellectual freedom, of young women feeling free to be, and live, as they wish, to refuse the dictates of obedience and conformity and fashion, to pursue civic and political action. There are darker themes at work in the 'XX factor' phenomenon with its so-called meritocratic insistence, from childhood onwards, on intense competitiveness, long working hours, ruthless networking, obsession with securing prestige, high salaries and high social status. I think back to the woman sitting in therapist Susie Orbach's office who 'has it all' and feels empty inside, or the young people that Melanie Strickland observes, desperate to have the right stuff, to 'keep up'. By definition, the intense competition among a growing pool of favoured individuals and families for access to elite institutions and occupations creates failures of the vast majority. This is not an argument for a reversal of female fortunes; it is an argument for more justice, in our public lives, and greater balance and genuine autonomy in our personal ones.

★

So many factors go into making a young person who she is, and shaping her future: temperament, schooling, financial backing (or lack of it), good or bad luck, mentors or friends, personal choice and individual courage. But family and social class is so often the key to all that follows, whether in rebellion or conformity. The writer Kamila Shamsie, who 'grew up in the harsh world of a misogynist military government in 1980s Pakistan – where women's freedom was severely threatened', has spoken of how she was nurtured by the support of the women in her family, and particularly her mother, who was, in her turn, buoyed up by the encouragement of Kamila's father. She writes:

> It impossible to underestimate the value of growing up the daughter of Muneeza Shamsie. My mother has always loved books, but for a long time thought her lack of university education meant she didn't have the qualifications to write or talk publicly about them. It was my father who first bought her a typewriter and encouraged her to write for the newspapers – often editing her articles in the early days. She was a feature writer, then a book reviewer, and is now a short-story writer and – I'm pretty sure I can say this without nepotism – the leading critic and expert on Pakistani Anglophone writing. When I think of all these women, I finally understand what was hidden from me in my 'take-everything-for-granted' childhood . . . my familial legacy enabled me to imagine, without pressure or expectation, a life centred around writing.

As Shamsie implies ('without pressure or expectation'), at the heart of real support for our daughters is that simple-complex process: letting our children be. Not pushing or prodding too much, not robbing them of their dreaminess or diminishing their dramas: believing what they say: giving their ideas and experience credence. We do them a disservice when we try to airbrush out the difficult emotions, such as anger and shame, boredom and silliness, shyness and vulnerability. By refusing to recognise weakness, in ourselves or others, we risk an emotional brittleness and callousness, blindness to the world as it really is. Any relationship, be it a friendship, love affair, partnership or parenthood, that deliberately

> At the heart of real support for our daughters is that simple-complex process: letting our children be.

excludes the experience of, or recognition of, vulnerability, is, at best, an exceptionally well-managed and largely empty deal. Any politics that disallows vulnerability is bound to have a nasty, authoritarian edge.

Josie Rourke, artistic director of the Donmar Warehouse, put it slightly differently:

> We've moved on a lot but what we don't yet own is the right to be uncertain. We can't walk into a room without having or representing an agenda. I don't know how we will get ourselves to a place where we can be uncertain, but that's my hope. It's my hope for careers, for relationships, and for so much more.

Gillian Flynn, the author of bestselling novel *Gone Girl*, phrases it is as follows: 'Is it really only girl power, and you-go-girl, and empower yourself, and be the best you can be? Isn't it time to acknowledge the ugly side? I've grown quite weary of the spunky heroines . . . soul-searching fashionistas that stock so many books.' Me too – and not just in books.

Sometimes it is the person who says 'enough is enough' – with all the emotional untidiness and anger that goes with it – who actually changes the world. It is a phrase I have heard a great deal while researching and writing this book. Sometimes it has come from women talking about economic crisis or the lack of female representation in politics, national and local. Or it has come from activists fuming at sexualised representations of women in advertising or the darker reaches of pornography or continued official inaction on male violence against women. Many – particularly older women – feel the need to fight for changes (or conservation of important rights) for the sake of future generations.

Throughout this book, I have talked about the rise of the Exceptional Woman. But I want to end by celebrating women who stand out for a different reason: in defence of justice or a concept of a wider human flourishing. In *Joining the Resistance*, Carol Gilligan discusses two women who have seen 'through the lies, and speak truth to power' in particular political circumstances:

Magda Trocme, the pastor's wife in Le Chambon-sur-Lignon who responded when Jews knocked at her door by saying, 'Come in'; Antonina Zabinska, the zookeeper's wife in Occupied Warsaw, who hid Jews in the zoo in the centre of the city – what they say when asked how they came to do this, is that they were human . . . I am haunted by these women, their refusal of exceptionality. When asked how they did what they did, they say they were human, no more no less.[3]

I am cheered by the paradox: the exceptional woman who 'refuses exceptionality' – in Gilligan's phrase – because she merely does what she thinks is right: she does the human thing. There are many contemporary examples of women (and men, of course) prepared to stand up and fight for what they believe in. But in the context of this book, and these arguments, I am thinking of women like Shelby Knox, the teenager who campaigned for genuine sex education in her Texas school district; Margaret Hodge, MP, who, in her late sixties, was appointed as Chair of the Public Accounts Committee, and began holding the Coalition government and its spending priorities to account; Enza Miceli, the Italian call centre worker, who was forced to resign her job because of the impossibility of both caring for her family and holding down a job, and who has joined a movement of protest against the misogynist culture of her nation, and who declared that 'I am only hopeful because I have young daughters and if I lost my hope I wouldn't know what to cling to'.[4] I want to celebrate the Twitter Youth Feminist Army, a group of articulate, self-possessed teenagers who take the feminist message to their sceptical peers; the brave female activists in Pakistan who organised protection for women who went to vote in the 2013 elections; Jody Williams, the Nobel Peace Prize winner who has tirelessly campaigned to ban anti-personnel land mines, and has become a harsh critic of the United States' overweening military might.

To young women, I would say: guard the pleasures and fight the pressures that will arise from the fact of your sex. You will need, too, to draw on a broader spirit, the ethic of consideration of others. I have every confidence that the best of you will do so, not in any self-denying way but as a part of a more generous self, a wider movement, that will surely help bring into being a better world for *all* our daughters.

# Acknowledgements

I had so many interesting conversations in the course of writing this book, as well as conducting more formal interviews, so thanks are due, in many different ways, to: Sohaila Abdulali, George Alagiah, Maryam Alkhawaja, Jill Armstrong, Chandni Asher, Rebecca Asher, Dawn Austwick, Kat Banyard, Barney Bardsley, Caroline Benn, Emily Benn, Pat Boles, Agnes Bolsø, Marina Cantacuzino, Clare Carter, Camilla Child, Rita Clifton, Chloe Combi, Shona Crallan, Pauline Crawford, Ragnhild Freng Dale, Miriam David, Rowenna Davis, Celia Dignan, Athene Donald, Helen Dunford, Lily Dunn, John Edmonds, Lucy Elgood, Cynthia Enloe, Kate Figes, Laura Flanders, Caryn Franklin, Nikki Gemmell, Ailsa Goodman, Tamsin Greig, Sian Griffiths, Gaby Hinsliff, Nigel Hobbs, Rosie Hobson, Dr Gabrielle Ivinson, Selma James, Gerard Kelly, Susan Kennedy, Marion Kozak, Tess Lanning, Kayte Lawton, Anna Llewellyn, Karen Mattison, Fiona Millar, Jane Miller, Cathy Moore, Estelle Morris, Kate Mosse, Helen Mott, Frances O'Grady, Ellie Mae O'Hagan, Lindsay O'Hagan, Susie Orbach, Miriam O'Reilly, Carrie Paechter, Shirley Palmer, Sumaya Partner, Louisa Pau, Nina Power, Kate Purcell, Emma Rich, Shelley Robinson, Anna Rowlands, Kate Ryan, Tom Schuller, Lynne Segal, Anthony Seldon, Yvonne Sharples, Sarah Shin, Alexandra Shulman, Valerie Stevens, Sue Steward, Henry Stewart, Melanie Strickland, Di Thomas, Lesley Thomson, Karen Townson, Eva Tutchell, Polly Vernon, Natasha Walter, Kate Williams, Denise Winn, Alison Wolf. Thanks, too, to the twittersphere for always coming up with such interesting responses to my various appeals for information and ideas.

I am particularly grateful to those who read, and commented on parts, or all, of the manuscript: Rebecca Asher, Margaret Bluman, Miriam David, Fiona Millar, Kate Purcell and Tom Schuller. Margaret Bluman gave me a wise piece of advice at the start of writing which kept me on the right track throughout.

Warm thanks to my editor Kate Parkin, who came up with the idea for the book – and the title! – and took such a close, careful and encouraging interest in both book and author from start to finish. My agent Faith Evans was similarly involved: a great friend both to the project and to me. Caroline Westmore, Isabel Miller and Nick de Somogyi at John Murray piloted the manuscript through to publication with exemplary skill and patience.

Last, but never least, love and thanks to my family, particularly to Tony Benn and Joshua Benn. Paul Gordon was, as ever, my first port of call, my ultimate reader. This book could not have been written without his steady, shrewd, loving support. But no set of acknowledgements would be complete, and particularly not for *this* book, without mention of my darling 'girls', Hannah and Sarah. Just as they have always shown affectionate and amused support for their mother's many projects so I now greatly look forward to doing the same for them as they finally embark on adult life.

The author and publisher would like to acknowledge with thanks the following for allowing the usage of copyright material: Lisa Appignanesi, Rachel Holmes and Susie Orbach, *Fifty Shades of Feminism*, Virago, London, 2013; Rebecca Asher, *Shattered: Modern Motherhood and the Illusion of Equality*, Vintage, London, 2012; Associated Newspapers Limited; Julian Barnes, *Through the Window: Seventeen Essays (and one short story)*, Vintage, London, 2012; Mary Catherine Bateson, *Composing a Life*, Grove Press, New York, 1989; Bauer Consumer Media; Leslie C. Bell, *Hard to Get: Twenty-Something Women and the Paradox of Sexual Freedom*, University of California Press, Berkeley, LA/London, 2013; Steve Biddulph, *Raising Girls: Helping Your Daughter to Grow Up Wise, Warm and Strong*, HarperThorsons, London, 2013, reprinted by permission of HarperCollins Publishers Ltd © 2013 Steve Biddulph; Amy Chua, *Battle Hymn of the Tiger Mother*, Bloomsbury, London, 2011; Kira Cochrane, *Women of the Revolution: Forty Years of Feminism*, Guardian Books, London, 2010; Anna Coote and Beatrix Campbell, *Sweet Freedom*, Blackwell, Oxford, 1982; Rachel Cusk, *A Life's Work: On Becoming a Mother*, Fourth Estate, London, 2001; Barbara Ehrenreich, Elizabeth Hess and Gloria Jacobs, *Re-Making Love: The Feminization of Sex*, Anchor Books/Doubleday, New York, 1986; Caitlin Flanagan, *Girl Land*, Reagan Arthur Books, New York, 2012; Betty Friedan, *The Feminine Mystique*, Penguin, London, 1965; Nikki Gemmell, *The Bride Stripped Bare*, Fourth Estate, London, 2011; Carol Gilligan, *Joining the*

*Resistance*, Polity Press, Cambridge, MA, 2011; Vivian Gornick, *Approaching Eye Level*, Beacon Press, Boston, MA, 1996; Guardian News and Media Limited; Independent Newspapers; Selma James, *Sex, Race and Class: The Perspective of Winning. A Selection of Writings, 1952–2011*, PM Press, Oakland, CA, 2013; Michael E. Lamb, *The Role of the Father in Child Development*, John Wiley and Sons, Hoboken, NJ, 2010; *The Nation*; *New Statesman* magazine; *The New York Times* Company; Peggy Orenstein, *Schoolgirls: Young Women, Self-Esteem, and the Confidence Gap*, Anchor Books, New York, 1994; Mary Pipher, *Reviving Ophelia: Saving the Selves of Adolescent Girls*, Ballantine Books, New York, 1994; Nina Power, *One Dimensional Woman*, Zero Books, London, 2009; Hanna Rosin, *The End of Men: And the Rise of Women*, Viking, London, 2012; Sheila Rowbotham, *The Past is Before Us: Feminism in Action since the 1960s*, Pandora Press, London, 1989; Sheila Rowbotham, Lynne Segal and Hilary Wainwright, *Beyond the Fragments: Feminism and the Making of Socialism*, Merlin Press, Pontypool, 2013; Sheryl Sandberg, *Lean In: Women, Work, and the Will to Lead*, Random House, New York, 2013; Jacqueline Scott, Shirley Dex and Heather Joshi, *Women and Employment: Changing Lives and New Challenges*, Edward Elgar Publishing, London, 2008; Taiye Selasi, 'On Discovering Her Pride in Her African Roots', *Guardian*, 2013; Laura Sessions Stepp, *Unhooked: How Young Women Pursue Sex, Delay Love and Lose at Both*, Riverhead Books, New York, 2007; extract from *Anne Sexton: A Self-Portrait in Letters*, reprinted by permission of SLL/Sterling Lord Literistic, Inc. Copyright by Anne Sexton; Helen Simpson, 'Hey Yeah Right Get A Life' and 'Lilies and Lentils', in *Hey Yeah Right Get A Life*, Jonathan Cape, London, 2000 © Helen Simpson 2000; Anne-Marie Slaughter, 'Why Women Still Can't Have It All', *The Atlantic*, 2012; Zadie Smith in *New York Times Book Review* courtesy of Rogers, Coleridge & White Ltd; Dale Spender, *Man Made Language*, Routledge and Kegan Paul, London, 1980; Telegraph Media Group Limited; Time Inc.; TSL Education Ltd; Natasha Walter, *Living Dolls: The Return of Sexism*, Virago, London, 2010; Alison Wolf, *The XX Factor: How Working Women Are Creating a New Society*, Profile Books, London, 2013; Naomi Wolf, *The Beauty Myth*, Vintage, London, 1990.

Every reasonable effort has been made to trace copyright holders, but if there are any errors or omissions, John Murray will be pleased to insert the appropriate acknowledgement in any subsequent printings or editions.

# Notes

## Introduction

1. http://www.guardian.co.uk/books/2013/jan/26/mary-beard-question-time-internet-trolls
2. http://www.telegraph.co.uk/women/womens-life/9827698/Jane-Austens-Pride-and-Prejudice-200-years-on-sons-expected-to-marry-for-financial-security.html
3. See *Guardian*, 19 January 2013
4. http://www.telegraph.co.uk/women/womens-life/9785537/It-has-never-been-harder-to-bring-up-a-daughter.html
5. http://www.newstatesman.com/v-spot/2013/03/how-do-you-get-teenagers-think-feminism-cool
6. Tess Lanning, 'Feminism and Democratic Renewal', *Soundings*, Issue 52, September 2012, p.1
7. Alison Wolf, *The XX Factor: How Working Women Are Creating a New Society*, Profile Books, London, 2013, p.1
8. http://www.independent.co.uk/news/uk/home-news/feminism-is-failing-working-class-women-says-ippr--study-8555264.html
9. http://www.independent.co.uk/news/uk/politics/majority-of-british-children-will-soon-be-growing-up-in-families-struggling-below-the-breadline-government-warned-8531584.html
10. Lynne Segal, 'All Shook Up: Bridging Generational Divides'. Paper presented to the 'Thinking Through Time and History in Feminism' Birkbeck Conference, 23 March 2012
11. http://www.guardian.co.uk/books/2013/mar/24/vera-brittain-testament-of-youth
12. http://www.guardian.co.uk/artanddesign/2012/nov/04/judy-chicago-art-feminism-britain
13. See for example Tess Lanning, 'Great Expectations: Exploring the Promises of Gender', IPPR, 31 March 2013

14. Linda Grant, 'Twitter's tales of sexism', *Guardian*, 12 March 2012

15. Margaret Stansgate, *My Exit Visa*, Hutchinson, London, 1992, p.12

16. Ibid.

17. Ibid., p.36

18. See Simone de Beauvoir (ed. and trans. H. M. Parshley), *The Second Sex*, Jonathan Cape, London, 1953

19. Melissa Benn, *Madonna and Child: Towards a New Politics of Motherhood*, Jonathan Cape, London, 1998, pp. 242–4

20. Lisa Campbell, 'Broadcasting gender imbalances is inexcusable after Expert Women's Day', *Guardian*, 21 January 2013

21. Ibid.

22. http://www.paulaprinciple.com/category/politics/

23. 'Gender pay gap twice as large for women in their 50s'. First findings/ report from *Age Immaterial*, a TUC project on issues facing older women at work, 20 February 2013

24. http://womeninjournalism.co.uk/the-lady-vanishes-at-45/

25. http://www.guardian.co.uk/commentisfree/2013/apr/21/nipple-tattoo-plastic-surgery

26. http://www.independent.co.uk/life-style/fashion/features/the-politics-of-pubic-hair-why-is-a-generation-choosing-to-go-bare-down-there-8539673.html

27. www.guardian.co.uk/books/2013/may/09/coverflip-maureen-johnson-gender-book?INTCMP=SRCH

28. http://www.guardian.co.uk/media/2012/nov/27/women-fighting-sexism-media-page-3

29. http://ukfeminista.handsupstaging.com/news/press-releases/men-still-on-top-in-the-arts/

30. Sheila Rowbotham, Lynne Segal and Hilary Wainwright, *Beyond the Fragments: Feminism and the Making of Socialism*, Merlin Press, London, 2013, p.24

31. See Nina Power, *One Dimensional Woman*, Zero Books, Winchester, 2009

32. http://www.guardian.co.uk/books/2012/feb/20/rachel-cusk-divorce

33. Lynne Segal, 'All Shook Up: Bridging Generational Divides'. Paper presented to the 'Thinking Through Time and History in Feminism' Birkbeck Conference, 23 March 2012

34. Natasha Walter, 'Beyond Autobiography', *Fifty Shades of Feminism*, Virago, London, 2013, p.268

35. http://www.iast.net/thefacts.htm

36. Laura Flanders, 'Eve Ensler Rising', *The Nation*, 7 November 2012

37. http://www.guardian.co.uk/society/2011/dec/03/pessimism-britons-things-worse
38. http://www.bbc.co.uk/news/uk-politics-18810248
39. http://www.fawcettsociety.org.uk/index.asp?PageID=1264
40. Selma James, *Sex, Race and Class: The Perspective of Winning. A Selection of Writings, 1952–2011*, PM Press, Oakland, CA, 2012, pp. 274–5
41. http://www.guardian.co.uk/world/2013/mar/07/men-women-unite-for-change
42. http://onebillionrising.org/
43. http://www.nytimes.com/2013/01/08/opinion/after-being-raped-i-was-wounded-my-honor-wasnt.html?hp&_r=o

## 1: Think Yourself Thin

1. http://www.independent.co.uk/news/uk/home-news/the-kids-are-all-right-survey-finds-that-most-children-are-happy-8560789.html
2. See Christine Howe, 'Gender and Classroom Interaction: A Research Review,' Scottish Council for Research in Education, 1997; Valerie Walkerdine, *Counting Girls Out: Girls and Mathematics*, Routledge, London, 2004
3. http://www.guardian.co.uk/education/2012/dec/13/gender-gap-university-applications-widens
4. http://www.guardian.co.uk/education/2013/jan/03/universities-working-class-white-boys
5. www.paulaprinciple.com
6. http://www.independent.co.uk/news/education/schools/better-people-make-better-students-bestselling-book-reveals-building-character-is-best-way-to-nurture-educational-success-8523295.html?origin=internalSearch
7. Vivian Gornick, 'What feminism means to me', *Approaching Eye Level*, Beacon Press, Boston, MA, 1996, pp. 62–70
8. Christine Barter, Melanie McCarry, David Berridge and Kathy Evans, 'Partner exploitation and violence in teenage intimate relationships', www.nspcc.org.uk/inform, October 2009, pp. 146–7
9. Polly Curtis, 'Dated attitudes towards gender "holding girls back"', *Guardian*, 8 June 2009. The article makes reference to Naomi Haywood, Sharon Walker, Gill O'Toole, Chris Hewitson, Ellen Pugh and Preethi Sundaram, 'Engaging all young people in meaningful learning after 16: A review', Equality and Human Rights Commission, 2009

10. http://www.guardian.co.uk/education/2013/jan/03/universities-working-class-white-boys

11. Peggy Orenstein, *Schoolgirls: Young Women, Self-Esteem and the Confidence Gap*, Anchor Books, New York, 1995, p.xx

12. Polly Vernon, 'Have We Become Size Blind?', *Grazia*, 16 April 2012

13. Nina Power, *One Dimensional Woman*, Zero Books, Winchester, 2009, p.24

14. http://www.news-medical.net/news/20120425/Rise-of-eating-disorders-among-men-and-boys.aspx

15. http://www.eatingdisorders.org.au/key-research-a-statistics

16. http://www.guardian.co.uk/commentisfree/2013/feb/07/uni-lad-sexism-teenage-stone-age

17. Barbara Fredrickson, Barbara L. et al., 'That swimsuit becomes you: sex differences in self-objectification, restrained eating and maths perfor-mance', *Journal of Personality and Social Psychology*, 75, 1998, pp. 1269–84

18. Natasha Walter, *Living Dolls: The Return of Sexism*, Virago, London, 2010, p.36

19. Naomi Wolf, *The Beauty Myth*, Vintage, London, 1990, p.217

20. http://www.20-firstblog.com/loving-sheryl-sandberg-and-wishing-she-would-lean-in/

21. See for example Sheryl Clark, 'A good education: girls' extracurricular pursuits and school choice', *Gender and Education*, Vol. 21, No. 5, 2009

22. Alison Wolf, *The XX Factor: How Working Women Are Creating a New Society*, Profile Books, London, 2013, p.273

23. See for example V. Walkerdine, H. Lucey and J. Melody, *Growing Up Girl: Psychosocial Explorations of Gender & Class*, Palgrave, London, 2002

24. See for example Sheryl Clark, 'A good education: girls' extracurricular pursuits and school choice', *Gender and Education*, Vol. 21, No. 5, 2009

25. http://www.psychologytoday.com/experts/leonard-sax-md-phd

26. Carol Gilligan, *Joining the Resistance*, Polity Press, Cambridge, MA, 2011, p.143

27. Ibid., pp. 144–5

28. Sara Rimer, 'Amazing! Driven to Excel; For Girls, It's Be Yourself, and Be Perfect, Too', *New York Times*, 1 April 2007

29. C. Maxwell and P. Aggleton, 'Becoming accomplished: Concerted cultivation among privately educated young women', *Pedagogy, Culture and Society*, 21(1), 2013, pp. 75-93

30. Emma Rich and John Evans, 'Now I am NObody, see me for who I am: the paradox of performativity', *Gender and Education*, Vol. 21, No. 1, 2009, p.2

31. John Evans, Emma Rich and Rachel Holroyd, 'Disordered eating and

disordered schooling: what schools do to middle-class girls', *British Journal of Sociology of Education*, 25, No. 2, 2004, p.126

32. Ibid., p.132
33. Ibid., p.131
34. Emma Rich and John Evans, 'Now I am NObody, see me for who I am: the paradox of performativity', *Gender and Education*, Vol. 21, No. 1, 2009, p.12
35. Ibid.
36. Alison Wolf, *The XX Factor: How Working Women Are Creating a New Society*, Profile Books, London, 2013, p.1
37. http://www.economist.com/blogs/banyan/2011/05/depressed_students_south_korea
38. http://www.guardian.co.uk/books/2013/feb/02/hilary-mantel-experience-fat
39. http://vagendamag.blogspot.co.uk/2013/04/samantha-brick-fat-is-not-failure.html
40. John Evans, Emma Rich and Rachel Holroyd, 'Disordered eating and disordered schooling: what schools do to middle-class girls', *British Journal of Sociology of Education*, 25, No. 2, 2004, p.135
41. Ibid.
42. Ibid., p.134

## 2: Name, Shame – and Blame

1. http://www.guardian.co.uk/lifeandstyle/2010/sep/10/kat-banyard-influential-young-feminist
2. http://www.guardian.co.uk/commentisfree/2013/feb/15/freedom-doesnt-mean-let-it-all-hang-out
3. 'Porn: the shocking truth', *Times Educational Supplement*, 5 October 2012
4. See http://www.dailymail.co.uk/news/article-2110257/One-teenage-girls-sexually-assaulted-boyfriends.html#ixzz2KbdcA5b4
5. http://www.bbc.co.uk/news/uk-politics-21127073
6. Caitlin Flanagan, *Girl Land*, Reagan Arthur Books, New York, 2012, p.184
7. Ibid., p.178
8. http://www.guardian.co.uk/lifeandstyle/2010/sep/10/kat-banyard-influential-young-feminist
9. http://www.dailymail.co.uk/debate/article-2286264/A-14-year-old-raped-boys-age-obsessed-online-porn-Welcome-nightmare-I-ve-warned-years.html

10. http://www.dailymail.co.uk/debate/article-2237909/Who-teach-boys-women-arent-meat-Men--means-footballers-singers-Top-Gear-presenters.html

11. 'Porn: the shocking truth', *Times Educational Supplement*, 5 October 2012

12. http://www.guardian.co.uk/commentisfree/2013/jan/24/children-enemy-sexism-not-sexualisation

13. http://www.telegraph.co.uk/news/worldnews/europe/iceland/9866949/Iceland-considers-pornography-ban.html

14. http://www.telegraph.co.uk/women/sex/9887800/Could-the-UK-really-block-internet-porn.html

15. http://makelovenotporn.com/

16. http://www.guardian.co.uk/books/2013/feb/09/lucy-ellmann-interview-mimi

17. http://www.dailymail.co.uk/debate/article-2237909/Who-teach-boys-women-arent-meat-Men--means-footballers-singers-Top-Gear-presenters.html

18. http://www.guardian.co.uk/commentisfree/2013/may/09/men-victims-of-male-aggression-speak-up

19. http://www.guardian.co.uk/commentisfree/2013/apr/26/protect-children-talk-rape-desmond-tutu

20. http://cas.uchicago.edu/workshops/racereligion/files/2010/03/Moffett-Bateau-Draft1.pdf

21. Ruby M. Gourdine and Brianna P. Lemmons, 'Perceptions of Misogyny in Hip Hop and Rap: What Do the Youths Think?', *Journal of Human Behavior in the Social Environment*, 21, No. 1, 2011, pp. 57–72

22. http://news.bbc.co.uk/1/hi/scotland/8516387.stm

23. Christine Barter, Melanie McCarry, David Berridge and Kathy Evans, 'Partner exploitation and violence in teenage intimate relationships', www.nspcc.org.uk/inform, October 2009, p.103

24. Ibid., pp. 58–9

25. Ibid., p.103

26. Ibid., pp. 132–3

27. Ibid., p.137

28. http://www.independent.co.uk/news/uk/crime/100000-assaults-1000-rapists-sentenced-shockingly-low-conviction-rates-revealed-8446058.html

29. Ibid.

30. John McCarthy, talk to school leaders

31. http://www.guardian.co.uk/politics/2011/may/04/nadine-dorries-teenage-girls

32. The latest data from the Office for National Statistics shows teenage

pregnancies are at their lowest rate since the early 1980s. The under-18 conception rate for 2009 was 38.3 conceptions per 1,000 women aged 15 to 17. This represents a fall of 5.9% compared with 40.7 conceptions per 1,000 women aged 15 to 17 in 2008.

33. http://news.bbc.co.uk/1/hi/health/6927733.stm
34. See Caitlin Flanagan, *Girl Land*, Reagan Arthur Books, New York, 2012, for a full discussion of the 'oral sex' moral panic
35. http://www.telegraph.co.uk/comment/columnists/allison-pearson/9821275/Our-daughters-are-abused-by-a-culture-of-porn.html
36. Ibid.
37. Christine Barter, Melanie McCarry, David Berridge and Kathy Evans, 'Partner exploitation and violence in teenage intimate relationships', www.nspcc.org.uk/inform, October 2009, p.154
38. End Violence Against Women Poll Results, October 2010
39. Christine Barter, Melanie McCarry, David Berridge and Kathy Evans, 'Partner exploitation and violence in teenage intimate relationships', www.nspcc.org.uk/inform, October 2009, p.154
40. Caitlin Flanagan, *Girl Land*, Reagan Arthur Books, New York, 2012, p.171
41. http://www.guardian.co.uk/commentisfree/2013/feb/04/sex-education-women-relationships
42. Leslie C. Bell, *Hard To Get: Twenty-Something Women and the Paradox of Sexual Freedom*, University of California Press, London, 2013, p.182
43. http://www.telegraph.co.uk/women/womens-life/9785537/It-has-never-been-harder-to-bring-up-a-daughter.html
44. *Observer Food Monthly*, February 2013, p.10
45. Caitlin Flanagan, *Girl Land*, Reagan Arthur Books, New York, 2012, p.7

## 3: The Myth of Perfection

1. See for example Carol Gilligan, *Joining the Resistance*, Polity Press, Cambridge, MA, 2011, p.132
2. Simone De Beauvoir, *The Second Sex*, Jonathan Cape, London, 1953, p.352
3. Ibid., p.360
4. Ibid., p.391
5. Ibid., p.383
6. See for example Peggy Orenstein, *Schoolgirls: Young Women, Self-Esteem and the Confidence Gap*, Anchor Books, New York, 1995; Mary Pipher, *Reviving Ophelia: Saving the Selves of Adolescent Girls*, Ballantine Books, New York, 1994

7.  Peggy Orenstein, *Schoolgirls: Young Women, Self-Esteem and the Confidence Gap*, Anchor Books, New York 1995, p.xxxi

8.  Mary Pipher, *Reviving Ophelia: Saving the Selves of Adolescent Girls*, Ballantine Books, New York, 1994, p.19

9.  Ibid., p.43

10. See Katha Pollitt, 'On Gilligan's Island', *Reasonable Creatures: Essays on Women and Feminism*, Vintage, London, 1995

11. Carol Gilligan, *Joining the Resistance*, Polity Press, Cambridge, MA, 2011, p.116

12. Ibid., p.115

13. Ibid., p.132

14. Ibid., pp. 146–7

15. Ibid., p.174

16. Ibid., p.163

17. Ibid, pp. 114–16

18. Ibid., p.145

19. Christine Howe, 'Gender and Classroom Interaction: A Research Review,' Scottish Council for Research in Education, 1997

20. 'Why a single-sex school was right for my daughters', http://www.boltonschool.org/senior-girls

21. http://www.guardian.co.uk/education/2009/dec/02/co-eds-or-single-sex

22. http://www.guardian.co.uk/world/us-news-blog/2013/feb/05/girls-science-gender-gap-fix

23. http://www.guardian.co.uk/science/blog/2013/feb/08/pseudoscience-stereotyping-gender-inequality-science?INTCMP=SRCH

24. http://occamstypewriter.org/athenedonald/2011/03/06/do-we-want-to-feminise-science-teaching/

25. Diana Leonard, *Single sex and co-educational secondary schooling: life course consequences?*, Full Research Report, ESRC End of Award Report RES-000-22-1085, Swindon: ESRC

26. http://www.guardian.co.uk/education/2009/dec/02/co-eds-or-single-sex

27. http://www.guardian.co.uk/education/2012/dec/30/why-dont-girls-study-physicsDonald

28. Robin Alexander, 'Neither National Nor a Curriculum?', Response to the Secretary of State's National Curriculum proposals for England, University of Cambridge, June 2012

29. http://www.theatlantic.com/magazine/archive/2012/07/why-women-still-cant-have-it-all/309020/6/

30. Carol Gilligan, *Joining the Resistance*, Polity Press, Cambridge, MA, 2011, p.152

31. Michael E. Lamb (ed.), *The Role of the Father in Child development*, John Wiley & Sons, Hoboken, NJ, 2010, p.9

32. Susan Harkness, 'The household division of labour: changes in families' allocation of paid and unpaid work', in Jacqueline Scott, Shirley Dex and Heather Joshi, *Women and Employment, Changing Lives and New Challenges*, Edward Elgar Publishing, London, 2008, p.264

33. Margaret Drabble, *The Millstone*, Penguin, London, 1966, p.9

34. Helen Simpson, *Hey Yeah Right Get a Life*, Jonathan Cape, London, 2000

35. Parts of this passage are reproduced, with thanks to Taylor and Francis, from Melissa Benn, 'Events, Dear Girl, Events', *Women: A Cultural Review*, Vol. 24, Issue 2–3, pp. 191–208

36. Steve Biddulph, *Raising Girls: Helping Your Daughter to Grow Up Wise, Warm and Strong*, HarperThorsons, London, 2013, p.206

37. Michael E. Lamb (ed.), *The Role of the Father in Child development*, John Wiley & Sons, Hoboken, NJ, 2010, p.3

38. Ibid., p.5

39. Ibid., p.11

## 4: Lean in – Or Lose Out?

1. http://www.guardian.co.uk/commentisfree/2012/jul/03/unemployed-female-graduate

2. http://www.independent.co.uk/news/business/news/women-in-their-twenties-smash-glass-ceiling-to-reverse-pay-gap-2154836.html

3. Ibid.

4. Chartered Management Institute: press release on pay rise

5. Jacqueline Scott, Shirley Dex, Heather Joshi, Kate Purcell and Peter Elias, 'Introduction: changing lives and new challenges', in Jacqueline Scott, Shirley Dex and Heather Joshi, *Women and Employment, Changing Lives and New Challenges*, Edward Elgar Publishing, London, 2008, p.7

6. Ibid.

7. http://www.independent.co.uk/news/business/news/women-in-their-twenties-smash-glass-ceiling-to-reverse-pay-gap-2154836.html

8. http://www.guardian.co.uk/commentisfree/2011/nov/27/young-women-earning-more-men

9. See http://www.time.com/time/business/article/0,8599,2015274,00.html#ixzz2M15CH6de

10. Ibid.
11. http://careers.guardian.co.uk/how-to-close-gender-pay-gap
12. Ibid.
13. http://www.aauw.org/files/2013/02/graduating-to-a-pay-gap-the-earnings-of-women-and-men-one-year-after-college-graduation.pdf
14. Annual Survey of Hours and Earnings, 2011, Provisional Results (SOC 2000), published by the Office for National Statistics
15. http://www.equalityhumanrights.com/uploaded_files/triennial_review/how_fair_is_britain_ch11.pdf
16. 'Girls Career Aspirations', report published by the Office in Standards of Education (OFSTED), April 2011
17. http://www.publications.parliament.uk/pa/cm201213/cmselect/cmbis/writev/womeninworkplace/m01.htm
18. Ruth Woodfield, *What Women Want from Work: Gender and Occupational Choice in the 21st Century*, Palgrave Macmillan, London, 2007
19. http://www.guardian.co.uk/society/2012/feb/20/female-unemployment-crisis-women
20. Sheryl Sandberg, *Lean In: Women, Work and the Will to Lead*, Random House, New York, 2013, p.34
21. Alison Wolf, *The XX Factor: How Working Women Are Creating a New Society*, Profile Books, London, 2013, p.284
22. Ibid., p.285
23. http://www.theatlantic.com/magazine/archive/2012/07/why-women-still-cant-have-it-all/309020/
24. Ibid.
25. http://www.independent.co.uk/voices/commentators/helena-morrissey-women-dont-need-quotas-to-get-to-the-top-7468794.html
26. http://www.washingtonpost.com/opinions/sheryl-sandbergs-lean-in-campaign-holds-little-for-most-women/2013/02/25/c584c9d2-7f51-11e2-a350-49866afab584_story.html
27. http://ideas.time.com/2013/03/07/forget-about-mentors-women-need-sponsors/#ixzz2QdVT49cP'
28. 'Teachers' pay rises to be based on performance, Michael Gove confirms', *Guardian*, 15 February 2013
29. http://www.guardian.co.uk/society/2013/feb/06/david-cameron-nhs-nurses
30. http://www.washingtonpost.com/opinions/sheryl-sandbergs-lean-in-campaign-holds-little-for-most-women/2013/02/25/c584c9d2-7f51-11e2-a350-49866afab584_story_1.html

31. http://www.guardian.co.uk/commentisfree/datablog/2012/jul/02/graduates-future-prospects-debt-unemployment

32. http://www.economist.com/node/21528614

33. http://www.guardian.co.uk/commentisfree/datablog/2012/jul/02/graduates-future-prospects-debt-unemployment

34. http://www.independent.co.uk/news/uk/home-news/feminism-is-failing-working-class-women-says-ippr--study-8555264.html

35. Sheila Rowbotham, *The Past is Before Us: Feminism in Action since the 1960s*, Pandora Press, London, 1989 p.166

36. A survey by the Industrial Relations Service suggests that 23% of employers now include zero hours as one of their employment options

37. Tess Lanning, 'Feminism and Democratic Renewal', *Soundings*, Issue 52, September 2012, p.3

38. Ibid., p.9

39. See for example Ferdinand Mount, *The New Few Or A Very British Oligarchy: Power and Inequality in Britain Now*, Simon and Schuster, London, 2012

## 5: Love in a Cold Climate

1. Leslie C. Bell, *Hard to Get: Twenty-Something Women and the Paradox of Sexual Freedom*, University of California Press, Berkeley, LA/London, 2013, p.113

2. Barbara Ehrenreich, Elizabeth Hess and Gloria Jacobs, *Re-making Love: The Feminization of Sex*, Anchor Books/Doubleday, New York, 1986, p.205

3. Ibid., pp. 199–202

4. Laura Sessions Stepp, *Unhooked: How Young Women Pursue Sex, Delay Love and Lose at Both*, Riverhead Books, New York, 2007, p.1

5. Ibid., pp. 1–2

6. Ibid., p.4

7. Ibid.

8. Ibid., p.5

9. Ibid., pp. 6–7

10. Ibid., p.16

11. Ibid.

12. Barbara Ehrenreich, Elizabeth Hess and Gloria Jacobs, *Re-making Love: The Feminization of Sex*, Anchor Books/Doubleday, New York, 1986, p.89

13. Ibid., pp. 89–90

14. Anna Coote and Beatrix Campbell, *Sweet Freedom: The Struggle for Women's Liberation*, Blackwell, Oxford, 1982, p.218

15. Barbara Ehrenreich, Elizabeth Hess and Gloria Jacobs, *Re-making Love: The Feminization of Sex*, Anchor Books/Doubleday, New York, 1986, p.102

16. 'Eva Ensler Rising', *The Nation*, 7 November 2012

17. See, for example, http://www.nybooks.com/articles/archives/2012/sep/27/pride-and-prejudice/?pagination=false

18. Anna Coote and Beatrix Campbell, *Sweet Freedom: The Struggle for Women's Liberation*, Blackwell, Oxford, 1982, p.211

19. Laura Sessions Stepp, *Unhooked: How Young Women Pursue Sex, Delay Love and Lose at Both*, Riverhead Books, New York, 2007, p.5

20. Hanna Rosin, *The End of Men: And the Rise of Women*, Viking, London, 2013, p.33

21. Ibid., p.23.

22. http://www.theatlantic.com/magazine/archive/2012/09/boys-on-the-side/309062/2/

23. Hanna Rosin, *The End of Men: And the Rise of Women*, Viking, London, 2013, p.29

24. Ibid., pp. 17–47

25. http://www.telegraph.co.uk/news/newstopics/howaboutthat/3685314/Young-women-have-more-sexual-partners-than-men.html

26. Alison Wolf, *The XX Factor: How Working Women Are Creating a New Society*, Profile Books, London, 2013, p.290

27. Elke D. Reissing, Heather L. Andruff and Jocelyn J. Wentland, 'Looking Back: The Experience of First Sexual Intercourse and Current Sexual Adjustment in Young Heterosexual Adults', *Journal of Sex Research*, 49, No. 1, 2012, pp. 27–35

28. Hanna Rosin, *The End of Men: And the Rise of Women*, Viking, London, 2013, p.25

29. http://www.orgasmsurvey.co.uk/pressrelease.htm

30. See http://www.dailymail.co.uk/femail/article-2179955/How-quarter-women-admit-faking-orgasms-EVERY-TIME-sex.html#ixzz2LMwf3bqh

31. Rhiannon Lucy Cosslett and Holly Baxter, 'In search of the female orgasm,' *New Statesman*, 21 January 2013

32. Leslie C. Bell, *Hard to Get: Twenty-Something Women and the Paradox of Sexual Freedom*, University of California Press, Berkeley, LA/London, 2013, p.3

33. Ibid., p.5

34. Ibid., p.7

35. Hanna Rosin, *The End of Men: And the Rise of Women*, Viking, London, 2013, p.31

36. Leslie C. Bell, *Hard to Get: Twenty-Something Women and the Paradox of Sexual Freedom*, University of California Press, Berkeley, LA/London, 2013, p.15

37. Ibid., p.17

38. Ibid., p.173

39. Ibid., p.183

40. Read more, http://www.dailymail.co.uk/femail/article-2259592/The-New-Rules-Revamped-dating-manual-says-initiate-contact-man.html#ixzz2PWII28QU

41. http://www.theatlantic.com/magazine/archive/2012/09/boys-on-the-side/309062/3/

42. http://www.thefword.org.uk/blog/2012/04/breaking_up

43. http://www.guardian.co.uk/commentisfree/2013/jan/18/traditional-nuclear-family-gay-marriage

44. Ibid.

# 6: Breakpoint

1. Helen Simpson, 'Lentils and Lilies', *Hey Yeah Right Get a Life*, Jonathan Cape, London, 2000, pp. 1–10

2. http://www.ft.com/cms/s/0/2ce8952c-922b-11e2-851f-00144feabdc0.html#axzz2TKtcZK6q

3. Rebecca Asher, *Shattered: Modern Motherhood and the Illusion of Equality*, Vintage, London, 2012, p.1

4. http://www.guardian.co.uk/money/2012/nov/13/parental-leave-flexible-nick-clegg

5. Rachel Cusk, *A Life's Work*, Faber and Faber, London, 1988, p.11

6. Ibid., p.15

7. Rebecca Asher, *Shattered: Modern Motherhood and the Illusion of Equality*, Vintage, London, 2012, p.1

8. Ibid., p.3

9. Rachel Cusk, *A Life's Work*, Faber and Faber, London, 1988, p.25

10. http://www.guardian.co.uk/money/2013/jan/01/merge-work-life-balance

11. Ibid.

12. Hanna Rosin, *The End of Men: And the Rise of Women*, Viking, London, 2013, p.67

13. http://www.dailymail.co.uk/news/article-2267393/Recession-causes-number-stay-home-fathers-soar-women-main-breadwinner.html

14. Fatherhood Institute research summary, 'Fathers, mothers, work and family', 18 January 2011, p.2

15. Fatherhood Institute, 'Supporting Employers: the "business case" for Paternity Leave in the UK', 7 March 2011, p.3

16. http://www.ippr.org/press-releases/111/9902/friendly-to-families-unfriendly-to-women

17. http://www.timewisejobs.co.uk/staticpages/11000/revealed-the-uk-s-power-part-time-top-50/

18. http://www.guardian.co.uk/lifeandstyle/2009/jul/10/mothers-wages-fawcett-society

19. http://www.telegraph.co.uk/finance/jobs/9659232/Women-earn-500000-less-than-men-over-working-lives.html

20. http://m.ippr.org/articles/56/8837/real-men-do-housework

21. http://www.demos.co.uk/press_releases/theotherglassceiling

22. Amanda Jayne Miller and Sharon Sassler, 'The Construction of Gender Among Working-Class Cohabiting Couples', *Qualitative Sociology*, 35, 2012, pp. 427–46

23. Susan Harkness, 'The household division of labour: changes in families' allocation of paid and unpaid work', in Jacqueline Scott, Shirley Dex and Heather Joshi, *Women and Employment, Changing Lives and New Challenges*, Edward Elgar Publishing, London, 2008, p.265

24. http://www.guardian.co.uk/world/2005/apr/09/gender.weekend7

25. Ibid.

26. Hanna Rosin, *The End of Men: And the Rise of Women*, Viking, London, 2013, p.74

27. *Great Expectations: Exploring the Promises of Gender Equality*, IPPR, 2013, p.31

28. http://www.telegraph.co.uk/news/uknews/8608855/Million-more-people-employ-a-cleaner-than-a-decade-ago.html

29. Mary Catherine Bateson, *Composing a Life*, Grove Press, New York, 1989, p.88

30. https://www.gov.uk/government/uploads/system/uploads/attachment_data/file/128778/think-act-report-annual-report.pdf

31. http://www.guardian.co.uk/law/2013/mar/09/women-on-maternity-leave-illegal-discrimation

32. http://www.guardian.co.uk/media/2013/mar/02/vogue-alexandra-shulman-working-home

33. http://www.stylist.co.uk/people/lucy-mangan/your-boss-cant-help-abusing-their-power#image-rotator-1

34. http://www.theatlantic.com/magazine/archive/2012/07/why-women-still-cant-have-it-all/309020/1/

35. Ibid.

36. http://www.ippr.org/articles/56/10613/childcare-and-flexible-work-key-to-21st-century-feminism

37. http://www.guardian.co.uk/commentisfree/2010/feb/17/21-hours-working-week

## 7: How Should a Woman Be?

1. http://www.independent.co.uk/news/education/schools/better-people-make-better-students-bestselling-book-reveals-building-character-is-best-way-to-nurture-educational-success-8523295.html?origin=internalSearch

2. Lennie Goodings, 'Immodest Power' in Lisa Appignanesi, Rachel Holmes and Susie Orbach (ed.), *Fifty Shades of Feminism*, Virago, London, 2013, p.77

3. Vivian Gornick, *The End of the Novel of Love*, Virago, London, 1999, p.31

4. Betty Friedan, *The Feminine Mystique*, Penguin, London, 2010, p.355

5. www.paulaprinciple.com

6. Mary Catherine Bateson, *Composing a Life*, Grove Press, New York, 1989, p.167

7. Stefan Collini, *What are Universities For?*, Penguin, London, 2012, p.92

8. Taiye Selasi, 'On Discovering Her Pride in Her African Roots', *Guardian*, 22 March 2013

9. Vivian Gornick, *Approaching Eye Level*, Beacon Press, Boston, MA, 1996, p.80

10. Carol Gilligan, *Joining the Resistance*, Polity Press, Cambridge, MA, 2011, pp. 131–2

11. Mary Catherine Bateson, *Composing a Life*, Grove Press, New York, 1989, p.206

12. Julian Barnes, 'The Deceptiveness of Penelope Fitzgerald', in *Through the Window: Seventeen Essays (and one short story)*, Vintage, London 2012, p.4

13. http://www.guardian.co.uk/commentisfree/2011/nov/09/talk-to-online-misogynist-bullies

14. Vivian Gornick, *Approaching Eye Level*, Beacon Press, Boston, MA, 1996, p.78

15. Ibid., p.81

16. Dale Spender, *Man Made Language*, Routledge and Kegan Paul, London, 1980 p.41
17. Ibid., p.43
18. Ibid., p.42

## 8: Stand Up and Stand Out

1. Rhiannon Lucy Cosslett and Holly Baxter, 'How do you get teenagers to think feminism is cool?', *New Statesman*, 4 March 2013
2. http://www.newstatesman.com/culture/2013/04/reviewed-fifty-shades-feminism
3. http://www.guardian.co.uk/theguardian/shortcuts/2012/sep/11/cam-paign-stop-page-3-succeed
4. http://www.guardian.co.uk/media/2013/mar/10/anti-page-3-the-sun-campaigner
5. http://www.guardian.co.uk/media/2012/nov/27/women-fighting-sexism-media-page-3
6. Liz Kelly, 'Changing It Up: Sexual Violence Three Decades On' in Lisa Appignanesi, Rachel Holmes and Susie Orbach (ed.), *Fifty Shades of Feminism*, Virago, London, 2013
7. http://www.newstatesman.com/global-issues/2013/03/are-black-feminists-too-defensive-about-violence-our-communities
8. Ibid.
9. http://www.guardian.co.uk/commentisfree/2013/apr/01/david-miliband-british-politics-mps
10. *Sex and Power 2013: Who Runs Britain?*, published by the 'Counting Women In' coalition, February 2013
11. http://www.guardian.co.uk/politics/2013/feb/24/shocking-absence-women-uk-public-life
12. http://www.guardian.co.uk/politics/2001/mar/16/women.labour
13. http://www.guardian.co.uk/women-in-leadership/2013/apr/17/tessa-jowell-thatcher-legacy-nonexistent
14. http://www.countingwomenin.org/wp-content/uploads/2013/02/Sex-and-Power-2013-FINALv2.-pdf.pdf
15. Lynne Segal, 'All Shook Up: Bridging Generational Divides'. Paper presented to the 'Thinking Through Time and History in Feminism' Birkbeck Conference, 23 March 2012
16. http://www.guardian.co.uk/commentisfree/2010/mar/24/women-politics-political-wives

17. Interview, *Woman's Hour*, 25 April 2013
18. http://www.guardian.co.uk/commentisfree/2012/mar/18/quotas-women-boardroom-equality
19. http://www.guardian.co.uk/commentisfree/2011/jul/18/diversity-boardroom-corporate-decisions
20. http://www.guardian.co.uk/politics/2013/feb/24/shocking-absence-women-uk-public-life
21. http://www.guardian.co.uk/commentisfree/2013/feb/26/feminists-sexy-funny-anger-changes-world
22. http://www.guardian.co.uk/commentisfree/2013/apr/04/where-are-the-activists-austerity
23. http://www.guardian.co.uk/society/2013/mar/11/generation-self-what-young-care-about
24. Ibid.
25. http://www.nybooks.com/blogs/nyrblog/2012/jun/02/north-west-london-blues/
26. Gary Younge, 'A Mitt Romney win would merely reward Republicans for bad behaviour', *Guardian*, 4 November 2012
27. Parts of this passage are reproduced, with thanks to Taylor and Francis, from Melissa Benn, 'Events, Dear Girl, Events', *Women: A Cultural Review*, Vol. 24, Issue 2–3, pp. 191–208

## Epilogue: What Should We Tell Our Daughters?

1. Nina Power, *One Dimensional Women*, Zero Books, London, 2009, p.66
2. http://www.guardian.co.uk/commentisfree/2013/may/01/welfare-wages-women-fight-market?CMP=twt_gu
3. Carol Gilligan, *Joining the Resistance*, Polity Press, Cambridge, MA, 2011, p.164
4. http://www.guardian.co.uk/world/2013/jan/31/italian-election-female-question-employment

# Select Bibliography

Lisa Appignanesi, Rachel Holmes and Susie Orbach, ed., *Fifty Shades of Feminism*, Virago, London, 2013

Rebecca Asher, *Shattered: Modern Motherhood and the Illusion of Equality*, Vintage, London, 2012

Sarah Bakewell, *How to Live: A Life of Montaigne in One Question and Twenty Attempts at an Answer*, Chatto and Windus, London, 2010

Kat Banyard, *The Equality Illusion: The Truth About Women and Men Today*, Faber and Faber, London, 2010

Julian Barnes, *Through the Window: Seventeen Essays (and one short story)*, Vintage, London, 2012

Michele Barrett and Mary McIntosh, *The Anti-social Family*, Verso/NLB, London, 1982

Mary Catherine Bateson, *Composing a Life*, Grove Press, New York, 1989

Leslie C. Bell, *Hard to Get: Twenty-Something Women and the Paradox of Sexual Freedom*, University of California Press, Berkeley, LA/London, 2013

Melissa Benn, *Madonna and Child: Towards a New Politics of Motherhood*, Jonathan Cape, London, 1998

Steve Biddulph, *Raising Girls: Helping Your Daughter to Grow Up Wise, Warm and Strong*, HarperThorsons, London, 2013

Leslie T. Chang, *Factory Girls: Voices from the Heart of Modern China*, Spiegel and Grau, New York, 2008

Amy Chua, *Battle Hymn of the Tiger Mother*, Bloomsbury, London, 2011

Kira Cochrane, ed., *Women of the Revolution: Forty Years of Feminism*, Guardian Books, London, 2010

Anna Coote and Beatrix Campbell, *Sweet Freedom*, Blackwell, Oxford, 1982

Ann Crittenden, *The Price of Motherhood: Why the Most Important Job in the World is Still the Least Valued*, Metropolitan Books, New York, 2001

Rachel Cusk, *A Life's Work: On Becoming a Mother*, Fourth Estate, London, 2001

—— *Aftermath: On Marriage and Separation*, Faber and Faber, London, 2012

Simone de Beauvoir, *The Second Sex*, Penguin, London, 1949

Margaret Drabble, *The Garrick Year*, Penguin, London, 1964

Nell Dunn, *Talking to Women*, Pan, London, 1965

Barbara Ehrenreich and Arlie Russell Hochschild, *Global Woman: Nannies, Maids and Sex Workers in the New Economy*, Granta, London, 2003

Barbara Ehrenreich, Elizabeth Hess and Gloria Jacobs, *Re-Making Love: The Feminization of Sex*, Anchor Books/ Doubleday, New York, 1986

Kate Figes, *The Big Fat Bitch Book: For Girls*, Virago, London, 2007

—— *Couples: The Truth*, Virago, London, 2010

Cordelia Fine, *Delusions of Gender: The Real Science Behind Sex Differences*, Icon Books, London, 2010

Caitlin Flanagan, *Girl Land*, Reagan Arthur Books, New York, 2012

Anne Frank, ed. Otto H. Frank and Mirjam Pressler, *The Diary of a Young Girl: The Definitive Edition*, Penguin, London, 2007

Emily Franklin, *A Wonderful Lie: 26 Truths About Life in Your Twenties*, 5 Spot/ Warren Books, New York, 2007

Nancy Fraser, *Fortunes of Feminism: From State-Managed Capitalism to Neoliberal Crisis*, Verso, London, 2013

Betty Friedan, *The Feminine Mystique*, Penguin, London, 1965

—— *Beyond Gender: The New Politics of Work and Family*, Woodrow Wilson Center Press, Washington DC, 1997

Nikki Gemmell, *The Bride Stripped Bare*, Fourth Estate, London, 2011

Lindsay German, *Material Girls: Women, Men and Work*, Bookmarks, London, 2007

Emma Gilbey Keller, *The Comeback: Seven Stories of Women Who Went from Career to Family and Back Again*, Bloomsbury, London, 2008

Carol Gilligan, *In a Different Voice: Psychological Theory and Women's Development*, Harvard University Press, London, 1982

—— *Joining the Resistance*, Polity Press, Cambridge, MA, 2011

Vivian Gornick, *Approaching Eye Level*, Beacon Press, Boston, MA, 1996

—— *The End of the Novel of Love*, Virago, London, 1999

—— *The Men in My Life*, MIT Press, Cambridge, MA, 2008

Germaine Greer, *The Female Eunuch*, Paladin, London, 1971

Catherine Hakim, *Work-Lifestyle Choices in the 21st Century: Preference Theory*, Oxford University Press, Oxford, 2000

Sheila Heti, *How Should a Person Be?*, Harvill Secker, London, 2013

Gaby Hinsliff, *Half a Wife: The Working Family's Guide to Getting a Life Back*, Chatto and Windus, London, 2012

Arlie Russell Hochschild (with Anne Machung), *The Second Shift: Working Parents and the Revolution at Home*, Viking Penguin, New York, 1997

Siri Hustvedt, *A Plea for Eros*, Hodder and Stoughton, London, 2006

Selma James, *Sex, Race and Class: The Perspective of Winning. A Selection of Writings, 1952–2011*, PM Press, Oakland, CA, 2013

Michael E. Lamb, ed., *The Role of the Father in Child Development*, John Wiley and Sons, Hoboken, NJ, 2010

Doris Lessing, *Walking in the Shade: Volume Two of My Autobiography 1949–1962*, HarperCollins, London, 1997

Angela McRobbie, *The Aftermath of Feminism: Gender, Culture and Social Change*, Sage, London, 2009

Susan Maushart, *The Mask of Motherhood: How Mothering Changes Everything and We Pretend It Doesn't*, Vintage Australia, Sydney, 1997

—— *Wifework: What Marriage Really Means for Women*, Bloomsbury, London, 2002

Juliet Mitchell, *Psychoanalysis and Feminism*, Pelican, London, 1975

Fiona Millar, *The Secret World of the Working Mother: Juggling Work, Kids and Sanity*, Ebury Publishing, London, 2009

Caitlin Moran, *How To Be a Woman*, Ebury Press, London, 2011

Abi Morgan, *Lovesong*, Oberon Books, London, 2011

Ferdinand Mount, *The New Few or a Very British Oligarchy: Power and Inequality in Britain Now*, Simon and Schuster, London, 2012

Susie Orbach, *Bodies*, Profile, London, 2009

Peggy Orenstein, *Schoolgirls: Young Women, Self-Esteem, and the Confidence Gap*, Anchor Books, New York, 1994

Rozsika Parker, *Torn in Two: The Experience of Maternal Ambivalence*, Virago, London, 1995

Karen Payne, ed., *Between Ourselves: Letters Between Mothers and Daughters*, Virago, London, 1994

Allison Pearson, *I Don't Know How She Does It*, Vintage, London, 2003

Laurie Penny, *Meat Market: Female Flesh Under Capitalism*, Zero Books, Winchester, 2010

Mary Pipher, *Reviving Ophelia: Saving the Selves of Adolescent Girls*, Ballantine Books, New York, 1994

—— *Letters to a Young Therapist: Stories of Hope and Healing*, Basic Books, New York, 2003

Katha Pollitt, *Reasonable Creatures: Essays on Women and Feminism*, Vintage, London, 1995

Nina Power, *One Dimensional Woman*, Zero Books, London, 2009

Janet Radcliffe Richards, *The Sceptical Feminist: A Philosophical Enquiry*, Penguin, London, 1982

Anne Roiphe, *A Mother's Eye: Motherhood and Feminism*, Virago, London, 1996

—— *Married: A Fine Predicament*, Bloomsbury, London, 2003

Katie Roiphe, *Uncommon Arrangements: Seven Portraits of Married Life in London Literary Circles 1910–1939*, Virago, London, 2007

Hanna Rosin, *The End of Men: And the Rise of Women*, Viking, London, 2012

Sheila Rowbotham, *Hidden from History: 300 Years of Women's Oppression and the Fight Against It*, Pluto Press, London, 1973

—— *The Past is Before Us: Feminism in Action since the 1960s*, Pandora Press, London, 1989

—— *A Century of Women: The History of Women in Britain and the United States*, Viking, London, 1997

Sheila Rowbotham, Lynne Segal and Hilary Wainwright, *Beyond the Fragments: Feminism and the Making of Socialism*, Merlin Press, Pontypool, 2013

Sheryl Sandberg, *Lean In: Women, Work, and the Will to Lead*, Random House, New York, 2013

Jacqueline Scott, Shirley Dex and Heather Joshi, *Women and Employment: Changing Lives and New Challenges*, Edward Elgar Publishing, London, 2008

Lynne Segal, *Straight Sex: The Politics of Pleasure*, Virago, London, 1994

—— *Making Trouble: Life and Politics*, Serpents Tail, London, 2007

Laura Sessions Stepp, *Unhooked: How Young Women Pursue Sex, Delay Love and Lose at Both*, Riverhead Books, New York, 2007

Andrew Simms, *Cancel the Apocalypse: The New Path to Prosperity*, Little, Brown, London, 2013

Helen Simpson, *Hey Yeah Right Get A Life*, Jonathan Cape, London, 2000

Curtis Sittenfeld, *Prep*, Transworld, London, 2005

Helen Small, *The Long Life*, Oxford University Press, Oxford, 2007

Dale Spender, *Man Made Language*, Routledge and Kegan Paul, London, 1980

Margaret Stansgate, *My Exit Visa*, Hutchinson, London, 1992

Carolyn Steedman, *Landscape for a Good Woman: A Story of Two Lives*, Virago, London, 1986

Susie Steinbach, *Women in England 1760–1914: A Social History*, Weidenfeld and Nicolson, London, 2004

Craig Taylor, *Londoners: The Days and Nights of London Now – As Told by Those Who Love It, Hate It, Live It, Left It and Long For It*, Granta, 2011

Jill Tweedie, *In the Name of Love*, Jonathan Cape, London, 1979

Natasha Walter, *The New Feminism*, Virago, London, 1998

—— *Living Dolls: The Return of Sexism*, Virago, London, 2010

Natasha Walter, ed., *On the Move: Feminism for a New Generation*, Virago, London, 1999

Ruth Woodfield, *What Women Want From Work: Gender and Occupational Choice in the 21st Century*, Palgrave Macmillan, London, 2007

Alison Wolf, *The XX Factor: How Working Women Are Creating a New Society*, Profile Books, London, 2013

Naomi Wolf, *The Beauty Myth*, Vintage, London, 1990

—— *Vagina: A New Biography*, HarperCollins, New York, 2012

Mary Wollstonecraft and William Godwin, ed. Richard Holmes, *A Short Residence in Sweden, Norway and Denmark* and *Memoirs of the Author of 'The Rights of Woman'*, Penguin Books, London, 1987

Virginia Woolf, *A Room of One's Own*, Penguin, London, 2004

# Index

24/7 society 63

Abbott, Diane 64, 267
Abbott, Tony 262–3, 269
Abdulali, Sohalia 29–30, 76, 77
abstinence: and oral and anal sex 87; as proposed sex education for girls 83–4, 86; Silver Ring Thing (SRT) 185
abuse *see* assault; child abuse; violence against women
academic achievement: girls' 33–61; and body anxiety 48–50; boys' vs girls' 35–6; rise in 34–5, 42
action: need for 24
Adams, Clover 230
adolescence: and separation of parent and child 28–9
adults: lack of involvement in young people's lives 85
advice to young girls: not welcomed 28–9
age-related discrimination: achievement 240
ageing: changes in perception 292; and stress 293
Aggleton, Peter 56
aggression and male desirability 80

Alexander, Robin 116
Alliance for Eating Disorders Awareness (US) 47
'alpha girls' 56
ambition: women 11–12, 227–8, 229–30, 231, 233; and conventional ambition 234; Eve Ensler 175; failure of 178; and fathers 126; and 'leaning in' 146–7, 151; Doris Lessing 227; loss of 154, 210–11; Estelle Morris on 235, 274; and mothers 128; and politics 232; rejection of 230; schoolgirls 104, 108, 264; and time for family and personal relationships 184, 203, 211; vs men's ambition 150
'ambivalence' towards women and their activities 10, 101, 115, 161, 167, 196, 201, 226
American Association of University Women: survey on gender and self-esteem 42, 101; report on pay gap 141
anal rape 70
anal sex: as substitute sexual experience 87
Anam, Tahmima 247
androgyny 42–3, 44; and success 60–1

Equal Opportunities Commission:
and rise in academic
achievement in girls 34–5
equal pay 155
equality: businesses 212–13;
domestic 209; and feminism 255,
282; legislation 64–5; prospects
for women 139; young people
117, 136
Equality Act (2010) 155
Equality and Human Rights
Commission (EHRC) 41
'erotic capital' 177–8
erotic life: empowerment 163
erotica: recent explosion 162
Evans, John 56–7
Everyday Sexism (Twitter
campaign) 256
exam boards: assessment objectives
28
exam results 40
exam success: male/female 35–9
Exceptional Mothers 201, 202–3
Exceptional Women 15, 25, 298–9
exceptionality: refusal of 299
'expectation gap' 194
expectations, academic: of girls 34
Expert Women (activist group)
256
Expert Women's Day 13–14

families: anger in 244–5; family or
career 11; importance to young
women 297; and politics 271;
transformation of family life
293, 294; variety 190; and
violence against women 76;
violence in, and peer violence
of teenagers 79

Fatherhood Institute 200
fathers: and female confidence
125–7, 128–9; and feminism 220;
as house-husbands 210;
ignorance of daughter's love life
169; role in child development
118, 128, 129–30
Fawcett Society 256; Bristol 285;
*Not Having It All* 204–5; *see also*
Bird, Anna; Mott, Helen
fear: and ambition 231; of
consequences of ageing 240;
and economic crisis 59, 282–3;
and family life 124; or fatigue
33; of powerfulness 295; and
sexual coercion 79; and
sexuality 86, 99, 165–7
feelings: commercialisation of 162
fees: effect on university
applications 36
female distress: and anxiety 46,
54–5; and pornification of
culture 63–4
female genital mutilation (FGM)
261
female obedience 33
Femen (Ukrainian group) 258–9
femininity: and career success
9
feminism 10, 21, 255–6, 279; and
advances in women's rights 8;
and careers 237–8; and equality
255, 282; and female sexuality
172; future needs 295–6; Vivian
Gornick on 251–2; ignorance of
7; and inequality 282; post-
feminism reaction 49; PR
problem 255; and social
movements 279–81; and